Reading for Life

READING FOR LIFE

developing the college student's lifetime reading interest

Edited with a Preface *by JACOB M. PRICE*

ANN ARBOR / THE UNIVERSITY OF MICHIGAN PRESS

Published in the United States of America by
The University of Michigan Press and simultaneously
in Toronto, Canada, by Ambassador Books, Ltd.
Library of Congress Catalog No. 59-9735
Designed by David Perkins

Printed in the United States of America
by The Haddon Craftsmen, Inc., Scranton, Pa.

Preface

BOOM AND CRISIS are a most common sequence in history. Rarely, however, have the two been so inextricably confused, if not merged, as in the present position of higher education. On the one side we see every sign of healthy boom: mounting enrollments, new foundations, constant building, etc. On the other, we hear incessant laments at the quality of the education received by today's college graduate. He lacks the "know-how" to build sputniks faster than other people; he is even more sluggish in pure science and mathematics; he knows practically nothing of foreign languages and little more about contemporary world problems. No one, of course, ever claimed he was particularly accomplished in the traditional humanistic disciplines.

Long before the "educational crisis" reached the front page, many persons concerned not with immediate technological problems but with the long-run health of American civilization became disturbed at the quality of the graduate product being turned out by the American university machine. Granted that most recipients of degrees were well-trained doctors, dentists, lawyers, engineers, accountants, agricultural extension agents, and television announcers—were they also educated men and women? Did they ever read a book meaningfully, analytically, perceptively, or sensitively? Did they in fact ever read a book? Were they in sum meaningful participants in that western lettered civilization of which universities fancied themselves the preservers and transmitters?

In the day of the golf course and the television set, of the longer weekend and the shorter attention span, of do-it-yourself and how-to-do-it, few could be complacent about the answer. Everyone had heard of too many undergraduates who boasted of never having entered their university library; everyone knew too many college graduates whose last reading preceded their last examination to look forward with any pleasure to the findings of Dr. Gallup and the library science surveyors. To those responsible for reading facilities on campuses and for reading disciplines, the problem appeared particularly pressing. Were they, their colleagues, and their institutions doing all they might to develop the campus atmosphere, the campus values, the curricular patterns, the study habits, and learning goals that made green freshmen from whatever background into educated men and women in whose way of life reading had a meaningful part? If not, why not? What might they do to start remedying the situation? When, where, how?

When at the University of Michigan, President Harlan Hatcher, University Librarian Frederick H. Wagman and the faculty planning committee began in 1953 and 1954 to plan for the new Undergraduate Library, they were more than aware of these problems. Each of them knew from experience much that was wrong with current teaching practices, current learning processes, and the current college product. They were resolved that their function should be not merely to determine how many square feet of floor space, how many books, how many chairs and tables were needed, but to create, if the art of the planner and architect could create, a new institution on the university campus with a new atmosphere and a new purpose, not simply a study hall or storage warehouse for books, but a place where students would go by choice, where reading of every sort would become a most natural and most vital part of every-

day living, and from which something more lasting might
be drawn than the answers for tomorrow's examination.

In the course of planning for the new Undergraduate
Library, Dr. Wagman and his associates entered into correspondence with librarians, teachers, and university administrators all over the country and with such organizations
as the National Book Committee that were concerned with
the problem of developing reading interest in America. It
soon became apparent to all that the questions being raised
and the answers being worked out at the University of
Michigan were by no means peculiar to it but were relevant
to the work of those thousands all over the country who
were concerned with the quality of college education today.
To analyze, compare, and publicize common problems, it
was suggested that the National Book Committee and the
University of Michigan might sponsor a national conference at which persons from a variety of institutions and
from outside the university world might exchange ideas and
try to come to more immediate grip with the challenge of
the nonliteracy of today's college graduate. At first it was
hoped to hold the conference at the start of construction
of the new building in late 1955 or 1956. It was later decided that it might more usefully be held after the comple-
tion of the structure in 1957 or 1958 when the building
itself might take a part in the conference.

The new Undergraduate Library of the University of
Michigan was completed late in 1957 and opened to students in mid-January 1958. The formal dedication was
held at a public ceremony on February 21, 1958. Side by
side with the dedication, the hoped-for conference was
held (February 21-22) on "The Undergraduate and Lifetime Reading Interest," sponsored jointly by the University
of Michigan and the National Book Committee. More than
thirty persons attended, representing many academic dis-

ciplines, college and university administration, librarianship, the publishing and bookselling professions, and several
interested national organizations. Seven papers were prepared and distributed in advance to the conferees. This left
the greater part of the actual conference sessions free for
discussion of the points provoked by the papers.

In this volume each of the seven working papers is
printed substantially as submitted by the author to the conference (chapters 1, 3; 5, 6, 7; 9, 11). A précis of the discussion follows each paper in Parts I and III as a separate
chapter (2, 4; 10, 12). In Part II, the discussion was more
general and has been combined in a common chapter at the
end of the section (8). Part I is concerned with the di-
mensions and character of the problem. Part II essays the
problem of what the individual teacher can do in his classroom to affect the lifetime reading interest of his students.
Part III examines the more general campus milieu with
special attention to the bookstore and the library.

The purpose of this volume is not simply to memorialize
the opening of the new Michigan Undergraduate Library
or to record for posterity some rather interesting papers
and discussion presented to the conference held at Ann
Arbor in February 1958. The problems raised at the conference are of the most pressing importance to all librarians
concerned with the function of the library in undergraduate education and undergraduate life, to all college teachers
and administrators concerned with the quality of the learning experience of undergraduates in American colleges
today, to all thoughtful persons concerned for the texture
of contemporary American civilization and for the place
of the book and the values transmitted by the book in that
civilization.

Such concern exists. It is the hope of all who have had
anything to do with the realization of this conference and

the reporting of its transactions that this volume will help to direct that concern into channels of fruitful investigation, reflection, self-examination, and action.

The editor should like to offer his thanks to all who have helped make this volume possible. First and foremost, he must acknowledge his indebtedness to Miss Margaret Dudley, executive secretary of the National Book Committee, Inc., and to Mr. Dan Lacy, managing director of the American Book Publishers Council for their constant and invaluable assistance from the initial planning of the conference through to the final editing of its transactions. Dr. Frederick H. Wagman, Director of Libraries at the University of Michigan, was not only the official sponsor of the conference but, in a very real sense, its guiding spirit. To him belongs the ultimate credit both for the original inception of the conference and for its successful realization. Valuable preliminary work was done by the University of Michigan Advisory Committee for the Conference (Dr. Wagman, chairman, Professors Arthur J. Carr, John A. Hanson, Roger W. Heyns, Wilfred Kaplan, Stephen W. Rousseas and Alfred S. Sussman). Mrs. Margaret Russell and her assistants in the director's office of the University Library worked long and hard on the immense mass of administrative work churned up by the conference. Finally, neither the conference nor its transactions would ever have seen the light of day without the financial assistance of the Council on Library Resources, Inc., the Lilly Endowment, Inc., and the American Library Association.

Contents

PART I:
The Nature of the Problem

1

A Survey of Recent Research

BY LESTER ASHEIM

REPORTING THE FINDINGS of research on reading is always a thankless task. The findings are invariably discouraging to those who are interested in promoting the use of the book, and in their disappointment, the readers of the findings tend to associate the bad news with the carrier of it. There is considerable evidence to show that many of my colleagues in librarianship assume that I am an advocate of limited reading because I have so often reported it. This is a little like holding Gibbon responsible for the decline of the Roman Empire, but there it is.

Certainly it must be admitted that the findings are discouraging. To the question, "Do you happen to be reading a book at the present time?" only 21 per cent of a random cross section of adults in the United States in 1949 could answer "Yes"; and by 1957 this percentage had dropped to 17. When we realize that the "reading" being reported here covers any kind of simple identification of black marks on white paper, we must acknowledge that reading in its fuller sense, reading as defined for example in Mr. Heckscher's paper, must be even more limited than these figures show.

On the other hand, in 1957, to a similar poll, 55 per cent of the adults in England reported reading a book; 34 per

3

cent in West Germany; 33 per cent in Australia; and 31 per cent in Canada. These international comparisons are embarrassing. The United States has a higher literacy rate, a higher average national income, a higher proportion of leisure time than do any of the other Western democracies, and over two-thirds of the adult population has attended high school or college. Yet in England, where three times as great a proportion of the adult population report book reading, only a negligible percentage has attended school beyond the age of fifteen.

On the surface it would appear that our educational system has been completely ineffective (at least in this area), and yet all of the studies of reading show something else: that education is the major correlate of reading. While it is true that 26 per cent of those who have attended college have not read a book in the past year, 57 per cent of those with only a high-school education, and 82 per cent of those with only a grade-school education have read no books in the past year. Or to put it another way, 43 per cent of those with a college education said "yes" to the question on current reading, as compared to 19 per cent of those with a high-school education, and 6 per cent of those with a grade school education.

The lifetime reading habit then would certainly seem to be influenced by the college reading experience, and if there is to be more and better reading in the United States, it is among the college educated that we shall have to look for it. An intensive look at what we know about the reading habits of college students may help us to understand a little better why the reading patterns in American society are so disappointing.

Numerous studies of the reading of college students have been made in the past thirty years. Despite the fact that they have been conducted at different points in time, in different segments of the academic year, in different kinds of schools, and for different levels within the academic program, the latest study almost invariably tends to support the findings of those that have gone before. And almost invariably too, when the latest findings are reported, librarians are shocked all over again. They are shocked because the amount of reading uncovered by objective studies usually appears to be nowhere near enough, although how much reading *is* enough nobody really knows.

The reason librarians take the facts about the reading of college students so hard is that we all subscribe, more or less, to the basic assumption that reading is a good thing, and therefore a lot of reading must inevitably be even better. Since the college and university student stands at the peak of our educational system, we feel that he ought to represent the best possible conduct in relation to reading, and when we find, let us say, that 15 per cent of the students withdraw no books at all from their college library in an entire academic year, and that 31 per cent withdraw less than one book per month, we shudder to think that this represents the best possible reading conduct. These figures describe those who are benefiting from what we call "higher education," but can there be any education at all where so little use is made of the library?

It seems that there can be—at least as we now define education—and this is quite a blow to the librarian who clings to his cliché conviction that the library is the heart of the university, and that the educated man is one who reads and has read widely, and with pleasure as well as profit. This much we do know from all our studies of reading: the college-educated person is likely to do much more book reading than a person without a college education. If 31 per cent of the college students read no more than one book a month, what possible conclusions can we draw about the

reading of the population at large? Small wonder that we
are disturbed by the data presented in the studies of the
reading of college students.

What are the facts that prove so disturbing? They come
in several categories related to the following questions:

1) How many books are read by the average college
   student?
2) How many students account for the books that are
   read?
3) From what sources does the student obtain the books
   he reads?
4) How great a proportion of the reading is in books
   placed on special reserve, and how much from the
   general collection?
5) How much of the reading is curriculum-related,
   and how much is "free choice" reading?
6) Do the "better" students read the most?
7) Do women read more than men?
8) Does reading increase as the student progresses
   through college?
9) In what subject areas is the most reading done?
10) What personal characteristics and what external
    factors seem to correlate with the reading?
11) Finally, given these facts, what can be done to in-
    crease the amount of reading by college and univer-
    sity students? (Note the underlying assumption:
    that the amount of reading—no matter what the
    figures are—should be increased.)

As I have said, many of the answers to these questions
still seem shocking to us although some of them can logi-
cally be anticipated and some are even fairly well known.
Putting them all together we come out with a reasonably
accurate over-all picture of the college student's use of the

library. That picture—a synthesis of the data gathered in the studies listed in the bibliography, with individual studies cited by number—is drawn in the following pages.

A mere count of the total number of circulation charges uncovered in most of these studies usually sounds impressive. A circulation of 2,519 books discussed in Ream's study (19),[1] of 6,833 in Todd's (26), of 15,300 in Hoole's (13) adds up to a lot of books. But there are, of course, a couple of obvious factors which must be considered before numbers overwhelm us: how many persons were responsible for this total circulation, and how long a period is covered? When we break down the figures by these necessary qualifications the totals are not so impressive. In study after study the average number of books per capita borrowed from the general collection during an academic year (not including reserve books) is somewhere around twelve: a figure which appeared in Branscomb's comprehensive summary of the early studies (4) and again in the latest of the studies of college library use by Knapp (15). This comes to slightly more than one book per month, and while we may not know how much reading is enough, certainly we can say that a book a month is not a lot of reading for a college student.

This figure, however, is neither as bad nor as good as it looks. It is not as bad because it represents only the circulation from the general collection; it does not represent the total reading done by the average college student. It does not include the books taken from the reserve book collections; if it did we should undoubtedly have to revise our reading figures upwards, for all the studies show that the major book use in the college libraries centers in the reserve collection.

Advocates of wide reading and "free" reading tend to

[1] See bibliography at the end of this chapter.

discount the use of reserve books because it represents required rather than free-choice reading, usually involves the
reading of parts of books rather than whole books, and ex-
aggerates the amount of circulation because the compul-
sory rapid turnover multiplies the number of charges (five
charges may stand only for a single reading of a single
book by a single person). While all of these criticisms are
true, reading of reserve books is still book reading, and if
it is a good thing for a college student to read *The Education of Henry Adams,* we should not discount that good
merely because the book was assigned, or because the student read it in five different two-hour periods. We shall
return to this problem later; our point here is merely that
many of the studies count general, nonreserve circulation
only, although assigned book reading, whatever its limitations in establishing the lifetime reading habit, represents by
far the largest proportion of the total reading done by college students.

The factor of the reserve book system—a special feature
of college book use—tends to make the reading of college
students look a little better. Another factor which characterizes reading behavior in all contexts—the concentration
of book use—tends to make it look a little worse. For the
figure of twelve books a year, attributed to the average
college student, is as high as it is because of the heavy reading of a few students. In those studies which show total
withdrawals for the total student body, there is a range of
about 8 to 15 per cent who withdraw no books at all;
about 35 per cent of the students withdraw no more than
one book a month; about 10 per cent no more than one
book in an academic year. For the quarter or the semester,
the mode in study after study is one book. Thus we find
that although the total circulation is fairly high, half of it
is accounted for by 20 per cent or less of the total student

body. And at the other end of the continuum about 15 out of every 100 students apparently can spend a whole year in college without looking at an unassigned book.

In the preceding sentence I have used the reservation "apparently" because we know that there is reading of which the college library has no record.[2] A few of the studies have attempted to find out something about this; to what extent do college students get their books from other sources—the public library, rental libraries, purchase, home collections, borrowing from friends, and so on? By and large the answer is: some, but not much. Here again the figure varies greatly from institution to institution. A prerequisite to borrowing from other sources is the convenient availability of good bookstores and public libraries, and only a few college communities can offer such facilities. Other factors also enter: in a small college town where the students live on the campus, use of off-campus sources is negligible; in the large, city university where the students live in town, their use of the local library is likely to be quite heavy. Students with part-time jobs which take them away from the campus are likely to make more use of the public library which is located near their job or on the route to it. For example, in a study of Chicago Teachers College it was found that a greater proportion of the students used the public library than used the college library. This was readily explained by the fact that the sample included a great number of students doing practice teaching in schools in the city who came to the college only once a week; that a number of the students lived in the city and found the public library branches more accessible than the library of the college; and that much of the outside reading was in

[2] There is indeed library use (reading within the library from open shelves, reference use, reading of personal books, multiple use of books by others on a single loan, etc.) of which the library has no record either.

current, popular, general titles which were more readily available in the public library. It is possible therefore that the so-called "nonreaders" who show up in these studies are actually only nonusers of the college's library facilities.

On the other hand, all studies of communication audiences show that the active users of one source are likely to be active users of others. This has been shown to be particularly true for book use. For example, library users are also book buyers. Wriston, in his study of faculty use of the college library, discovered a similar fact: "The more active buyers are also the more active borrowers . . ."[3] In other words, even within the campus community there exists a "communications élite" (as the concentration of book use has already demonstrated). It is much less likely that a student who never borrows a book from the college library will read extensively from other sources than it is that the student who employs all the other available book sources will also be a user of the college library.

One reservation should be made in this connection to take into account the paper-bound book, which was a negligible consideration in the 1930's when most of the studies were made. As more and more quality titles are being made available in soft covers, increasing use is being made of them by college instructors. Many publishers of paper-bounds make a deliberate effort to provide the titles which will lend themselves to college use. Dr. Knapp's study (15), for example, reflects essentially the same patterns in proportions of book use as do the studies made twenty years ago in every category except that of the reserve book collection: here her figures show a decided decrease. It is thus quite conceivable that in the 1950's

---

[3] Henry W. Wriston, "Objective Indices of Faculty Scholarship Obtainable Through the Library," *Association of American Colleges, Bulletin*, XVIII (March, 1932), 185.

many students actually are buying the books in paper-
bound editions that in the 1930's they would have had to
borrow from the reserve book collection. The purchase of
paperbacks may well be cutting into general circulation,
particularly in the area of recreational reading, but no
figures as yet exist to support this hypothesis. As far as
we can tell, although the reserve book use no longer reflects
course-related reading, the general, free, collateral reading
by college students on a high and serious level is still pretty
accurately reflected in the general circulation statistics of
the college library.

As we have seen, the peculiar organization of the college
library forces a separate analysis of reserve book reading,
and reading from the general collection. Automatically
such a dichotomy raises the question of "required" versus
"free" reading, and several of the studies have made this
distinction in the report of their results.

The major finding in this connection and one which
could be anticipated, is that the greatest proportion of
student borrowing is course-related. In the earlier studies
(2, 17, 22) around 85 to 90 per cent of all reading done
by students was found to be required curricular reading.
In the latest study by Knapp (15), 94 per cent of the total
circulation is course-related. Since, in the Knapp study,
each borrower indicated the specific course for which the
book was borrowed, her definition of "course-related"
reading is probably more valid than that employed in the
earlier studies and probably reflects the reality of the
situation more accurately. In other words, the earlier
studies were correct in pointing out that most of the reading done by college students is course-related; if anything,
they underestimated the proportion.

The findings on course-related readings are reported in
several different ways. Gerberich and Jones found that 56

per cent of their sample had done no optional book reading
(11). They found also that of the twenty-six hours per
week reported as the average for all types of reading and
study, 74 per cent was spent in required reading and study,
only 26 per cent in optional reading. In Gaskill's study
of use of the library (i.e., use of any library facility,
not just borrowing), it was found that 76 per cent of all
those who entered the library building were using it for
class-assignment reasons (10). Thus whether the fact is
described in terms of the total number of loans, the total
number of students, or the total hours spent, curriculum-
related reading accounts for most of the reading done by
college students.

As we have suggested, an accurate indicator of "course-
related reading" is difficult to establish. Some investigators
have compared the titles on reserve lists and course bibliographies with the titles actually borrowed, and have assumed that titles not on any of the lists may be taken as
voluntary reading. Others have added to this procedure
a comparison of subject matter of the borrowed book and
the subject major of the student (or the subject matter of
the courses in which he is enrolled), and have assumed that
a book on a subject for which the student is taking a course
should be counted as course-related. Such arbitrary measur-
ing devices may well underestimate in some cases, over-
estimate in others. The literature major will seldom be
credited with extracurricular reading if he is reading any
of the better fiction, for example. On the other hand, a
term paper in literature may require the student to borrow
many titles in the social sciences which do not appear on
his reading list or in the literature classification, but which
certainly should be counted as course-related. In one study,
for example, Keller's *Digest of Books* was considered an
example of free reading because it was not on the instruc-

tor's reading list, but there is every reason to believe that the student's use of the book was, to put it mildly, "course inspired." As we have seen, Knapp's more accurate gauge of course-related reading turns up a higher proportion than most of the other studies. In other words the fact that college students do more reading than do other groups in the population may reflect not so much personal interest in reading as a conviction that academic success depends upon it.

We have suggested that students read because they think they must in order to make a respectable academic record. The studies show, however, that although there is some association between scholastic standing and library use, the correlation is low. The comparison of the distribution of grades among heavy users of the library with that of those who withdraw one or less books per month reveals no significant differences; both exhibit a normal distribution curve. Even more disconcerting, some students receive high marks although they borrow few or no books from the library; other students use the library a great deal and receive low marks. In either case, among the better students and among the below-average students, distribution of student reading is heavily skewed in the direction of little reading, and the mode is consistently about one book per quarter or semester.

That students may read a great deal and still get poor marks, or read very little and get good ones, can be explained in several ways. It may be that the poorer student is a slow reader, and therefore must withdraw books more frequently and spend more time reading in order to cover the course assignments. It may be that the better students, in addition to reading quickly and easily, will also have read rather widely, and may already have done much of the reading assigned for the course. It may be that the brighter student can grasp the essentials from class lectures and has mastered the technique for taking examinations without reading the assignments. Or it could be that the assigned readings are on a kind of dead level which does not appeal to the best students, and that the library itself does not attract the alert reader who keeps his library use to a minimum and gets most of his reading elsewhere.

One interesting characteristic of reading patterns does appear: the students with the higher scholastic rating tend to do more "free" reading. The student on the lower end of the scholastic scale, although he often does quite a bit of the assigned reading, does almost no noncurricular reading on his own. This would seem to support the hypothesis that the poorer student is a slower reader and that the good student finds the assigned readings comparatively dull. One study revealed a different pattern: Sister Melania Grace's investigation of the recreational reading of 405 students in Seton Hill College (12) showed that the five students with the lowest scholastic standing read more books than the five students with the highest scholastic ratings, but that the proportion of quality books was much lower among the poorer students. In this case, it appears that the poorer students were neglecting their studies for a poor grade of recreational reading.

It is well known from the general studies of reading that women are generally heavier users of the public library than men, and especially of the fiction and recreational collections. The studies of college library use support this finding, but in strange ways. Women students consistently take out more books than men in every category of use; men take out more newspapers and magazines. Yet oddly enough, the optional reading of the men is significantly greater than that of the women, although the women do more required reading than men. Thus women seem to be more conscientious about assigned reading, but less imaginative about selecting books on their own. The optional reading of the men is not necessarily recreational—indeed, it is primarily course-related and functional rather than cultural or recreational—but it is directly related to their interests, and chosen with their own needs in mind, whereas the reading of the women tends to stay more strictly within the prescribed lists. In a sense, the reading of women in the public library is like this too; the best sellers and the books-everyone-is-talking-about make a kind of recommended list of readings which the women conscientiously follow, whereas the men, although they read fewer titles, read more in line with their own specific and technical interests. In college, however, although the women withdraw more titles than the men, the difference is not statistically significant and there is almost no difference between men and women in the amount of time spent in reading.

More important as an influence on amount of reading than either sex or scholastic achievement is the level of schooling. All of the studies indicate that reading increases as the student progresses through college, although the increase from class to class does not proceed at a uniformly significant rate. The significant increase as the student progresses from the freshman to the senior year is in non-required reading, and there is less and less use of reserved books. This does not necessarily mean "free" reading; the books chosen are still primarily course-related, but they are selected from the general collection, from more flexible bibliographies, or on the basis of individual needs.

Reasons for this are several, and they are probably inter-related. As the student progresses through college he presumably is maturing academically and is becoming more sophisticated in his use of books and scholarly materials. As the classes move into the upper divisions, the instructors' use of books and reading changes also: there is more emphasis on wide reading on an optional basis and much less use of reserved lists. It may be also that the poorer readers are eliminated before they reach the upper academic levels, although there is little evidence yet to support this. On the basis of her analyses, Knapp (15) found that class level is more significant than the individual in accounting for the changes, but actually both aspects are reflected: increasing use of books by the academic program and increasing maturity on the part of the student.

Many hypotheses have been put forward in an attempt to explain the kinds of reading patterns that prevail among college students, and a few studies exist which attempt to examine each of the hypothesized factors. Some of these factors (in addition to sex, scholastic achievement, and academic level) are:

age	occupation of the parent
intelligence	size of the home library
occupational choice	proposed degree
field of subject concentration	fraternity affiliation
amount of extracurricular activity	type of preparatory school

Because little evidence of significant correlation has been uncovered in these studies, we shall not analyze them in detail here. Suffice it to say that the most significant differences appear between different schools, different courses, different instructors, and different class levels. These are differences of degree, however, and not of kind. In other words the over-all pattern is very much the same in all of the studies: a considerable proportion of the student body borrows no books at all; a small proportion are responsible for a great part of the total circulation; assigned reading and course-related reading account for the major part of the circulation; men borrow more generalized readings, while women borrow more of the reserve-assignment readings. Within these patterns however the average number of books borrowed varies greatly from school to school and from course to course. Thus it seems quite clear that the amount of reading can be increased where the course is so designed as to motivate more reading and in those schools where the tradition of wide reading is established.

The study by Knapp (15) devotes particular attention to the effect of courses and instructors upon the amount of reading done by college students. Through a special call slip which asked for the course for which each book was borrowed, through examination of reading lists and reserve lists, and through interviews with instructors, Knapp was able to provide a much more detailed analysis of this relationship than any of the previous studies. This is what she found:

The uneven distribution of library use among students results, not so much from the individual differences among students as from the fact that they are enrolled in courses which vary as to the amount of library use they stimulate. Out of the 160 courses offered during the quarter investigated, Knapp found that 11 accounted for more than half, and 40 accounted for almost 90 per cent of all the withdrawals for course work. To put this another way, more than half of the courses accounted for less than 3 per cent of the loans; 95 per cent of the courses accounted for less than 60 per cent of the loans.

Nor was this distribution of library use as closely tied to subject matter as might have been anticipated; although the humanities and the social sciences are more frequently represented among those courses which stimulate the most library use, seventeen of the nineteen subject departments in the college under investigation were represented among the courses for which library use was recorded. Certain courses in the sciences outranked certain courses in the humanities in the total number of books borrowed, the number of books per student borrowed, and the proportion of the class who borrowed books. The aims of the particular course and the methods of instruction employed by the instructors are more important as an influence upon reading than is the general subject matter.

That wide reading is not stimulated by all the courses should not automatically be interpreted as a reflection on the effectiveness of the instructor. In many instances, wide reading is not his goal: intensive reading of one or two texts, emphasis upon laboratory work rather than upon reading, other methods of instruction are often deliberately chosen. On the other hand, there are very real differences in the effectiveness of instructors in guiding students to reading even among those who take wide reading as one of the goals in their teaching. One thing appears to be fairly constant, instructors almost invariably expect more reading from their students than they get. "The average student . . . is devoting less than one hour to reading and study for each class period, or less than one-half the amount of time that is ordinarily assumed" (7). It is seldom that much reading occurs on the initiative of the student unless the instructor has provided the motivation.

Courses which stimulate the most use of the library were found to be almost exclusively advanced courses (usually elective rather than required) with small enrollments. Courses of a special nature which permit individual student-faculty conferences such as independent study and honors courses were high on the list as stimulators of library use. This may bode ill for future use of the college library. As the teaching load becomes heavier, as the schools become more crowded, the opportunity to work with the individual students, to prepare special reading lists, and to devise a variety of special assignments will appear less and less frequently. Already, to handle the increased teaching load, the colleges are beginning to turn to such mass teaching devices as television, reducing even more the kind of personal influence and contact which has been shown to be the most effective means for stimulating the student's use of the library and the resources of print. Even now "in general, the library does not have a role which is pervasive throughout the curriculum. Its contribution is important for a minority of the courses offered" (15).

Before we become too discouraged by this kind of finding, it would probably be well for the librarian to look closely at his own assumptions concerning library use by college students. The widely held view among librarians is that a love of books is "one of the criteria of a liberal education and should be developed among all students during their college career or . . . the program for higher education must be admitted at fault."[4] Even more strongly, many librarians and educators would claim that without fairly wide voluntary reading to supplement the assigned readings, "students are learning what to think, they are not learning how to think . . . the adjective 'well read' is synonymous with those other adjectives 'intelligent' and 'educated'. That is the most important benefit of a college education . . . to train students in the appreciation of worthwhile works and to broaden their interests so that after they leave college they will be equipped to do their own thinking."[5] To most of us this kind of reasoning seems

[4] Russell I. Thompson and John B. Nicholson, Jr., "Significant Influences on General Education in a Small College Library," *Library Quarterly*, XI (April, 1941), 179.

[5] Idair Smookler, "A Report on the Voluntary Reading Habits of Students of the Women's College," *Delaware Notes*, 12th series (1939), 59-60.

irrefutable, and when we discover that two-thirds of the
college courses motivate no voluntary reading, and very
little assigned reading, we are much concerned. We are
particularly disturbed because the differences among classes
and the differences among schools make it clear that this
low level of library use is not inevitable.

The truth of the matter is that not all courses require
library use. As a matter of fact, there is no logical reason
why they should. The nature of the course content and the
instructor's objectives for his course may dictate other
emphasis. There are certain subject fields, like the sciences
for example, where laboratory work and actual practice are
more desirable ways for the student to master the content
than through reading. There are some subjects, music and
art for example, where only through performance can
course objectives be reached. And even where the subject
matter is primarily handled through books, for example
philosophy or literature, the instructor may defensibly feel
that he prefers to have his students read intensively in one
or two texts rather than to range widely through commen-
taries and secondary sources. The college course which requires its students to read Aristotle instead of reading about
Aristotle is not without its defenders.

The crux of the conflict is that the librarian is talking
about the overall aims of a total college education, while
the instructor is talking about the aims of his particular
course. Most instructors would proclaim their belief that
the total program should result in the establishment of
lifetime reading habits over a wide range of interests. But
the instructor whose first objective is to teach a speaking
knowledge of French, will find it necessary to leave the
freewheeling, voluntary reading program to other courses.
More than that, even the staunchest advocate of voluntary
reading would probably have to admit that indiscriminate

reading is not always more desirable than guided reading. The librarian might be hard put to it to demonstrate that a broad program of free reading is better than a prescribed program of carefully chosen "core" works, to create that love of books, that power of discrimination, that appreciation of the "worthwhile" which is one of the aims of education. Should not quality rather than quantity be the goal in reading too?

Unfortunately these reasons sound convincing, but they are often produced after the fact. The limited use of library facilities results all too frequently from the ignorance or indifference of the instructor rather than from a deliberate decision based on an analysis of the library's potential education contribution. The interviews with faculty members made by Dr. Knapp (15) reveal that many instructors hold a narrow view of the value of library use, not only for a particular course or subject matter, but in general. The library, for many of them, has only two functions to serve: it provides a readily available and limited collection of prescribed readings for the undergraduate, and it acts as a storehouse of esoteric resources for the researcher on the advanced level. In very few instances did the instructor seem to recognize any very important, permanent, educational value in having all students know how to use the library and all of its facilities. The heaviest emphasis on library use is in the upper division courses where it is seen as useful primarily to those subject majors who plan to go on to graduate work. The purpose of the emphasis is to introduce them to the methods and the matter that they will need for their academic research, not to establish lifetime habits of reading and library use. For those for whom the college degree is terminal, such training and experience is seen as nonessential. Thus, while the instructor pays lip service to the more general objectives of the educational program, he has not yet translated the professed goals into the structure of his courses. This is not surprising, since most of the faculty members do not themselves seem to use the full resources of the library for their own purposes, they can hardly be expected to visualize the ways in which others could so use it.

The general patterns of college library use are now well known. More studies which ask only "how many books" and "how many readers" are not likely to uncover any very startling deviations. But there is still much to be learned about the "why" and the "what can we do about it." Dr. Knapp's study points the way to one fruitful area of research: the relationship between the instructor (his philosophy of education, his attitude towards books and the library, the nature of his assignments, and the structure of his courses) and the use that his students make of the library facilities. There are other things we should want to know also: how is it that teaching personnel know so little about the role that the library can play in the teaching program? Why is it that where books are equally accessible and similar motivations obtained, some people read widely and others not at all? Which is the better way to establish the habit of reading: through a program of widely ranging, free choice reading, or through a limited list of carefully selected readings, intensively studied? Why does the habit of reading drop off so sharply at the school-leaving point? What, exactly, are the benefits of wide reading, since they do not appear in academic success or scholastic standing?

The questions may seem to emphasize the gloomy side of the reading picture, but they need not do so. As a matter of fact, the most fruitful research may well be that which concentrates on the bright side, studying the "good" reader, the avid reader, the reader who continues, even after the pressure of school assignments is removed, to turn to books for information, recreation, and continuing education. We should study more intensively, in a series of case studies in depth, that small percentage of readers who account for the largest proportion of books borrowed. We should analyze more imaginatively the courses which do stimulate library use, extracurricular reading, and continuing book use beyond the limits of the assignments and the duration of the course. In other words, future studies of reading might well concentrate on why the best readers do so much reading, rather than on why the poorer readers do so little. Since our goal is the creation of more "good" readers, it would seem to be basic that we know all that we can about who the good reader is and how he gets that way. The beginnings have been made by Gray and Rogers in their study of the mature reader;[6] it is to be hoped that more studies will follow which will tell us even more.

My assignment was to summarize the findings of research on the reading of college students; not to conjecture on the proper role of the college library in the promotion of lifetime reading habits. Nevertheless, at the risk of usurping the tasks assigned to other working papers for this conference, I cannot forbear to underline one important implication of what has been reported here. The conflict between the long range objectives of the total program and the immediate objectives of the individual course certainly suggests that the course assignments alone cannot be expected to fulfill all of the objectives of the total program. The library, on the other hand, is more free than any subject department or any sequence of courses to concentrate on the creation of lifetime, as opposed to schooltime, reading habits. It follows that a more dynamic role could properly be played by the college and

[6] William S. Gray and Bernice Rogers, *Maturity in Reading; Its Nature and Appraisal* (Chicago: University of Chicago Press, 1956).

university library, not only in support of the specifics of
the curriculum but also in an active program of its own
designed to increase the student's reading and his knowledge of books. This is a contribution as important to the
student's education and as relevant to the objectives of the
parent institution as the provision of duplicate copies of an
assigned reading. In the library's experiments with such
programs lie the data for another area of fruitful research.

BIBLIOGRAPHY

1. Armstrong, Hazel E., "A Study of Library Use," *Teachers College Journal,* XIV (November, 1942), 36-37.

2. Armstrong, Mary Kathryn, "A Comparison of Student Library Use," Unpublished Master's thesis, Graduate Library School, University of Chicago, 1938.

3. Bowles, Minnie Redmond, "Library Activities for the Stimulation of Reading Among College Students." Unpublished Master's paper, Graduate Library School, University of Chicago, 1945.

4. Branscomb, Harvie. *Teaching with Books.* Chicago: Association of American Colleges and American Library Association, 1940.

5. Carnovsky, Leon, and Hazel A. Johnson, "Recreational Reading of Graduate Students," *Journal of Higher Education,* VII (January, 1936), 7-12.

6. Cuff, Noel, and H. L. Donavan, "What Freshmen Read in a Teachers College," *American Association of Teachers Colleges Quarterly* (September, 1931), 8-14.

7. Eurich, Alvin C., "The Amount of Reading and Study Among College Students," *School and Society,* XXXVII (January 21, 1933), 102-4.

8. Eurich, Alvin C., "The Significance of Library Reading Among College Students," *School and Society,* XXXVI (July 16, 1932), 92-96.

9. Eurich, Alvin C., "Student Use of the Library," *Library Quarterly,* III (1933), 87-94.

10. Gaskill, H. V., R. M. Dunbar, and C. H. Brown, "An Analytical Study of the Use of a College Library," *Library Quarterly*, IV (1934), 564-87.
11. Gerberich, J. R., and Charles Jones, "The Optional and Required Reading of College Students," *School and Society*, XXXVIII (July 15, 1933), 93-96.
12. Grace, Sister Melania, "An Analysis of the Extra-Curricular Reading of College Women in Relation to Their Personality Traits and Other Characteristics." Unpublished Master's thesis, Graduate Library School, University of Chicago, 1942.
13. Hoole, William Stanley, "A Cross-Section Survey of the Reading Habits and Library Usage of Birmingham-Southern College Students," *Peabody Journal of Education*, XV (January, 1938), 216.
14. Hoole, William Stanley, "The Reading of Birmingham-Southern College Students," *Peabody Journal of Education*, XIV (November, 1936), 151-57.
15. Knapp, Patricia B., "The Role of the Library of a Given College in Implementing the Course and Non-Course Objectives of That College." University of Chicago, Graduate Library School, Unpublished doctoral dissertation, 1957.
16. Knox, Lois Bennett, "Reading Interests of Students of North Texas State Teachers College in the First Semester of the Year 1942-43." Unpublished Master's thesis, North Texas State Teachers College, 1944.
17. McDiarmid, Errett Weir, Jr., "Conditions Affecting Use of the College Library," Unpublished Ph.D. dissertation, Graduate Library School, University of Chicago, 1943.
18. Neiser, Lois, "A Study of Factors Involved in Undergraduate Use of the Library," *Vanderbilt University Abstracts of Theses*, XII (August, 1943), 35-36.
19. Ream, Bessie, "The Reading of Students and Faculty at Chicago Teachers College." Unpublished Master's paper, Graduate Library School, University of Chicago, 1943.
20. Reeves, F. W., and J. D. Russell, "Relation of the College Library to Recent Movements in Higher Education," *Library Quarterly*, I (1931), 57-66.

21. Severance, Henry O., "What Do University Students Read?" *School and Society,* XXIII (June 5, 1926), 726-28.
22. Smith, George Donald, "The Nature of Student Reading." Unpublished Ph.D. dissertation, Graduate Library School, University of Chicago, 1946.
23. Smookler, Idair, "A Report on the Voluntary Reading Habits of Students of the Women's College," *Delaware Notes,* Twelfth Series (1939), 55-68.
24. Stieg, Lewis, "Circulation Records and the Study of College-Library Use," *Library Quarterly,* XII (January, 1942), 94-108.
25. Thompson, Russell I., and John B. Nicholson, Jr., "Significant Influences on General Circulation in a Small College Library," *Library Quarterly,* XI (April, 1941), 142-85.
26. Todd, Ann McKinney, "Undergraduate Student Reading at the University of Missouri." Unpublished M.A. thesis, Graduate Library School, University of Chicago, 1948.
27. Waples, Douglas, et al. *The Library.* (Vol. IV of The Evaluation of Higher Institutions.) Chicago: The University of Chicago Press, 1936.
28. Whitcomb, Ruth Twining, "A Study of the Nonrequired Reading Done By a Selected Group of Hiram College Students over a Four Year Period, 1950-1954." Unpublished M.S.L.S. thesis, Western Reserve University, School of Library Science, 1957.

2

The Character of Modern Reading

SOME PROBLEMS SUGGESTED BY DEAN ASHEIM'S PAPER

CAUTION, Dean Asheim stressed in introducing his paper, must be used in interpreting the statistical material thus far available. None of it was methodologically unimpeachable or definitive in coverage; much of it was rather limited in scope and sophistication. The over-all picture it presented was, however, remarkably consistent and discouraging. If anything, the methodological weaknesses tended to err on the side of generosity in estimating the amount of reading done both by college students and by the general public. The only hopeful sign was the general correlation of volume of reading with extent of formal education. Despite glaring exceptions at the college level and below, people with more education do tend to read more than people with less.

Mr. Ellsworth, however, noted a marked statistical bias in those sections of the surveys that reported increasing reading as students proceeded through college. In state universities, only about 45 per cent of entering freshmen in liberal arts colleges ever graduate. In comparing freshmen and senior reading patterns, one is thus not really comparing equivalent groups. Dean Asheim agreed that researchers in this field ought to make more allowance than they have hitherto done for the weeding out of nonreaders by academic attrition.

In a similar vein, Mr. Guinzburg questioned whether we might not be putting the cart before the horse by too readily assuming from the statistics that people who have been to college read more because they have been to college. Might it not very well be that young people go to college because they already have reading interests? The non-readers to a considerable extent eliminate themselves. Thus, colleges may be too complacent in assuming from the statistics that they are developing readers. The cause and effect relationship is not clear.

This weeding-out process was, according to Dean Odegaard, confirmed by the experience of college administrators. Every admissions officer working with incoming college students notices the effect of family background not only in determining which student goes to college but also in selecting to a considerable extent the curriculum the student will pursue when he gets to college. Certainly, the fact that a student comes from a family where there are books on the shelves and where there has been some inducement to read, or, better yet, where the mother and father have done some reading, has a definite effect. One cannot escape from the fact that some students become users of books or are made users of books before they ever come close to college.

Professor Gjelsness reported that there is significant evidence that, as Mr. Odegaard suggested, lifetime readers can be identified early in life, but he did not seem to think that this interest, once established, was immutable. If, as seems to be the case, reading interest emerges at the grade school level, then its development is vitally connected to subsequent opportunities for reading presented by the whole educational program and the place of libraries in that program. There is actually evidence of a drop off in reading, often at the high school level. This may come from other emphases in the curriculum, from inadequate library facilities or from a failure of the library and book facilities to meet the interest of the student—and also from a lack of interest on the part of high school teachers. Elementary school teachers are much concerned about this problem and are worried lest they are developing readers who are later lost.

Mr. Heckscher, however, was quite disturbed by the too-ready acceptance of imperfect statistics. Their seeming "lessons" could easily lead to misunderstanding, complacency, and passivity on the part of many. Whatever they might show about the importance of background, children from the same background did not necessarily develop identically. One of his own older boys was a great reader, the other did not read at all. Similarly, despite the statistics that seemed to show that readers went to college, there were still exceptions. The best-read individual he knew, a disciple of Thoreau, decided that he could manage his own life and education by himself, and had not chosen to go to college. On the other hand, there were all the thousands of people who bought, gave and borrowed books without actually reading them.

Dean Asheim agreed with the general tenor of the criticism of the research: it did tend to be overly optimistic. He did not think, though, that present research methods could answer the "chicken and egg" problem raised by Mr. Guinzburg and Dean Odegaard. Whether a process of self selection put them in college or whether college made them readers, the research revealed only that college graduates were the most likely to read. Even though you could in isolated instances show that a person who never went to college was a good reader—even though he had to have a

dictionary beside him—Mr. Asheim did not think that
this upset the general picture.

A quite different and very active line of discussion was
stimulated by the distinction made in the research reported
by Dean Asheim between "assigned" and "free" reading,
or between "course-related" and "personal" reading. This
seemed to raise the questions: What do we mean by reading?
What kind of lifetime reading habits are we actually concerned with encouraging?

Mr. Guinzburg felt that a striking inadequacy in all the
surveys was that they characteristically contented themselves with a question like, "Have you read a book lately?"
without asking what in fact the answerer had read. Reading
of sorts was a pretty common time-consumer. The "book"
covered by a "yes" answer might be absolute junk or it
might be a practical manual of some sort.

Dean Asheim and others stressed the fact that the average
business or professional man today, far from being a non-
reader, was a continuous reader—in the sense that he cast
his eyes over print. His reading is not only professionally
oriented but job related. The amount of paper that goes
over any executive's desk today is tremendous. One must
not forget this in trying to understand why, if a business
or professional man has an hour or two in the evening for
relaxation, he might not choose to read. Provost Gross told
of a committee charged with drawing up recommended
general reading lists for engineers. After some study and
considerable recrimination from defenders of the harassed
engineers, it was decided that an engineer could not reasonably be expected to read more than four nonprofessional
books a year. And, Mr. Heckscher noted, when the weary
business or professional man does allot a moment for reading, as often as not, it goes in a random and purposeless

sampling of newspapers, magazines, digests, etc. that serves no literate purpose and leaves little behind.

In Dean Asheim's paper, it was explained that research generally reveals a greater purposiveness in men's reading as compared to women's. Professor Buck pointed out that in this purposiveness, the characteristic reading patterns of professional men are presaged far in advance by their reading patterns as undergraduates. The most intelligent and most highly motivated students, the ones that we should like to think would do the most general reading, are also the ones with the most clearly defined career goals. Thus, whatever the college's ideas of a well-rounded liberal education may be, they have their private curricular requirements to fulfill. Some of the best students go into law, an exacting profession that takes its toll. Both in law school and in practice, lawyers read a lot. But do they read anything but law? He could only think of one lawyer acquaintance who read, a distinguished judge, whose nonprofessional reading was provided by his membership in a Lincoln Book Club. Another spent all his free time turning wood on various machines. He wondered what research on this level might reveal.

Not only preprofessional training, but academic zeal in its most disinterested forms may prove inconsistent with general reading as commonly understood. Mr. Wormald remembered how the senior tutor of his college at Oxford advised him to devote all his free time before coming up to reading everything he could lay his hands on in modern literature because his honors work in Greats (classical literature, philosophy, and history) would make it impossible for him to do any such reading in the four years he would be at Oxford. In the same vein, Professor Buck wondered whether the best students in an American university today, taking an honors degree in a narrow field of specialization, are accustomed, prepared or even able to read important literature in any field but their own. How much science or social science does even the most widely read literary student ever read?

Professor Buck's hunch that course work might in fact get in the way of general reading was born out by Professor Angell. He reported that (although the studies covered by Dean Asheim showed that over-all book withdrawals increased as the student proceeded from the freshman to the senior year) a survey conducted in the Literary College of the University of Michigan by his colleague, Morris Janowitz, was less encouraging. Through student self-evaluation, it concluded that as the student went through college the amount of nonrequired, recreational reading he did diminished. Although Professor Angell felt certain that the amount of required reading increased, students gave not this but campus and social activities as the reason for the decline in their recreational reading.

Dean Asheim agreed that it was quite possible that as a student progressed through college, his independent reading might decline as his course-related reading increased. He was unhappy, however, about the category "course-related" commonly used in the surveys. If a student in a course in the twentieth-century American novel reads some novels by Faulkner as assigned reading and others on his own initiative, is it meaningful in a survey to label the reading of any one novel "course-related" and by implication less desirable?

Mr. Hamlin thought that the term "course-related" as used in the surveys was too vague. He suggested instead the use by future researchers of the more precise category "course-required." Anything not specifically required should be considered part of the student's independent reading, whether course-related or not. He cited research with freshman physics and chemistry students which showed that the difficulty of the material and the interest of the students led them to "independent" but almost universal outside "course-related" reading.

Mr. Heckscher would go even farther. The distinction between "course-related" and more general reading was misleading. All recreational reading ought to be related to an interest or major concern of the reader. If you assume that the courses a student is taking in college represent the dominant focus of his interests or feelings during that period, then it is only normal that his personal reading should be related in one way or another to those courses. "Noncourse-related reading" unfortunately suggested reading of only minor or secondary importance.

Mr. Heckscher further wondered if the senior might not have developed a wider sense than the freshman of what is and is not course-related. The freshman with a narrower conception of what is course-related may indulge in more indiscriminate sampling; the senior with a more highly developed sense of the interrelatedness of his interests may give his reading a clearer interest focus.

One of the pitfalls librarians fell into in the thirties, Mr. Vosper noted, was talking too much about recreational reading as being something quite separate from studying. This developed a difficult and dangerous dichotomy that has carried over into the terminology of subsequent research and writing. He was interested in the suggestion of Mr. Heckscher and others that there was an extension and richer use of reading as one goes from freshman to senior year. His own rather limited investigations suggested, however, that a major proportion of undergraduate reading—the same unimportant magazines, etc.—continued unchanged from the freshman to the senior year.

Dean Odegaard felt that "course-related" reading was a

most vital category that in some ways was a test of the
success of the curriculum. We have failed as teachers if, in
teaching, we have left the student so unchallenged that he
prefers going out and running the *Daily* instead of spending his time reading more sociology or more literature.
Professor Angell and he, in working on the Michigan honors
program, had come to recognize that through this extra
"course-related" reading bright students used up some of
the time not actually taken up by their curriculum. If,
therefore, one intensifies the opportunities and stimulation
of the curriculum, one would expect that more of the
student's free reading would be course-related. This he
would regard as an evidence of some degree of success in the
curriculum.

The sense of the meeting seemed to suggest that too
much of a distinction ought not to be made between course-
related and independent reading, with the imputation of
greater esteem to the latter. A pattern of random, independent reading might only imply immaturity of interest
and/or an unstimulating curriculum. As a student matures,
his interests should become more clearly defined and more
integrally related to his current curriculum. Thus, the sup-
planting of purely independent reading by course-related
reading need not imply the death of curiosity but rather
the maturity and definition of curiosity.

There was, however, a dissident element in the discussion
that preferred to follow other lines of analysis. Provost
Gross suggested a more significant classification of reading
might be the purposive distinction between cognitive and
aesthetic reading, between reading done for the functional
purpose of acquiring specific data whether for vocational
or avocational purposes, and reading done for its intrinsic
aesthetic merit and pleasure.

Mr. Ellsworth was unhappy about most of the distinctions thus far made. For him the important thing was that reading books should be a pleasure, whatever other functional motivation might bring the reader to his book. Professor Goldberg, also, felt that the joy of reading was too frequently neglected. Juniors and seniors frequently complained to him that the joy they had found in reading as freshmen was lost by their later years. Dean Asheim saw no reason why there could not be a considerable element of pleasure in the reading done for training, professional, or business purposes. However, these were not practical distinctions to make in research.

To Mr. Harwell, all the distinctions thus far made missed the point. He thought we were worrying excessively when we asked whether books bought, borrowed, or given were in fact read. For him the important thing was to have books about one in the home, whether one sat down and read any particular volume through or not. Buying books is enough, one doesn't have to read them. It is a sign of a mature reader that he knows when to put down a book after he has read ten, twenty-five or fifty pages and found that it isn't worth reading. People who buy books and have them in the home are likely to be book users as opposed to book readers. They turn to their books regularly, if only briefly at times, for the widest range of purposes. Between them and the many who do not "use" books there is a great gulf that is not revealed by such questions as "What have you read this month?"

The remainder of the discussion of Dean Asheim's paper surveyed areas for future research. Mrs. Smith pointed out that we know very little about the actual mechanical reading ability of the average college student. How can we be sure that a student will get the pleasure out of a pleasurable book or the information out of a cognitive one if he doesn't read very easily. She suggested that more colleges ought to experiment with testing incoming freshmen in reading skill, speed and comprehension. Subsequent examinations might follow reading progress through college. Mr. Pattillo thought this very much to the point. The Lilly Foundation had recently made a grant to five contiguously situated colleges for reading development. They found that the average reading ability of the entering students in these particular colleges was about eighth-grade level. Instructors found the *New York Times* too difficult for actual entering freshmen. If these figures were thought shocking, he could cite others that showed reading ability at reputable American colleges ranging as low as the level of the fourth grade.

Reading ability tests, however, were already widely used. Much less was known about other conditioning factors. Dean Odegaard wished we knew more about "course-related" readings: what courses stimulated this sort of reading? What kinds of curricula? Is there any demonstrable relationship between such reading and the deliberate objectives of the course, or the way in which it is conducted? Dean Asheim answered that Mrs. Knapp's study had attempted to deal with some of these questions.

Mr. Pattillo and Mr. Lacy also wished we had more careful comparative research statistics. Do reading patterns vary with the type of institution? Is there any demonstrable correlation with the emphasis the institution gives to teaching? What effects have such curricular features as independent study plans, senior comprehensive examinations, etc.? Mr. Lacy was particularly concerned with correlating reading evidence with such data as the size of classes, the method of teaching used (lecture, discussion, etc.), the organization of the material. Do large lecture courses always fail to stimulate reading?

Mr. Guinzburg and Dean Steere suggested, and Mr.

Pattillo concurred, that some attention might also be given to the type of student attracted to the institution. Dean Steere pointed out that we are constantly citing studies taken at specific institutions or making generalizations based upon experience with a limited number of institutions without realizing how widely the intellectual interests of students vary from institution to institution. Few realize how bad the worst are. The enormous difference in atmosphere between institutions, of course, may be more difficult to handle statistically.

President Hard suggested that library science researchers might attempt to analyze the answers to the "What have you read in the last year?" sort of question used on the admissions applications of many smaller colleges. He wondered whether any impact on reading could be detected from the great current undergraduate interest in all forms of recorded sound, the greatly increased number of poetry and drama records released and the extension of listening facilities in college libraries. Dean Asheim answered that no investigations had so far been made along these lines, though he suspected that most students who listened to recorded readings had been led to it by previous silent readings of the material, rather than vice versa.

The horizons for future research were surveyed by Mrs. Knapp in her extended remarks on Dean Asheim's paper. She stressed that the research we have so far is notable mostly for its superficiality and incompleteness. We really know very little except obvious surface facts about the nature of the reading of college students or their use of the library. Library research in general has not developed as fast as it should have and has not kept pace with the newer methods and concepts characteristic of the vanguard of general sociological research. The most exciting recent work suggested the concept of "social role" as the most important

variable in determining the maturity of reading—more
important than the level or type of education. If then the
quality of reading of the random person is best predicted by
his sense of social role and the place of reading in that role,
shouldn't we investigate the college student's sense of his
own social role? How does reading figure in that image?
Does that image embrace the "lifetime self-educators" we
hope colleges produce?

Provost Gross reminded the conference of Stendhal's
image of his own countrymen, "Instead of a diet of love
and amusement you will find in the French, reason, benevolence, economy and a great love of reading."

3

Reading in America:
Its Social and Cultural Background

BY AUGUST HECKSCHER

READING TAKES PLACE in every civilized society; but the
particular forms which it assumes depend upon a number
of factors, including the class structure, the level of technology, the major objectives and ideals of the common life.
Certain people read, and read in a certain way, in eighteenth-century England; it would be foolish to expect a
similar pattern in twentieth-century America. The style in
which books are written, as well as the format in which they
are produced are determined by the social context. The way
they are sold and distributed is shaped by, and in turn
shapes, the outer form and the inner content. These generalizations may well be stressed at the beginning, for I
conceive my task to be that of pointing out what is characteristic and special about reading in this country and in this
epoch—not to write a familiar essay on the well-read man,
as he has appeared in a disembodied form through the ages.

The America of this mid-century is marked by a number
of striking developments, some of which we have only begun to chart and to measure in their full impact. We have
our own style of education, our peculiar form of family
life. We are making over our cities, or at least letting them

make *us* over, as they sprawl incontinently across the countryside. We are creating an economy which puts an enormous emphasis on consumption, while we are providing the
leisure which makes possible consumption on an unprecedented scale. Many older predilections, such as our predilec-
tion for action rather than thought, remain, and business
leadership, though in a changing form, continues to domi-
nate our society. Over all this hangs the vast transformation
brought about by the accelerating rate of technological
change and by America's new position in the world. It is
within such a framework that we must look at reading today. The plan of this paper, after some preliminary discussion, is to deal more or less chronologically with reading
habits through the life span, as they are affected by such
considerations as I have mentioned.

America is not a book-reading country: I would hazard
that as a generalization at the start. To support it I shall
try to avoid statistics, though a good many are available,
and they could be cited to support the thesis. Mr. George
Gallup can show that in the United States we read less than
in Australia, far less than in Canada, far less than in Great
Britain; that our college graduates, though reading more
than those who went no further than high school, still in a
disconcerting proportion can go through a year without
(in the old phrase) having "cracked" a book. It can be
shown that the amount of the recreation dollar which is
devoted to books has declined substantially since the First
World War, and disturbing comparisons can be made between the amount spent on books with the amount spent
on betting on dogs and horses. If I keep clear of statistics, it
is not because of any desire to minimize the importance of
significant research which has been done in this area, but
because the point I wish to make is essentially one of definition, not quantitative measurement.

In brief, I want to attach a somewhat special meaning to
the word "book," and a special meaning to the word "reading." The old distinction between poetry and prose—in
the former the lines come out unevenly at the right hand
margin while in the latter they do not—may be extended
to mark the difference between a book and a nonbook. Thus
it could be argued that what is between hard covers is a
book, and what is between soft covers is a magazine or
something else. But the paper-bounds break down this convenient categorizing, and they help remind us of the ob-
verse: that not everything is necessarily a book which
appears between hard covers. Thus there are bound pamphlets, and manuals, and theses, and tracts, a whole series
of productions in prose which, however serviceable, do not
belong in the honorable company of books. The distinction
eludes the collector of statistics, and I am not certain that
it should not at best be left somewhat shadowy and vague.
It is enough for my purposes to argue that what America
does not do is to nurture and cherish to a notable degree
the kind of reading matter which deals with general ideas
and with the deeper relationships and moods and customs
of men and women.

A book in the sense I am using it can be defined as a
creation, rather than a concoction; it holds the mirror to
events, either true or imagined, but it makes sure that these
events have passed through an ordering and seeing mind.
It is designed to have a life beyond the season or the year
in which it is published, and it is aimed at some part of man
that is general and basic, so that its potential audience is
wider than any particular group in society. I am not argu-
ing that it must necessarily be a *good* book, or succeed in
all its aims. "We owe a great deal to bad books," says so
discerning a critic as Virginia Woolf; "indeed we come to
count their authors and their heroes among those figures

who play so large a part in our silent life." A detective
story or a western can, I suppose, figure more vitally in
the imagination of a growing boy than many a classic read
under compulsion, and it may provide for his elders a more
somnolent influence than perusing Tennyson's *Lotus Eat-
ers*. But even in these lesser works some elements must appear, some gift of transfiguration and harmony, which the
do-it-yourself manual or the textbook does not possess.

Secondly, I would attach a particular sense to the word
reading. To show how paradoxical are these seemingly simple terms, we might begin by saying that reading is not
necessarily done with the eye. To be read to aloud is certainly to be on the way to being made (in Bacon's phrase)
a "full man," or perhaps more significantly, a "full child."
Whether poetry is best read by the ear or the eye is an open
question. Whatever else we may deplore in the wilderness of
present-day technical gadgetry, there is certainly no reason
for looking with anything but satisfaction at the development of spoken recordings which now form an important
part of any library. Having said that reading may be by
ear, we must now say that not everything is reading that is
taken in by the eye. We learn many things, we analyze
them, we consult and dissect printed materials. But when
we read them we apply a kind of reflection and judgment,
a detached and critical spirit, which gives the experience a
quality of its own. What has been called "the humane passion for disinterested reading" is something we recognize
instinctively when it flowers in ourselves or in others; it is
the factor without which books cannot exist, or exist merely
as dead things.

No statistics can count the circulation of books in the
form to which I have limited them, and no polling can really
measure reading. There are, to be sure, suggestive approaches. The poll conducted by *Life* magazine (of which

the results have not been decoded and released) has an interesting breakdown, which tries to get at the motives and objectives of reading, asking the individual whether he reads for self-improvement, for recreation, or "because he has nothing better to do." Yet without statistics, we can surely agree that Americans have their shortcomings in this field. They live in a sea of printed matter, they flounder in sensations; their eye is continually assailed and their mail burdened with printed material. But they still do not do much in the way of reading books. It is interesting to note that even with the widest definition, book publishing consumes less than 1 per cent of the paper used in this country in a year. Book reading may well consume no greater proportion of the free hours available to the population.

We do not draw much encouragement from looking at the more obvious manifestations of the reading process. Our bookstores are few, and are usually combined with the selling of other lines of goods running from antiques to greeting cards. They will do as much as a third of their year's trade in the Christmas season. Are we really to suppose that gift books are read? Are they not often both given and received as indications of status or marks of a not-necessarily existing intellectual appetite? Most of us remember separating out as children the books from the "real presents" we received. It is recorded that Gibbon, on presenting one of the numerous volumes of the *Decline and Fall of the Roman Empire* to his patron, the Duke of Gloucester, received only the gruff comment: "What? ah! Another damned big square book, eh!" No doubt but many of those who receive in the Christmas season books from friends and business associates would, if they were candid, acknowledge the gift in the same way.

Libraries are a supplement to the bookstore, but roughly a fifth of the population is estimated to have no access to either a local bookstore or a library. Like museums, libraries in recent years have been humanized and have let in the light. Where modern buildings exist, there is no longer the long flight of marble steps to make the approach hazardous and ceremonious. A profusion of books about, accessible and inviting, takes the place of the secret stacks and grottoes from which, under conventional systems, the sought-for volume mysteriously and at long last emerged. All this is to the good, and it never has seemed better to me than when exported, as it has been in the Free Library given by the Americans to the people of West Berlin. Yet libraries in this country not only are out of reach of too many, but they are lacking grievously in financial support. They are fighting a hard battle for a place in the community, and the library staff receive scant signs, either monetary or otherwise, of the appreciation which should be their due.

If the possession of books is a sign of bookishness, the United States must be acknowledged to make a poor showing. A population so constantly on the move as ours can scarcely be expected to amass large quantities of what are undoubtedly the heaviest, most difficult and most costly of all things to transport. It is true that there has been a recent tendency to re-establish books as a desirable element of interior decoration, and there are now, as I suppose there have always been, those who are ready to buy books by the yard in order to fill their waiting shelves. Yet how few households have any collection of books at all or any place to put one! The plans of present-day homes shown in the popular magazines usually include a "den" or a "study"; but this room turns out on closer inspection to be for sheltering the television set. In other periods and in more bookish societies it was not uncommon to rate wealth in terms of books. "So and so is well off," Thomas Carlyle would say; "he is worth at least 3,000 volumes." The bibliophile

Holbrook Jackson estimates that according to this criterion Montaigne when he died was worth 1,000 books, Robert Burton, 1,700, Samuel Pepys, 2,474—and so on.

To have books around is itself a virtue, and I do not mean to run down those who possess them because they give a pleasant warmth of color and diversity to their walls. Francis Meynell, in a paper read last spring before the Friends of the Columbia Libraries in New York, reminds us that books in the past have not infrequently been put to a variety of odd uses. Sydney Smith found "no furniture as charming as books"; the artist Burne Jones maintained that their principal merit was "to prop up models in difficult positions." All that the wise teacher and the good librarian can do will never be a substitute for the books which the child comes upon at home, perhaps long neglected and unread by his elders, yet offering to him not only the thrill of discovery but a sense of entering into wilderness which he can subdue and conquer for his own. It is a pity indeed that so few of todays' children have that advantage. A survey taken in the twenties reveals that in a particular area of Ohio the average number of books owned per family was 120, with the average rising to 148 outside the metropolis with its numerous cramped apartments. This was considered a small number at the time. But I wonder how many homes in today's suburbia have a dozen volumes, far less a hundred.

The physical aspects of books in America further reveal the essential unbookishness of the population. The techniques of packaging and of industrial design have largely colored the once sacred field of typography. A volume is expected to have a satisfactory "bulk," rather than a legible and inviting type page. It puts infinitely more emphasis on the jacket, which will be soon discarded, than on the binding, which will presumably remain upon the shelf. English trade books manage to retain the capacity to invite reading, to tempt one into perusal and digestion, one opens them still with something of the emotion of a William Hazlitt. "O delightful," he exclaims, "to cut open the leaves of a book, to inhale the fragrance of the scarcely dried paper, to examine the type." I suppose our modern publishers could find ways of injecting a synthetic scent into their volumes, but I am not really advocating that. I would only maintain that when books come to seem mere products, turned out like other products in the industrial society, they lose something important. They lose the sense of creating a world of their own, of establishing values peculiar to them, of being (as I believe at their best they should be) a kind of secret, disruptive force, working away at the foundations of things and dissolving the pretense and falsity and ugliness which always threatens to engulf the world.

The paperbacks, with their bright and appealing covers, are legitimately sleek and should look machine-made. It is often argued that the wide distribution they attain compensates for whatever decline there may be in the more traditional type of book. I would not want to be in the position of those sixteenth century humanists who lamented the coming of the printed book, on the grounds that it vulgarized learning. Yet it may be asked whether the paperback can ever be a substitute for the true book, or whether, for that matter, it can accomplish a diffusion of reading on any new and spectacular scale. We had hoped that a wholly untouched audience would be opened up by these accessible and inexpensive volumes. But in practice it has been found that the cheap novels are bought by those who had been reading cheap novels in the magazines, while the good fiction and nonfiction are being consumed by those in the colleges and elsewhere who have been providing all along the market for this fare. The paperbacks are a valuable supplement; but unless the true books, with their special aura and printing style, keep the flame going at the center, the art of reading will suffer.

I do not wish to catalogue here the many well-known and obvious factors which combine to render the United States an uncongenial soil for reading; they should emerge in my discussion of reading in the various stages of the life cycle. But I would like to take two concepts basic to political theory and sociology, seeking their relationship to the rather pessimistic point of view of the status of reading which I have been expressing. Community and Authority: they have been vital elements in all going societies, and yet in the United States they are either seriously undermined or else they are appearing in new guises so that it is difficult to acknowledge them.

The sense of community makes reading, in the true sense, possible. This may appear strange, for reading is characteristically pursued in solitude and finds its devotees among those who are least susceptible to the pressures of the day. But is not solitude itself related to community—to a feeling of shared values, to the conviction of being sustained and nourished by a wide and permanent framework of civilization? An atomistic society breeds the loneliness of the individual lost in the crowd. The viable community breeds the solitude of the mature human being, withdrawn for purposes of renewal and refreshment yet still one with an enduring company.

Reading is always close to conversation; it involves a shared experience, a give-and-take with the minds of one's own age and of past epochs. The writer requires a kind of resonance to be able to do his work; the reader requires the conviction that he is both receiving and giving. Because the physical act of reading is so quiet and solitary it may be assumed that the lines of communication run only in one

direction, and that of all pleasures it is that which remains
even when the foundations of the world fall apart. Our
experience, however, tells us this is not so. Every decisive
moment of influence or regeneration has come with the
awareness of intimate communication, of oneness not alone
with the author but with kindred spirits widely scattered
in time and place. For a while a society in the process of
rapid change or of dissolution may survive on stored memories and habitual affinities; the wise men of the time retreat
to go over in silence the accumulation of art and literature
with which they are familiar. The citizens as a whole, however, can no longer recreate the mood in which reading is
fruitful, and cut off from the vital forces uniting them
with their own kind, they fall back on crude sensationalism
or frivolous entertainment.

The sense of community has been strained in the United
States today, and indeed throughout the whole Western
world. The social order in which men and women have
lived, where they have found their values expressed and
transmitted, has been changed irreversibly under the impact of vast wars, the surge of population, the onrush of
technology and the changed patterns of family and community life. There are new communities emerging, but
these have not yet been warmed by experience or even
defined by insight and prophecy. There is a passage in the
writings of John Jay Chapman which expresses well this
sense of alienation and its effects on reading and culture.
He speaks of New York in the years before and after the
turn of the century; what he says of the great city is true
today on a scale as broad as Western civilization.

The young person born in New York during the past quarter
century [writes Chapman] has been like a rat in a bag which
the rat-catcher keeps agitating lest the creature's teeth get a
purchase on the prison. The New York youth cannot be ex-

pected to get hold of any idea while the kaleidoscope is turning so furiously. He is numb and dizzy. He cannot connect his reading with his environment; for the books of the world have been projected out of quietude. They reflect stability, depth, relaxation, and all those conditions of peace and harmony which make thought possible. The youth, therefore, discards books as incomprehensible—foolish, in fact. Education has for the time being lost its significance.

It is not only the communities of town and village, of farm and city, which have been disrupted by the turbulent years since Chapman wrote. The wider community of the nation has ceased to have the meaning it once had. Can a geographical unit that cannot suffice for economic viability or for self-defense be made artistically relevant? The region still maintains a wholeness and harmony, after the social class and the national state no longer provide the framework within which significant experience takes place; and at the other end of the scale an international community waits to be born. But for the present we should be hard put to it were we compelled to read or to write exclusively about the men of this new community—airmen, and international civil servants, and a few other stray figures who seem homeless and even faintly subversive. Moreover, we should find it hard going if the literature of the Orient were to be made our daily fare. Yet in time there will surely be a circulation of books all around the globe. There will be a new community, and new writers and readers to match its scope.

Related to the breakup of community is the undermining of authority in the United States and in a comparable degree wherever industrialization has done its work. Settled authority is essential in a society where reading is a familiar art. The work has got a bad name among us, being too often associated with tyranny or compulsion. Yet in fact it is

the opposite of these, and involves rather an assent and recognition springing from below than constraint imposed
from above. Authority may be defined for our purposes as
being a power that is more than persuasion but less than
force; it rests on legitimacy and tradition in matters of
state, and in habitual deference to what is known to be
tried and excellent in matters of art and culture. Authority
is always a two-way process. The best teacher in the world
is without this saving gift, except as there resides in the
student a readiness to acknowledge the possibility of de-
cency and the validity of the search for truth.

The authority of books rests likewise in their capacity
to evoke agreement, not to their views, but to their intrinsic
merit and their underlying claims of integrity. In settled
ages there is an aristocracy in these spiritual and artistic
matters, and men go confidently among the known giants.
Where the achievement fails of greatness, or even of success
on its own terms, there are standards by which its shortcomings can be judged and by which its attainments, such
as they are, can be enjoyed. Pride and pity—both in the
best sense, a sense so rare as almost to have made the words
unintelligible to the present day—are given a stage to express themselves.

It seems unnecessary to labor the point that authority has
been corroded in the society we know. It leads a threadbare
existence in the home, in the school, in the political order.
Individuals here and there still possess the power to wake
it, and still find those who will gladly respond. But the in-
stinctive and habitual submission to ways and methods, to
standards of judgment and tests of truth, is not an ordering
principle of our condition. In terms of reading, this means
that the family and the school do not possess in the degree
they once did the capacity to bring young people along the
paths where intellectual and imaginative adventuring

lie. It means that men and women are afterwards cast loose amid a bewildering profusion of literary products, all more or less equal, or all thought to be equally bad. The exceptions are the so-called classics, but these hold what sway they do more by convention than by shared understanding. Their "authority" is of the debased kind which equates the word with death and pedantry.

There is no use bemoaning unduly what appears to be the loss of order and degree in the world, for order and degree have their own ways of returning among men, usually through channels where they are least sought. What looks like chaos to one generation is often an emerging harmony which the next generation will take for granted. Yet the ages where reading is an art, and where books are cherished, have been ages when the basic assumptions of society were not challenged and differences were achieved within the framework of accepted values and familiar themes. We ride the whirlwind, and books can only exert their spell by winning afresh, from each individual on each reading, a recognition of their worth. It is not surprising that they do not have the quiet, universal influence we would ask for them, an influence which, if it existed, would subtly transform our libraries, our bookstores, the physical appearance of our printed volumes, and in time give its color to the whole cast of the modern mind.

Our culture puts its emphasis on youth. The child is urged forward in paths of self-expression and self-development, and no effort is spared to give him the tools through which he may find himself. Children's books are brighter, clearer, more resourceful in the use of text and picture than they have perhaps ever been before. Yet there is another side to the picture, for the same society that stresses self-development puts a premium on adjustment in human relationships and ultimately on conformity. We want our children to be themselves, yet not to be very different from our neighbor's child; to be fulfilled, yet not to be led into byways or thickets; in short, to be readers, but not to be bookish. We see books as tools, reading as a means; but worry a good deal lest reading should become something done for its own sake, or as an end in itself. Much of the folklore of American youth deals in disparagement with the bespectacled boy, the outsider, the bookworm. Today's parents, while paying lip service to the need for more and better reading, are a little worried lest their enthusiasm carry too far. "It's all very well," said one parent of my acquaintance to her son's principal, "—it's all very well for you schoolteachers to be saying that reading books is important, but what would you do if your child swallowed it hook, line, and sinker!"

The schoolteachers themselves encourage, it seems to me, a kind of reading short of the ideal through their anxiety to hitch on to the child's natural interests. Wisely enough they avoid seeing the child as a bag to be stuffed, a maw to be crammed full of what somebody has decided children ought to be familiar with. They look for a developing tendency, and they seek to satisfy it. Material is keyed to take advantage of the curiosity aroused by everyday surroundings, by the child's concern with knowing how and why in the crucial years of growth. All this is to the good. The danger is that they will indeed satisfy the child, will tell him what he wants to know, without giving him the added challenge which could make of him a reader of books, and not merely a consulter of the printed page. A child's questions need to be answered, but more than that, his interests need to be evoked, to be steadied and enlightened, to be enlarged and related to his personality, I would guess that the weakest link in the chain of getting children to read is precisely here: at the moment when a passing curiosity must be

turned into a permanent interest, when the carefully prepared reading material must be superseded by the true
book. Too many children never make that leap. The factual materials of their early grades give way to the do-it-
yourself manuals of their later life; the artfully concocted
stories of their reader give way to the stories which are
similarly concocted by the editors of the mass-circulation
magazines.

A myth common to our American culture is that men
and women are born having interests. The young people
grow up with the idea that at some moment there will
develop within them an interest which will determine their
choice of a career and shape their path through life. I have
known students at college who were as appalled to discover
that they had no clear and decisive interest as they would
have been to discover that some vital organ was missing
from their makeup. My own guess is that interests are not
the cause of what people do, so much as they are the result.
What we pass through, what we experience and learn and
feel and read, gives us our sense of direction and priority.
The man who waits around to be interested in some particular job is likely never to take a job at all. So it is that at some
point in the development of reading habits there must be
a jump beyond what the child thinks he wants; there must
be immersion in a new condition, with the child gently, but
perhaps not too gently, prodded by such remnants of discipline as today's teacher retains.

There is much to be said for this kind of prodding and
almost nothing, it seems to me, to be said against it. The
healthy young American animal is not likely to be turned
into a bookish recluse. As for being turned into a reader,
all our experience suggests that the boy or girl who reads
easily and widely moves with confidence through the realms
of life, naturally interested in all that is going on, naturally

a leader among peers. "The true reader is essentially young," says Virginia Woolf. "He is a man of intense curiosity, of ideas; openminded and communicative, to whom reading is more in the nature of brisk exercise in the open air than of sheltered study; he trudges the high road, he climbs higher and higher upon the hills until the atmosphere is almost too fine to breathe in; to him it is not a sedentary pursuit at all." I wish that this picture could be got across to worried parents and made more prevalent among youth itself.

Like every form of skill, reading must be acquired, and acquired with a degree of perfection if it is to take us "higher and higher upon the hills." The emphasis now placed upon reading techniques seems to me one of the hopeful elements in secondary education. As I understand what is being done, "techniques" is actually too narrow a word, for the child is made to master not only words but ideas, to see the relation between art and life, and to understand (as the good reader must) what is the calling and task of the writer. I remember analyzing sentences in school, but it was not until much later that the structure of paragraphs was part of my English courses. Now from the earliest grades there is stress upon what the author is really saying, what point he is trying to get across. The ability to separate the central theme from subsidiary and qualifying considerations is brought out almost as soon as the child can spell.

Much can be done at this stage also in giving children a feel for books as entities—a combination of soul and body, of form and content. The child is a natural collector, and with a little encouragement books can seem as natural an object of his passion as soldiers or sea shells. He is quick to appreciate pictures, and can be led to an appreciation of type and binding. At the Scribner bookstore in New York

I was told recently that the children of a particular school are always welcomed and allowed to handle and peruse books on their own, for they show a consistent respect for the volumes. I do not know how this is achieved, but if the secret were shared we might see a generation in this country with a new attitude toward books and reading.

I was myself greatly influenced by having done some printing while still at school. It is a difficult and meticulous craft, and I am not sure whether it could be recommended for the majority of students. But if we are going to see a revival of handicrafts in this country, as I believe we may, printing should take its place among those which are being taught. The increasing leisure to which men and women can look forward in life makes the provision for some secondary enterprises almost essential, and carpentry, ceramics, printing, etc., can be made to serve liberal, as opposed to vocational, ends. Certainly the setting of type and the development of typographic style gives to a young person a feeling he could not otherwise acquire for the nature of words and the meanings they seek to convey. The good printer realizes how modest, at best is the role he plays; it is his function to transmit what others have dreamed and wrought, and the little pieces of lead which he marshals are to him the witnesses of insights and spiritual forces.

If things go well in youth the moment carries when all is forgotten in the thrill of reading for its own sake. The good teacher, the careful steps by which skill is cultivated and enhanced, the graded reading materials, the lure of volumes as valued acquisitions—all give way to the sheer enjoyment of the quest itself. A fire has been lit, and it consumes everything in its path. This is the mood in which whole shelves are devoured, the most varied subject matters falling into place in the mind's expanding universe. The mood passes, other ventures exert their spell, but if something of the original excitement can be preserved, perhaps in a new interest that persists to order his life, perhaps even in a few volumes which are felt to contain a light of their own, the young person has graduated with honors from the school of reading. From then on he is a citizen of the free city of books.

The college years should be the time, above all, for reading. The college library should be the heart of the university; indeed in a real sense it should be the university itself, around which everything else revolves and circulates. The college graduate should form the element of the population which provides a steady and widening market for the best books. All these things should be, but as everyone knows they are only very partially achieved. With vastly more college graduates in proportion to our population than Great Britain we read proportionately fewer books. I remember one of my classmates at Yale who boasted that up to his graduation day (and he did graduate) he never had been in the library. I could also give the name of a college president whom the library was not to glimpse during his tenure. These are admittedly unrepresentative cases, but it does seem that some other means of communication than books, some other art than reading, suffices too often for getting a college education.

The United States is about to witness a vast expansion in the college population. It is easy to assume that this will mean a comparable expansion of the demand for books. At the very least it could be expected that textbooks will have an unprecedented circulation, as well as paperbacks, which now are spread out in such an enchanting array in every college bookstore. These things will undoubtedly happen, but perhaps not in quite the degree mere numbers of college students would suggest. It is possible, moreover that if we simply expand existing institutions, making everything more crowded and hurried, narrowing the function of a college and making its aims more vocational, there will be less reading rather than more.

The complaint of the American college has been, incongruously enough, lack of leisure. The refrain one invariably hears is that there is not enough time for reading, not enough for thinking or for pursuing the quiet errands of the mind which should be at the heart of the educational process. The extracurricular activities absorb a student; coeducational diversions distract him. Courses are numerous and the required hours in the classroom restrict, both for him and his professors, the periods of free inquiry. What ought to be a life apart, organized on its own lines to achieve its special ends, has become more and more a replica of the world outside, subject to the world's pressures and submissive to its standards. The modern college is the American community writ small. This is especially true now that married students represent so substantial a part of the college population—14 per cent, according to figures just issued. Is it not almost certain that the influx of the next college generations will increase the sense of haste and pressure?

Yet while it is possible I must make the argument in favor of leisureliness at college—the quality that is inseparable from true reading and true learning. At the Twentieth Century Fund we have been doing some thinking on this subject of leisure, and though we are not ready to state conclusions, I can tell you something of how our minds have been moving. One of the questions we have to decide is where, in different circumstances, the line is to be drawn between leisure and work. Are the years of college, for example, to be put in one category or the other? What aspects of college life are to be considered the activities of leisure? Without stopping to give the steps in our reasoning let

me say that a liberal education, aimed at the pursuit of virtue and truth and the development of the whole man, seems
to be the very essence of leisure. Conversely, education
aimed at preparing a person specifically for a job is an adjunct of work, and indeed work itself. If a liberal arts training *is* leisure, then how can the students complain that they
have no leisure? Either their training has been subtly nar-
rowed and professionalized, or else they misconceive leisure
to be mere relaxation and aimlessness.

For a man to complain that at college he has no leisure for
books is, therefore, a contradiction in terms. While he is
true to the liberal arts he is pursuing the life of leisure in its
ideal form, and the essence of that life is reading. Experience plays its part in the attainment of wisdom; the formal
lecture, the pervasive influence of the wise teacher, are important. But within the framework of the college, and at
the time of life when college education takes place, books
are the chief instrumentality by which the student finds
himself, defines his interest and reveals to himself his place
in the world. I do not know what but books you can put at
the center of a university. I do not know how you can have
a university if this center is blurred.

How we are going to keep this emphasis through the
years and changes ahead is a problem; yet it is conceivable
that the new conditions will compel us to put more reliance
on books, rather than less. It may well prove impossible to
advance along the line of small courses, individual tutoring,
and round-table seminars. The press of numbers will work
against them; we can expect to produce neither the teachers
nor the physical installations essential for fulfilling many of
the most agreeable of present-day reforms. Numbers will
force solutions of their own, and perhaps one of the solutions will be a greater reliance than hitherto on the student's
own capacity to read.

The development of our colleges has been toward a more humane and enlightened organization of learning, combined with surroundings constantly more bizarre and distracting. Now some of the improvements of recent decades may be sacrificed, but at the same time greater care and attention may be devoted to the atmosphere and environment of learning. Large lecture courses or even courses by television need not frighten us if the rest of the student's time is spent amid circumstances which encourage his private intellectual pursuits. What would be fatal, on the other hand, are large courses and impersonal teaching carried on in the midst of a little society where fraternities, athletics and various business enterprises set the tone of living and thinking.

This image of students going their own way, urged and pressured only by the inner drive toward truth, necessarily implies a rethinking of the role of a college library. That this is actually going on is evidenced by the new student library here, as well as by comparable experiments elsewhere. The need is for books accessible to all the students, in great numbers and variety—books that can be taken down from the shelves and felt and handled; all this in a place lit by the bright day, easily entered, pleasantly accommodating in the comforts and amenities which it offers. The need is also for books that can be carried away and made serviceable to the student in his own haunts. The paperbacks serve this function supremely well. They can be quite literally consumed and disembowelled without anything irreplaceable having been lost. I understand that some college libraries are making available to students books on long term loans, so that they can in effect have personal collections during their period at the college.

A college education focused on the library, with its days leisurely and its leisure finding expression in reading, could

hardly fail to produce graduates who would go on reading
in later life. The habit of books is at least as catching as
other habits of a less useful kind. Yet it seems to me that it
could do more than it now does toward keeping its alumni
informed about current literature. Might it not be assumed
that graduates would be interested in knowing the latest
developments and the newer contributions in areas where
their major studies had been pursued? A list of the year's
outstanding books compiled by the faculty of a man's Alma
Mater should be at least as important to him as similar lists
compiled by book reviewers and journalists.

This brings us to reading during the active period of a
man's life. I have already indicated a few of the difficulties
in the way of continuous reading, and indeed the whole
development of American life could be cited in this connection, from the first appearance of the automobile to the
latest suburb superimposed upon a vanishing countryside.
Most of the specific social changes have reduced the influence of books, though there is usually a certain compensa-
tory action. Thus the movies and TV provide a competing
form of entertainment, but they also stir up interests which
books alone can satisfy. This is similar to what I have seen
happening in the field of newspapers. One might suppose
that having seen a national convention televised, people
would not be anxious to read about it in the next morning's
paper. Actually they like most of all to read about something which they have directly experienced. The press on
these occasions plays something of the role of a piece of
dramatic criticism, evaluating the play one has seen the
night before. And all books are, in the deepest sense, a
criticism of life. It is significant that when people have
been most involved in the realities of their fate, as in periods
of war and depression, the amount of reading in our society
has mounted. This is not merely because there is then more

time, or greater need for economy, or less competition from consumer goods. It is also because people have felt themselves immersed in events, and in books they have found their own experience made comprehensible and deepened by art.

The steady tendency toward classlessness in American society has also had ambivalent effects on reading. The rise in the income of the average family has created a vast market for culture which has been only partially tapped by booksellers and publishers. More significant from our point of view than the new millions of literate and well-off suburbanites has been the erosion of the comparatively small literary elite, which once set standards for all those coveting admission to its circle. There was formerly, no doubt, a great deal of snobbishness and pretense among cultural climbers, with people in the least likely circumstances affecting a degree of learning which they had by no means attained. But at least these people bought books, and acted as if they had read them. Perhaps on occasion they even did read them. Today there is less pretense if only because there is no established elite and no ladder with firm rungs to mount.

What has taken the place of the moderately hierarchical society which America maintained through the first years of the century is a congeries of shifting groups, not readily defined or identified. Men and women are nervous because they cannot decide to which they should hope to belong, nor how to get in when they do decide. Their nervousness does not lead to any consistent plan of self-improvement. The marks which qualify them for one group or another have very little to do with wealth (since wealth tends to be roughly equal for so many of them). They have less to do with culture, or with the books they read and the authorities they quote. They have to do, rather, with the games they play, the cars they drive, all the mysterious subtleties of consumer choice. Books that tell people how to get over their nervousness, or how to cope with the practical questions of daily living, therefore attain an audience in suburbia which more purely literary works cannot match.

Labor unions in the United States have never seriously tried to inspire in their members that desire for self-cultivation which has been conspicuous in the labor movement of England and the Continent. As for the business community, it has not, at least up to the present, put book-reading upon the list of virtues which the successful executive should possess. But this may be changing. Despite the present wave of enthusiasm for scientific education, there is a new value being set upon the liberal arts, especially for practical men. The tasks of administration and executive action are found to be so complex under modern conditions, and to mix questions of ends and objectives so inextricably with the humdrum questions of means, that the wells of true wisdom seem not too deep to draw upon. Experiments have been made by several companies in subjecting their top men to the influences of a liberal training. These cannot but have the effect of putting books and reading on the map for an important and highly influential segment of the population. To associate reading with action, and books with business, is to open a new highway through the American cultural scene.

Many of the separate elements of contemporary society are working against the cause of books and reading. But taking this society as a whole, one finds much that should strengthen that cause. The depth and rapidity of current change, of which I have already spoken, imposes constant tests. We are called to master ourselves and our environment in ever-new circumstances. The answers we need are not in books, but the qualities necessary to attain the answers—a basic wisdom, an alive sense of life's meaning and direction—will be found through the use of books, or probably not found at all. Certainly these qualities will not be discovered in any remembered dogma or easily summed up formula. Adult education, in the form of genuinely liberal studies for adults and not merely vocational training, is a promising development. But something even more important is the capacity of men and women to gain for themselves, through their own reading and reflection, a feeling for the things of their changing world that count and that must be carried forward. Flexible minds and strong spirits can alone be equal to the contemporary challenge; and these are not attained where books are neglected and intellectualism is disparaged. The statesmen who rode out the storms of another revolutionary age—men like Adams, Jefferson and Madison who imposed the pattern of their thought upon our early history and institutions— were among the best-read men of their own or of any period.

For another reason the age drives us in the direction of more and deeper reading. It is an age of subtle powers and pressures, bearing down upon men at a thousand points so insistently that they are scarcely felt; and the only hope of withstanding them is the cultivation of an inward world of being. These powers are not political but social; they come from the community, not from the state, and they are basically related, it seems to me, to the emphasis on consumption which marks our economic system. The economic need is for men and women to keep buying at all costs, to replace last year's model and to take on something new whether they like it or not. The myth that they do like it must be fostered and encouraged. The citizens must be made to believe that happiness is the object of existence and that their true happiness is in the unending acquisition of material things.

The nightmarish extension of tendencies we see at work about us is sketched in Huxley's *Brave New World*. I am indebted to a recent article in the *Political Science Quarterly*, by Martin Kessler, for pointing out what distinguishes Huxley's grim Utopia from Orwell's *1984*. Orwell saw a society of scarcity, in which the power of the state was used for deliberate oppression and for rooting out the elements of discontent which were bound to appear. But Huxley was writing of something that touches much nearer home—a society of abundance. Here power was used to condition the nature of men and women's desires, to persuade them that they were happy and that true happiness depended on the state.

The conditioning of desire and the propagation of the myth of happiness—these are, unhappily, not alien to our culture. We shall never arrive, let us hope, at the methods Huxley described; but we must be on our guard against the underlying drift. For this reason I spoke earlier of books being "a kind of secret, disruptive force." It is through them that a society finds the way of escape from what otherwise must appear an unbreachable net of circumstance and pressure. Books speak directly to the individual; what they have to say comes as from another region, carrying the accents of disinterestedness and freedom. Through reading men regain the chance to become disengaged and to assert themselves against the outside world. The totalitarian society must, in the nature of things, burn books, or else rewrite them. While they exist, and while men and women have the wit to enter with the right spirit into the domain they create, there is always the possibility of being a little apart from things, of standing up and very firmly and quietly saying *no*. "No, this is not what I desire, even though you insinuate very cleverly that it is. No, this is not happiness; and besides, happiness as you conceive it is not the chief end of life."

There are two ways of looking at the implications of Change and Power as they may show themselves in our society. One may conclude that together they undermine the basis of judgment and the capacity for independent thought. Where Whirl is King, and where unseen forces eat away at the free mind, books may be thought to have only the dusty upper shelf of the world for their place. Or it is possible to take the more optimistic point of view and to say that these very compulsions, by making books necessary to our continuance as a free society, will ensure that they are given a larger role among us. For my own part I do indeed incline to the brighter view. Human societies, like individual human beings, have an instinct for survival. If the reading of books will save them—why, then they will even read books.

I have threatened to go through the ages of man, and so I must deal briefly in conclusion with reading in the later years. This is a real problem and a real opportunity, given the tendency toward early retirement and the boon of added years through medical advances. In this field we see another genuine contribution by machines to the reading process (I spoke earlier of the advantages of *listening* to poetry); for older people may have books on tape and records. I am not aware of whether study has been given to the kind of books older people should read, comparable to the work on appropriate reading for children. I rather hope it may not be done, for the essence of reading for older people is, I should think, that it be precisely the same as in all the other periods of maturity. Indeed it may be said that so long as a man reads he is young, and that, if he judges himself to be old, then there is no longer any motive or desire for books.

It is impossible, I would suppose, for a person to begin reading in the later years. He may have loved books and neglected them, and return to them as to a woodland of his youth; or he may never have stopped reading, and go on with zest unabated to the end. But a man cannot "take up" reading, when other delights and occupations have begun to fail. The need for preparation is unescapable, and the habit once found, is an insurance and a proof of security.

At best one reads little enough of the books of this world. Van Wyck Brooks in a jotting from his recently published notebook debunks the claims which have been made for the omnivorousness of certain famous men. Thus Hitler is said by one historian to have read all the 7,000 military books in his library; Lawrence of Arabia is said to have read 40,000 and Thomas Wolfe, 20,000. Indeed Wolfe, no doubt with himself in mind, described Eugene Gant in *Look Homeward Angel* as "pulling books out of a thousand shelves and reading them like a madman. . . . He read insanely by the hundreds, the thousands, the tens of thousands." But, says Van Wyck Brooks: "How tiresome all this and how untrue." He figures that he himself for the last twenty years has been obliged to read six or seven hours a day, every day. And how many books has he read in all? "Something less than 6,000."

Where the field is so wide, and a mortal life is so brief, is there any choice but to begin at once, and to read on, and to keep reading as long as one can? The years and books fly by, and the world, perhaps, turns out to be not quite so disheartening a place as we have sometimes been inclined to imagine it.

4

Healthy Reading in a Sick Society

SOME COMMENTS ON MR. HECKSCHER'S APPROACH

THE DISCUSSION of Mr. Heckscher's paper concentrated on his two fundamental criteria of *authority* and *community*, the latter getting the bulk of the group's attention. Professor Heyns in his comment on the paper declared himself frankly puzzled by the concept of authority as used by Mr. Heckscher, and by its applicability to present reading patterns.

Mr. Ellsworth alone was sympathetic to the concept and its utility. He felt, however, that by inferring that one should go back to older standards of authority if one wanted to encourage more reading, one was simply putting old wine in new bottles. The authority you find in society today, the commonly accepted source for acquiring knowledge, is obviously science. Science is the tremendous authority in this country. Its cult starts in the school when children are taught that through laboratory work and the methods of science we shall find out certain things about our physical world. Similarly, they are taught that when psychology becomes scientific enough, we shall learn about human relations through scientific psychology and not through the traditional humanistic traditions of the western world. We are fooling ourselves if we think that

our educational institutions (our new bottles) are made
for carrying on the humanistic reading tradition (the old
wine). They fundamentally are not oriented that way;
the students they produce are not looking for the older
humanistic pleasures we are talking about.

Professor Henderson saw the problem of authority most
immediately met in the "tone" that governs so much life
on the campus. Without a strong effort to establish an
intellectual tone, undergraduate life becomes swallowed
up in a heavy round of rather inconsequential activities
coming pretty directly out of the typical American environment. The effort to establish a tone more conducive
to learning can be established through the leadership of a
few effective figures on the campus. Without such intellectual leadership, however, colleges of the most respected
accomplishments can run down hill within a generation and
lose entirely the old tone that once made them so successful.

Community, however, rather than authority attracted
the greatest attention in the discussions. Professor Heyns
wondered whether within the large state university it
might not be possible to do more to build up small valuable
communities of students. We are impressed with the ano-
nymity of the large and variegated activities of the university; what we now have to do is to think very, very
self-consciously about promoting communities of shared
experiences among students, including the wonderful experience of having read the same book. How often does a
freshman have the exciting experience of reading a book
with his peers and then getting a chance to talk about it
outside the classroom? We musn't forget that some of the
reinforcement of the habit of reading, some of the rewards
of reading, come from the conversations one has about the
reading, the assimilation of the provocative ideas that come
out of discussion based on a common focus.

Professor Heyns felt that too little attention had been given to the possibility of organizing students into educational units that would share a common residence hall, a common curriculum and a common time table. Through such arrangements a large university can approximate some of the intimacy one expects to find in small colleges and thus provide for its students the common sharing of experiences and standards emphasized by Mr. Heckscher. In so doing, a university should increase for its students the social rewards of reading. After all, Professor Heyns pointed out, it is not necessarily self-evident to a freshman that every time he reads a book, he is going to get a kick out of it. Though we may like to think so, it is not intrinsic to the reading process itself. There are, however, social rewards—and part of them come from the group.

Professor Henderson reminded the conference that where the university fails to assume the responsibility for creating educationally desirable groupings among its students, the students will themselves form groups not always of a desirable kind. He told of his visits to continental universities where instruction consisted almost exclusively of the large, formal lecture with subsequent examination at a remote period on the contents of the lecture. This left the students with little incentive along the way to do any reading or studying in the subject of the lectures. Since the subjects of the lectures were themselves frequently formally prescribed and rather detached from the life of our time, many students had little interest motivation to read more in them. Many of these countries were undergoing considerable social change at the present time. Students imbued with great curiosity about the factors involved in social change, about political systems, etc. found very little in the formal curriculum to satisfy their curiosity. As a result, they gathered at cafés for discussion about contemporary

issues, forming informal groups in which the leadership
was frequently assumed by interested persons, organized
agitators, communists, etc.

Mr. Vosper noted that within a university there are all
kinds of small communities. Many students find theirs by
working on the student *Daily* or intramural basketball. We
here are concerned with developing communities of readers.
This can perhaps be done through curriculum planning, or
by the development of the physical plant of the library
into an environment that helps engender communities of
readers.

Mr. Marshall noted that this function has been and can
be performed by almost any good bookstore on a college
campus. Such bookstores develop their own communities,
often of lost souls. If one could come and sit by his fireplace, one would see the informal groupings based in part
on his store. He knew twenty to fifty students who came
into his store a minimum of once a week. There were four
or five who come in twice a day. That was where they met
their friends, the locus of some of their most stimulating
intellectual relationships.

Professor Brower thought that much more attention
could be paid to the student's immediate environment. The
most important loss that we have suffered in providing an
ideal student environment is the loss of a room of one's
own. This is particularly important in teaching literature.
It is only natural that a student of literature might want
it quiet some day to spout Shakespeare aloud. Yet today, if
one wants to read or just to stop and think, one finds three
roommates about. Some years ago, a Harvard freshman
asked Professor Brower, "Could I find a place where I
could read aloud? I like to read aloud. I even like to read."
Mr. Brower was very much embarrassed to admit that he
couldn't assure the student that he could find such a place.

This is not a problem that can be solved easily. Yet all persons thinking about planning for a better student environment should insist on the principle that each student should have some place to which he could retreat entirely alone.

Dean Odegaard felt that in general the discussion had given too narrow a focus to the concept of community. By community, we tend to envisage a small group of people together in one room preferably around a fireplace. Community can, however, be viewed in another sense, the sense he believed Mr. Heckscher had in mind. Community in this wider sense, implies a shared experience, extending perhaps over a continent.

A year or so ago, there was a meeting here in Ann Arbor of some foreign professors who had been spending a year in this country. One of the visiting professors, an Egyptian, in the course of some remarks at the closing luncheon, noted that he had been visiting professors in Great Britain and around the Continent. He found out that if he wanted to learn about an Italian, he would go to Rome; if he wanted to learn about a Frenchman, he would go to Paris; for an Englishman, to London; but, if he wanted to find out what a European is, he would have to come to the United States.

We are a multicultural country now in the process of achieving our distinctive culture. We are struggling to find ourselves as a nation out of an inheritance of many languages, many religions. All of the orthodoxies of Europe, all the heterodoxies are over here in the mainstream of American life. We are still in the midst of what would be a great cultural problem for any people. Twenty or thirty years ago, it was hardly decent in our colleges and universities to mention our own literature. We face perhaps the problem of making a first approximation of what we are as a people through our own idea of ourselves. Don't the larger approximations and the deeper meaning that we hope to get out of books depend in part on our starting with at least something that is familiar? Our first look at ourselves in the mirror has to be perhaps strictly trial and error. Perhaps the easiest way to get a rough definition of what we are would be through our vernacular. This may involve some rather humble beginnings pedagogically. The end, however, is basically consistent with Mr. Heckscher's concern—the definition among modern men of what they are and where they are going.

Mr. Heckscher would agree with Mr. Odegaard as to process, though he did doubt in his paper whether the dean's national community in fact existed.

PART II:
The Problem as Seen from the Classroom

5

The Humanities: Reading in Slow Motion

BY REUBEN A. BROWER

THE QUESTION, "How shall we encourage and influence the lifetime reading habit?" brings to mind the words of Solon that Croesus recalled on the funeral pyre: "I shall not call you fortunate until I learn that the end of your life was happy too." Call no student a lifetime reader until . . . No teacher can be quite sure that he has a lifetime habit of reading, and if asked whether his students have acquired it or formed good reading habits, he will probably feel most uneasy about making an answer. But assuming that we could see each student's life as a whole, *sub specie aeternitatis*, we should have to ask the further question: What reading habit are we evaluating? In the age of the New Stupid (a term Aldous Huxley once used for the age of mass literacy), nearly everyone has a reading habit of some sort. Everyone runs through the morning newspaper or *Time* and *Life* strictly as a matter of daily or weekly routine. Each social group has its "great readers," a term of admiration used to cover a wide range of activities that have little more than the printed page in common. There is, for example, reading as anodyne, and reading as extended daydream. There is reading as pursuit of fact or of useful technical know-how, and reading that may or may not be useful, when we are interested solely in understanding a theory or a point of view. Still more remote from immediate usefulness, comes reading as active amusement, a game demanding the highest alertness and the finest degree of sensibility, "judgment ever awake and steady self-possession with enthusiasm and feeling profound or vehement." Reading at this level—to borrow Coleridgean terms a second time—"brings the whole soul of man into activity." Coleridge was speaking of the poet and the power of imagination, but his words describe very well the way we read when we enter into, or rather engage in, experiences of imaginative literature. I say "amusement," not "pleasure," to stress the play of mind, the play of the whole being, that reading of this sort calls for. I am hardly suggesting that literary experience is not a "good," that it is not in some indirect and profound way morally valuable. But if it is to do us any good, it must be fun. The first line of a poem by D. H. Lawrence offers an appropriate motto for teachers and students of literature:

> If it's never any fun, don't do it!

Active "amusement" is the reading habit I am concerned with here and more especially with the role played by the teacher of literature in encouraging students to acquire it. I prefer to speak of the "teacher of literature," not the "humanities," because that noble term has become so debased in current usage, and because teachers of texts in humanities courses are or should be teachers of literature. The teacher of Plato or Hobbes or Hume is not only interpreting a system but an expression, an expression that uses many resources of language and uses them in ways that profoundly influence how we take the writer's radical meaning. We cannot subtract from our interpretations the effect of Platonic comedy or of Hobbesian metaphor or of

Hume's dispassionate irony. But it remains true that the teacher of literature in the conventional sense has a special interest in encouraging students to respond actively to all the uses of language, from the barely referential to the rhythmic. He is always more or less consciously urging his students to make themselves readers of imagination.

How will the teacher go about reaching this noble aim? By a method that might be described as "slow motion," by slowing down the process of reading to observe what is happening, in order to attend very closely to the words, their uses, and their meanings. Since poetry is literature in its essential and purest form—the mode of writing in which we find at the same time the most varied uses of language and the highest degree of order—the first aim of the teacher of literature will be to make his students better poetry readers. He will try by every means in his power to bring out the complete and agile response to words that is demanded by a good poem.

But in order not to create a wrong impression, a word needs to be said here about method, a term liable to please some and displease others for equally bad reasons. There is certainly no single sacred technique for teaching reading at the level I have in mind. In teaching literature—unlike science, one may suppose—no holds are barred, providing they work and providing that the injury to the work and to the student does not exceed the limits of humanity. The most distinctive feature of the kind of literature course I am about to describe is that the teacher does have some "holds," some ways of reading that he is willing to demonstrate and that his students can imitate. In this respect "Literature X", as I shall call it, differs from the old-time appreciation course in which the teacher mounted the platform and sang a rhapsody which he alone was capable of understanding, and which the student memorized, with the usual inaccuracies, for the coming examination.

But why a course in slow reading? The parent who has a son or daughter in college may well feel confused, since almost certainly he has at least one child with a reading difficulty, the most common complaint being that the child cannot read fast enough. As the parent himself watches the mounting lists of important books, and as he scans the rivers of print in the daily paper, he may well feel that like Alice and the White Queen, he and his children are going faster and faster but getting nowhere.

The difficulties of parent and child point to conditions that have led to the introduction of how-to-read courses in our colleges and universities. We might note first the sheer mass of printed material to which we are exposed—not to mention the flood of words and images pouring through radio and television. If by temperament or principle we resist the distracting appeals of the press and other media, we must nevertheless read a great deal as we run if we are to perform our tasks as citizens and wage earners. Add to such facts the changes in family life that have altered reading habits of both parents and children. Memorization of Bible texts and poetry is hardly common in school or home, and the family reading circle where books were read aloud and slowly, has all but disappeared even from the idyllic backwaters of academic communities. Yet many if not all of the writers of the past, from Homer to novelists like Jane Austen and Dickens, have assumed reading aloud and a relatively slow rate of intellectual digestion. Literature of the first order calls for lively reading; we must almost act it out as if we were taking parts in a play. As the average high school student reads more and more with less and less wholeness of attention, he may become positively incapacitated for reading the classics of his own or any literature. Incidentally, the parent of the slow reader should take heart: his child may not be stupid, but more than ordinarily sensitive to words. He may in fact have the makings of a poet.

Another change in precollege education is almost certainly connected with the decline in the ability to read literature of the first quality, a change that points also to profound changes in the literary public of the past century and a half. Up until thirty or forty years ago a high proportion of students of literature in our liberal arts colleges had received a considerable training in Latin or Greek. If we move back to the much smaller reading publics of the seventeenth and eighteenth centuries, the audiences for whom much of our greatest literature was written, the relative number of readers trained in the Classics becomes much higher. The principal method of teaching the ancient languages, translation into English or from English into Latin or Greek, may have had disadvantages compared with the direct method of today, but as a basic preparation for the study of literature it can hardly be surpassed. It may be doubted whether learning of a foreign langauge can take place without some translation, at least into what experts in linguistics call the "meta-language" of the learner. To translate from Latin and Greek demanded close attention to the printed word, and since the ideas being communicated and the linguistic and literary forms through which they were expressed were often quite unlike those in English, translation compelled the closest scrutiny of meanings and forms of expression in both the ancient and the modern language. Although the oldtime Classicist may not always have been successful as a teacher of literature, he cannot often be accused of lacking rigor. His students had to spend a good many hours in school and college reading some pieces of literature very attentively. One purpose of a course in

slow reading is to offer a larger number of present-day undergraduates an equivalent for the older classical training
in interpretation of texts.

It might be noted that Coleridge, who harshly criticized
the practice of Latin versemaking in English schools, paid
the highest tribute to that "severe master, the Reverend
James Bowyer":

> At the same time that we were studying the Greek tragic
> poets, he made us read Shakespeare and Milton as lessons: and
> they were the lessons too, which required the most time and
> trouble to *bring up,* so as to escape his censure. I learned from
> him, that poetry, even that of the loftiest and, seemingly, that
> of the wildest odes, had a logic of its own, as severe as that of
> science; and more difficult, because more subtle, more complex,
> and dependent on more and more fugitive causes. In the truly
> great poets, he would say, there is a reason assignable not only
> for every word, but for the position of every word; and I well
> remember that, availing himself of the synonymes to the Homer
> of Didymus, he made us attempt to show, with regard to each,
> why it would not have answered the same purpose; and wherein
> consisted the peculiar fitness of the word in the original text.

> In our own English compositions (at least for the last three
> years of our school education) he showed no mercy to phrase,
> metaphor, or image, unsupported by a sound sense, or where the
> same sense might have been conveyed with equal force and dig-
> nity in plainer words. *Lute, harp,* and *lyre, Muse, Muses,* and
> *inspirations, Pegasus, Parnassus,* and *Hippocrene* were all an
> abomination to him. In fancy I can almost hear him now, ex-
> claiming: "Harp? Harp? Lyre? Pen and ink, boy, you mean!
> Muse, boy, Muse? Your nurse's daughter, you mean! Pierian
> spring? Oh aye! the cloister-pump, I suppose!"

The Reverend James Bowyer and not Coleridge, it appears, was the original New Critic, which is to say that
much New Criticism is old criticism writ large. Bowyer's
example suggests another important point to which I shall

return: that teaching of reading is necessarily teaching of writing. The student cannot show his teacher or himself that he has had an important and relevant literary experience except in writing or in speaking that is as disciplined as good writing.

To teach reading or any other subject in the style of the Reverend Bowyer demands an attitude toward the job that is obvious but easily overlooked in our larger universities, where increasing numbers of students often impose mass production methods. The most important requirement for teaching an undergraduate course—beyond belief in what one is doing—is to keep this question in mind: What is happening to the student? Other questions soon follow: What do I want him to do and how can I get him to do it? Planning and teaching from this point of view makes the difference between a course that engages the student and one that merely displays the teacher. The perfect model for the teacher of literature as for the teacher of science is Agassiz, who would come into the laboratory, pour out a basket of bones before the student, and leave him alone to sort them out. We learn that after this introduction to the "material" of the course, Agassiz limited his teaching to infrequent visits, when he checked on the learner's progress by an occasional nod or shake of the head to say "That's right!" or "No, not that!" The great thing in teaching is to get the basket of bones before the student and get him to sorting them for himself as soon as possible. What we must avoid at all costs is sorting out all the bones in advance. Agassiz' principle is of great importance in the teaching of literature, where far too often we present the undergraduate with the end products of literary scholarship without being sure he has read or has the capacity of reading the works we are interpreting.

If we are interested in fostering a habit of reading well,

we must set up our introductory courses on a principle
very different from that underlying the older survey or
the now more fashionable history-of-ideas course. We are
not handing the student a body of knowledge, so much
"material"—the history of the Romantic Movement or an
anatomy of the concepts labelled "Romanticism"—however useful such knowledge may be at a later stage in
literary education. Our aim rather is to get the student in
a position where he can learn for himself. If we succeed,
we have reason to believe that he may acquire a lifetime
habit of learning independently. The teacher who is working toward this noble end will always be working *with*
the student, not *for* him or *over* him. Whitehead used to say
that the student should feel he is present while the teacher
is thinking, present at an occasion when thought is in
process. Those who knew Whitehead in the classroom will
know what he meant and why he never seemed to be lecturing, even before a class of a hundred or two hundred
students. His listeners never knew exactly where he was
coming out. Not knowing where one is coming out is an
essential part of the experience of thinking.

To get the student to a point where he can learn for himself requires therefore a redefinition of a "lecture." It asks
the teacher to share his ignorance with his students as well
as his knowledge. Or if professors shrink from admitting
less than omniscience, it calls for at least a Socratic simula-
tion of ignorance. What is wanted is the "nonlecture," to
borrow E. E. Cummings' happy term, an action performed
by the teacher but clearly directed to the next performance
of the student. The ideal nonlecturer is setting a job for
the student and showing him how he would go about doing
it. If he is not in fact setting a job, he will clearly indicate a
relevant kind of job to be done. A proper job means setting
a question and offering a way, not a formula, for answer-

ing it. Student and teacher must clearly understand that a course in interpretation is a course in "right answering," not a course in "right answers."

Let me now attempt to describe Literature X,[1] a course in slow reading that aims to meet the general requirements I have been outlining, and that is designed also to meet the needs of young readers in our colleges and universities. I have said that we want students to increase their power of engaging in imaginative experience, and we assume—this was implied by our earlier reference to Coleridge—that a work of literature offers us an experience through words that is different from average, everyday experience. It is different in its mysterious wholeness, in the number of elements embraced and in the variety and closeness of their relationship. When Othello, just before Desdemona's death, says "Put out the light, and then put out the light," we feel not only the horror of his intention, but also a remarkable concentration of much that has gone on before: the moving history of the relations between the lovers and between them and Iago, the echoed presence of earlier moments of "lightness" and "darkness."

We all agree that such experiences in literature are wonderful, but what can a teacher do to guide a student to discover them? He will of course start from his own excitement, and he will do everything he can to infect his students with it: he will try to express in other words what Othello and the audience are experiencing; he will read the passage aloud or get a student to do it; he will exhort and entreat. But finally he cannot hand over his feelings to

---

[1] The description of this imaginary course is based on courses given at Amherst College and Harvard University. The particular exercises and devices described are all drawn from these courses, but all were not used in any one course. My colleagues in both institutions will best know how much I owe to their ingenuity and their cheerful support in making many experiments in slow reading.

his students; he cannot force them to be more sensitive than
they are. What can he do that the students may also do and
that they can imitate when they read another scene or another play? He can do a great deal if he remembers that
while he and his students do not have a common nervous
system, they do have the same printed page and they share
some knowledge of the English language. He will therefore
direct their attention to the words, to what they mean and
to their connection with other words and meanings. In
considering the "put out the light" speech from *Othello,*
the teacher may begin by asking what the words mean in
terms of stage business. He may then call for a paraphrase:
for "put out the light" someone may offer "bring darkness," or "put an end to." The class can next be asked to
connect this expression with others used elsewhere in the
play. Someone may recall Othello's earlier line associating
Desdemona with darkness and death: ". . . when I love thee
not,/Chaos is come again." The reader can now begin to
appreciate the poignancy and the irony of Othello's pictur-
ing his action as "putting out the light." So by directing
attention to words, their meanings, and relationships, the
teacher may put his students in a position where they too
will feel the pity and terror of this moment in the play.

We might describe Literature X as a "mutual demonstration society," the work of the course being carried on
mainly through student-teacher explorations of the kind
I have been attempting to illustrate. For the students the
most important and most strenuous demonstrations will be
the exercises that they write on their own after being suit-
ably prepared by the teacher. *Othello* may serve as an example once more. After several classes of reading aloud and
exploring connections in the earlier acts of the play, an
exercise will be set on a speech or scene from the last act.
The students now have an opportunity to show whether

they can practice independently the sort of interpretation they have been attempting in class. To guide them, they will be given an exercise sheet with a very carefully planned series of questions. Beginning with queries on words and phrases, the exercise goes on to ask about relationships of various kinds, and it concludes with a question demanding a generalization about the work as a whole or about a type of literature or experience. An exercise on *Othello* might finally call for a statement about the nature of Othello's tragedy and for a tentative definition of "tragic" as used in Shakespearean drama. But the words "tragic" or "tragedy" will not necessarily appear in the directions; rather, the students will be impelled to talk about these concepts because they are relevant. In the class on the exercise papers the students and his teacher will be admirably prepared to consider what is meant by tragic literature and experience. These discussions of the exercises should be among the most valuable classes in the course. Here the student can learn by comparing where he succeeded or failed as an interpreter, and frequently he may have the pleasure of finding that he has taught his teacher something, an event that can give satisfaction to both parties and that can take place more often in a course where the student is an active participant, not a passive member of an audience.

Literature X as a whole will consist of a series of these exercise-waves, with some more terrifying than others, the seventh and last coming when the students are given two or more weeks without classes in which to read new material—poems, plays, or novels—with no teacher to guide them.

The course will not begin with Shakespeare, although Shakespeare is the necessary measure of imaginative experience and of the capacity to engage in it. We shall begin rather with the smaller model of the short poem, because

as I have said it offers literary experience in its purest form.
By beginning with poems we can be reasonably sure that
the student learns early to distinguish between life and
literature and not to be unduly distracted by questions of
biography and history or by social and psychological problems of the type raised so often by the novel. Most important, the student will learn at the outset to deal with
wholes, since within the limits of a class-hour or a brief
paper he can arrive at an interpretation of a whole literary
expression. Poems may come to stand in his mind as Platonic
forms of true and complete literary experience.

Beginning with poems has another advantage if students
are to learn the value of attending closely to language and
if they are to see the satisfactions that come from alert and
accurate reading. In the small world of a sonnet, a reader
can see how a single word may cause a shift in the equilib-
rium of feeling in the whole poem. So when Shakespeare
says:

> For thy sweet love remember'd such wealth brings
> That then I scorn to change my state with kings.

"state" carries connotations of Elizabethan *state,* and as a
result the speaker's voice takes on a tone of grandeur, a
somewhat stagey grandeur that reminds us of gestures in a
play. But the word "state" would hardly impart that quality
without the reference to "kings." This fairly simple example brings home the importance in interpretation of considering the context. A course in interpretation is a course
in definition by context, in seeing how words are given rich
and precise meaning through their interrelations with other
words. The student who acquires this habit of definition
will be a better reader of philosophy or law or any other
type of specialized discourse, and he may learn something

about the art of writing, of how to control context in order to express oneself.

Reading poems also offers one of the best ways of lifting the student from adolescent to adult appreciation of literature. The adult reader realizes that reading a work of literature is at once a solitary and a social act. In reading we are alone, but we are also among the company of readers assumed by the poem or play or novel. The poem is more than a personal message, it invites us to move out of ourselves, to get into an "act," to be another self in a fictive drama. The sonnet of Shakespeare we have just quoted seems to call for a very simple identification of the actual reader with the imagined speaker,

> When in disgrace with fortune and men's eyes
> I all alone beweep my outcast state . . .

(Many will recall their own youthful readings of the poem.) Yet even this simple if not sentimental sonnet asks something more of us in the end; it asks us to take on the demonstrative air of the theatrical lover, to protest in language we would never actually use in our most romantic moments.

In Literature X we shall start by reading poems with no apparent method or at least with method well concealed. We begin, as Frost says, with delight, to end in wisdom. "What is it *like*," we say rather crudely, "to read this poem?" "With what feeling are we left at its close?" "What sort of person is speaking?" "What is he *like*, and where does he reveal himself most clearly?" "In what line or phrase?" We may then ask if there is a key phrase or word in the poem, and we can begin to introduce the notion of the poem as a structure, as an ordered experience built up through various kinds of meaning controlled in turn by various uses of language.

Remembering our questions about the speaker, we first
direct attention to dramatic uses of language, to the ways
in which the words create a character speaking in a certain
role. We may ask, for example, who is speaking in Keats'
sonnet on Chapman's *Homer*. An alert student may point
out that he is a traveller (many do not see this), and that
he uses idioms with a medieval coloring: "realms," "goodly,"
"bards in fealty," "demesne." But the speaker does not
continue to talk in this vein:

> Till I heard Chapman speak out loud and bold.

He has changed, and the drama moves into a second act.
We hear a voice that is powerful and young, the voice of
the New World discoverer and the Renaissance astronomer.
We now point out to our young reader (if he is still listening) that the poem is indeed an "act." The poet is speaking
as if he were a traveler-explorer, and the whole poem is
built on a metaphor. So, while reading many poems, we
may introduce a few basic notions of literary design and
some useful critical terms. But our emphasis will always
be on the term as a tool, as a device for calling attention to
the poem and how it is made. In time we can turn to study
of the poem as an experience of ordered sounds, but not,
we hasten to add, of sounds divorced from sense. Our aim
in talking about rhythmic pattern, as in considering dramatic and metaphorical design, is to show how the poem
"works" and what it expresses. We see, for example, that as
Keats's sonnet moves from the medieval to the modern
speaker and as the metaphor also shifts, the rhythm changes
from the "broken" couplets and inversions of the octave to
the long and steady sweep of the sestet. The whole sonnet
in its beautiful interaction of parts gives us the sense of discovery and release into a new world of literary and aesthetic
experience.

Following a period of reading poems, the course will move ahead to a play by Shakespeare so that students can see at once that the way in which they have read poems works also for a poetic drama and that there are some basic similarities between the structure of these different types of literature. They may see, for example, that the man speaking in a poem corresponds to the character in a play, that Shakespeare has his large metaphors just as Keats has his smaller ones.

From drama we go to the reading of a novel, often via short stories. The short story like the poem gives us literary experience in microcosm and makes it easier to see analogies between fiction and poetry, to see that a tale by Hawthorne is the unfolding of a single metaphorical vision, or that the narrator in a story by Joyce controls our sense of being within the child's world, exiled from adult society. The novel, especially as we have it in its classic nineteenth-century form in Dickens or George Eliot, demands a very different reading from a Shakespearean drama, but by putting the same questions to both genres their likeness and the unlikeness can be defined, and the exact quality of a particular work can be discovered. The student will find, for example, that the "marshes" and "mists" of *Great Expectations* are nearer to the fixed symbols of allegory than to the fluid metaphors of Shakespeare. But he can also see that in a novel as in a poem the narrative voice is of immense importance. Comparison of the opening scene in the film of *Great Expectations* with Dickens' telling shows that when the sanely humorous, entertaining voice of Dickens is removed, we are left with images of pure nightmare. The major themes of *Great Expectations*, guilt and innocence, justice and injustice, are not un-Shakespearean, but we can hardly read the novel without an awareness that unlike *King Lear* and *Macbeth* and like most novels, the imagina-

tive world of *Great Expectations* has a date. Jaggers is an
awesome symbol of the link between criminality and legal
justice, but he also embodies a sharp criticism of the actual
court and prison world of mid-nineteenth-century England.

Reading a novel forcibly reminds us that literature is
embedded in history, that the meaning of the work in itself
changes when we view it in relation to other works and to
the social situation in which it first appeared. Literature X
will move on in its later phases to some experiments in
historical interpretation, historical being used here to include the relation of a work to its time, especially to more
or less contemporary works, and to literary tradition. If
we return to *Othello* or *Coriolanus* after reading the *Iliad*
and after gaining some familiarity with the heroic tradition
in Renaissance epic and drama, we find that both plays are
clearer and richer in their meaning. We see in *Coriolanus*
what happens when an Achilles enters the Roman forum:
the simple absolutes of the hero, the code that makes Coriolanus prefer a "noble life before a long" one, bring confusion in a civil society. The teacher of our ideal course will
not merely lay a comparison of this sort before his students,
he will try to get them into a position where they can make
the comparison for themselves. He will use all the ingenuity
he can muster to devise assignments in which the student
can practice thinking historically about works of literature.

In a year in which the class has made some study of the
hero in Homer and in the Renaissance, a project might be
focussed on Fielding's *Tom Jones*. While the students are
reading the novel outside class (it takes time!), they would
study with their teacher readings useful for interpreting
the novel in relation to the heroic tradition and to the
climate of moral opinion in the eighteenth century. They
could observe in Dryden's *Mac Flecknoe* the shift from the

Renaissance "heroick" to the mock-heroic, and in the *Rape of the Lock*, they could see how allusions to the ancient heroic world are used to satirize eighteenth-century high society while giving the world of the poem splendor and moral seriousness. After comparing the mock-heroic in Pope and Fielding, they might attempt a definition of the hero in *Tom Jones*. By skillful prodding (in an exercise) they could be led to see that Fielding has created a new type of hero, a youth who is at once ridiculous and charmingly "good-natured," that although he finally gains a modicum of "prudence," he wins his way largely through "benevolence" and "goodness of heart."

As a final step in this experiment, there might be a series of readings in Chesterfield, Hume, and Dr. Johnson, all concerned with social "goodness," and more especially with "prudence" and "benevolence." The students would then be asked to define and place the moral attitudes expressed in *Tom Jones*, through comparing them with similar attitudes expressed in these eighteenth-century moralists. By projects of this type undergraduates could be given some practice—at an elementary level—in writing intellectual history. At the same time their earlier practice in interpretation would protect them from reducing the experience of the novel to the abstracted idea. But they would also begin to see that a purely literary judgment is finally impossible, that we are impelled to move back from literature to life. Dr. Johnson's famous comparison of Fielding and Richardson might be used to show that "liking" or "disliking" a novel is an act of moral evaluation. At the end of Literature X, by returning to poetry we could make the point that a choice between poems is a choice between lives.

You may be asking by now what the connection is between our ideal course and the lifetime reading habits of undergraduates. I should reply that Literature X attempts to influence future reading habits by keeping to the principle of student activity. No test or exercise or final examination asks the student to "give back" the "material" of the course. On the contrary, each stage of the work is planned with a view to how the student reads the *next* work, whether poem or play or novel. At the end of the first half of the course the student is sent off to read and interpret on his own another play of Shakespeare and another novel. He is given leading questions that impel him to do likewise "differently." An appropriate midyear examination in the course might consist of a sight poem to interpret and an essay-exercise on a longer work read outside class. The test for the second half-year (whether an examination or a long essay) would ordinarily be based on a set of texts to be used in interpreting a work in the manner of the project on *Tom Jones*.

But the teacher of a course in slow reading will always be haunted by the question once asked by a colleague of mine: "Our students learn *how* to read, but *do* they read?" Do they, for example, ever read an author, read every one of his books they can lay their hands on, with an urge to know the writer's work as a whole? Can we do anything in our ideal course to stimulate this most valuable habit? Some modest experiments can be made, I believe, and with some assurance of success. A model can be set by reading generously in a single poet, preferably a contemporary, such as Frost, Yeats, or Eliot. Or the teacher can give the class a start by reading a few poems in each of a number of writers, and then send the students off to read one of the poets independently. After some weeks they might write an essay "On Reading So-and-so." The essay must have a point (surprisingly few students know what a point is) supported by deft and apt interpretation of particular poems. The novel, the most important form for habitual readers in this generation, presents a problem, since we can hardly read all or even several novels of the same writer within the limits of an introductory course. But two novels and some stories by a single writer may rouse some readers to go ahead on their own, and sometimes the discovery that a difficult writer—James or Joyce—is understandable and rewarding or that an old-fashioned writer—Fielding or Jane Austen—is amusing, will start a student along the right path. The best way to influence later habits is the natural way: recommending without system books we have read with pleasure and without ulterior motives. Students recognize the difference between love and duty, and they will respond to genuine enthusiasm and avoid books that they "ought to" read or—and this is the lowest of all academic appeals—that "fill a gap" in preparing for general examinations or graduate school placement tests.

If we turn our attention from lifetime reading habits to the larger educational influence of courses in slow reading, we can note some possible correlations between classroom and later performances. In this connection we should recall the value for close reading of practice in equally close writing. The student who looks at poems as carefully as we have suggested will understand that poetry begins in grammar and that to express a just appreciation of a poem demands fine control of grammar on the part of the appreciator. But to help the student make such discoveries calls for guidance in small classes or at least careful criticism of written exercises. Good writing is an art not amenable to mass production methods.

Attentive criticism of written work is almost certainly of much more value for teaching good reading and writing than the usual discussions or section meetings. The value of a discussion meeting does not depend primarily on size, as many assume, but on the planning that precedes the

meeting and the direction of the conversation to a defined
goal. In our course in slow reading the discussion is not an
addendum, but the culminating act toward which the
teacher's demonstration and the student's exercise have
been directed. Under these conditions student and teacher
are fully prepared to say something meaningful to one
another, since they have before them well-defined questions
to pursue and alternative expressed answers to compare and
judge.

But the discussion of this type need not be vocal. The
student can carry it on internally during a lecture, if the
lecture is an exercise in how to ask and answer a question
of interpretation. The indispensable requirement for an
active course in literature is not "sections," but some form
of independent performance for an attentive critical audience of one. Here is where large-scale production methods
break down, and limitations in size are necessary. Very few
readers can handle more than twenty to twenty-five papers
of the type I have been describing and maintain the necessary vigilance and the power of viewing them as individual
performances. A reader can handle them in the usual
fashion—grade them and add a complimentary or devastating comment—but he cannot give them critical attention
at a high level. The student who is to rise to the kind of
reading and writing called for in our ideal course must feel
that he has a responsible reader, one who addresses himself
to this essay and to this mind. The most valuable discussion
a teacher can give is a comment surely directed to an individual written performance. Here we have the ideal section: two actors engaged in a Socratic dialogue. A teacher
who is not bewildered and dulled by reading too many
papers on the same topic will be able to judge the student's
present achievement in relation to what he has done in the
past. He can also help him keep track of his development

and show him where he is going, and when he has failed, show him how to build on an earlier successful performance. Again Coleridge's Reverend Bowyer may serve as a guide:

> . . . there was one custom of our master's, which I cannot pass over in silence, because I think it imitable and worthy of imitation. He would often permit our exercises, under some pretext of want of time, to accumulate, till each lad had four or five to be looked over. Then placing the whole number abreast on his desk, he would ask the writer, why this or that sentence might not have found as appropriate a place under this or that other thesis: and if no satisfying answer could be returned, and two faults of the same kind were found in one exercise, the irrevocable verdict followed, the exercise was torn up, and another on the same subject to be produced, in addition to the tasks of the day. The reader will, I trust, excuse this tribute of recollection to a man, whose severities, even now, not seldom furnish the dreams, by which the blind fancy would fain interpret to the mind the painful sensations of distempered sleep; but neither lessen nor dim the sense of my moral and intellectual obligations.

The marker of an English paper, as Coleridge realized though with "painful sensations," is a very important person indeed; he becomes the higher literary conscience, the intellectual guardian angel of his students.

It is evident that education in literature of this kind must be personal, and expensive, though scarcely more expensive than education in the sciences. Let us have at least as generous a supply of readers and conference rooms as we have of laboratory assistants and laboratories. The Humanities cannot flourish without *humanitas*. A protest is in order against the inhumanity of the Humanities when in some of our larger institutions the study of Great Books is reduced to display lectures before audiences of five and six hundred, and when the individual performance is measured by machine-graded examinations.

The teaching of great literary texts in Humanities courses has also had other if less depressing results which the teacher of literature should note if he is to fulfill his proper educational role. Because many works are taught in translation and taught often by staffs including many non-specialists in language and literature, and because the texts are often presented in some broad historical framework, a work of imaginative literature tends to be treated either as a document for studying the history of ideas, or as a text for illustrating and enforcing desirable moral and social attitudes. Though neither of these approaches are in them-selves harmful or inappropriate to a university, they may involve serious losses, especially in courses in which many students are reading for the first time—or for the first time at an adult level—masterpieces of European literature. There is a danger, which is increased by the large amounts of reading assigned in Great Books courses, that rich and special experiences will be too readily reduced to crude examples of an historic idea or a moral principle. Though the reductions may be necessary and useful for certain pur-poses, we must not let students make them too soon or too easily, not if we are seriously concerned with lifetime habits of reading. The undergraduate who masters the trick too early and too well may in the process suffer real damage. He may have acquired the dubious art of reading carelessly, of making the reduction *before* reading, and he may have lowered rather than increased his capacity for responding precisely to a particular work and for making fine dis-criminations between works.

Hence the special function of the teacher of literature, which is not to be confused with that of the historian or the moral philosopher. The teacher of literature in a Humanities course must feel he has betrayed a trust if he has not given the lay reader what he is best qualified to give: training in the literary disciplines of reading and writing. It is pertinent to recall the historic definition of the Humanities as it stands in the Oxford English Dictionary: "Learning or literature concerned with human culture, as grammar, rhetoric, poetry, and especially the ancient Latin and Greek classics." I suspect that some of the more enthusiastic general educators may be surprised by the words that follow "human culture": "as grammar, rhetoric, poetry . . ." (The order of items in the list is instructive, too.) The disciplines named are the ones that the teacher of literature has a special responsibility to impart. He is like Horace's poet a guardian of the language who shows (as Pope translates it) "no mercy to an empty line." His prime object is to maintain fineness of response to words, and his students rightly assume that he will be adept in discovering and illustrating refinements in writing whether in a great book or a student essay. This guardianship, once performed by teachers of the ancient Latin and Greek classics, now falls to the teachers of English and other modern literatures. Why is this so? Because they are committed to the principle that the study of letters is inseparable from the study of language.

Study of literature based on this principle can hardly be carried on in a course based mainly on texts in translation. Translations have their place in a course in interpretation, but only as ancillary to the main business of close reading in the original. The finer distinctions, the finer relationships which we are training our students to discover and make are almost invariably dulled or lost in the process of translation. We want the student to acquire the habit of recognizing and making such distinctions in his *own* language, and we can hardly teach him to do it if the examples before

him are relatively crude. Whitehead once remarked when
discussing Plato's cosmology, "After all, the translators
of Plato have had B+ philosophic minds." With rare exceptions the translators of literature have had literary
minds of similar quality. There are of course the handful
of translations that are masterpieces, such as Pope's *Iliad*,
North's *Plutarch*, and Dryden's *Aeneis*, texts that can bear
the close study necessary for literary education. Ironically
enough, these are the very translations avoided in most
Great Books courses.

In speaking of the necessity for close attention to language I am not forgetting that teachers of literature are
also teachers of human culture, and that they are therefore
guardians of important values. But they do not set out to
teach these values, although they inevitably impart them
by the way they talk and act in the presence of works of
literature. But they are especially concerned with another
task, with teaching ways of discovering and experiencing
values expressed through literary objects. The most precious
thing they can give their students is some increase of power,
some help however humble in getting into Shakespeare or
Dr. Johnson or Joyce.

We may hope that a student who has learned how to get
into these writers will go back for further experiences
after he has left the classroom and the university. That he
surely will we cannot say. Even if he does not return to
Shakespeare or Johnson, the experiences in the classroom
almost certainly have their value and their effect in determining the quality of his later reading. One play well read
with a good teacher and well digested in a reflective essay
may serve as a touchstone of what literary experience can
be. But finally, our belief that students' habits of reading
are permanently affected is Platonic. The model for most

cultural education is to be found in the third book of the *Republic*:

... our young men, dwelling as it were in a healthy region, may receive benefit from all things about them; the influence that emanates from works of beauty may waft itself to eye or ear like a breeze that brings health from wholesome places, and so from earliest childhood insensibly guide them to likeness, to friendship, to harmony with beautiful reason.

In the effort to realize this Platonic vision in a modern university the undergraduate library plays its part by surrounding our youth with fair works of literature through which they may come into "harmony with beautiful reason." No one knows how born readers are produced, but we can put books in their way and in the way of the less happily born in the hope that proximity will have its effect as it does in the formation of more mundane habits. Of one thing I am convinced: that a born reader on a library staff can have a tremendous effect on young readers who come his way. I remember with gratitude two librarians of that description, one in school and one in college, who led us to read books we might never have looked into by sharing their love for what they had read. If I were to found a library dedicated to influencing the reading habit, I should place a half dozen of these enthusiasts at strategic points to ensnare wandering students. They would not necessarily be trained librarians, and they would surely waste students' time and occasionally disturb their colleagues, but like great authors they would create an ever-widening circle of readers. Mere teachers of literature could hardly hope to compete with them and might in time quietly disappear from the academic scene.

6

Reading in the Social Sciences

BY ROBERT COOLEY ANGELL[1]

THE "LIFETIME READING HABIT" with which we are concerned is not, I take it, *any* kind of reading habit—say a taste for Mickey Spillane, whodunits and tabloids—but a habit of "good" reading. I thought Dr. Wagman's letter of invitation struck the right note when he asked whether the college graduate is a participant in western "lettered" culture. This strongly suggests reading of high quality and —what is the same thing—lasting significance. Now it is true that there is much good to read in the special sections of the best Sunday papers and in magazines like the *Atlantic, Harper's* and the *New Yorker;* but it is inconceivable that a truly cultured person would be wholly content with such abbreviated fare. He wants to get hold of life in larger slices too. In short, he reads books. What distinguishes the lifetime reading habit we are talking about is that its possessor is an avid consumer of significant books.

Among the many benefits from a habit of serious reading are several that appeal especially to the social scientist. As the store of knowledge grows with every passing decade

[1] I am indebted to Professors Robert F. Haugh of the English Department, Morris Janowitz of the Sociology Department, and Kenneth Boulding of the Economics Department, all of the University of Michigan, for helpful suggestions in the preparation of this paper.

a larger and larger proportion of the population must be able to act as bearers of the intellectual culture if the civilization is to continue. Sheer survival requires that each generation master the heritage which has been bequeathed to it. The books that fill our libraries are so much waste paper unless the truths contained in them energize new readers' minds.

But it is a pitiful goal merely to keep from slipping back. There are so many inadequacies and imperfections in life today that humane men will wish to press ahead. Survival may require greater technological skill but what the advanced nations most need for a sense of fruition is moral and spiritual enrichment. Where is this to arise if not from cultural leaders, men of imagination and breadth? Only a lifetime habit of good reading will produce such a man as Alfred North Whitehead.

Serious reading is also necessary for the daily practice of democracy. Gone are the days when a citizen could keep abreast of affairs by gossiping in the market place or frequenting the general store on Saturday nights. Nor are tabloids, radio, television and the newsreel adequate substitutes. The problems that confront modern democracies are too complex for cursory and sporadic attention; and they have to be studied not just by statesmen and political pundits, but by large sections of the general public. We cannot acquiesce in the inevitability, proclaimed by Ortega y Gasset, of political apathy among the masses. But their interest can hardly be aroused and maintained by popular media. These must be supplemented by magazine commentary, books on public affairs, and fictional analyses of current problems.

Finally, reading is important because it is a personal and private act. It helps to preserve individuality in an age

when mass communication threatens to sweep all before
its levelling tide.

The development of a lifetime habit of good reading has
been much more difficult since World War I. First the
movies, then radio, and finally television have presented
competing, and often exciting, temptations. Most of us,
no matter how well educated, have succumbed in some
degree. How well I remember, if I may be allowed a personal aside, the contentment with which my parents settled
down to read after dinner when I was a child. They often
read to each other—Trollope was their favorite—and my
mother especially read to me. It is hardly credible today
that she read aloud twelve of Scott's *Waverly* novels to me
before I went to high school, but that is the fact. Alas,
I cannot claim that my own children were equally exposed
to good books in their childhood. The movies and the radio
were taking their toll. With the seduction of television
added, we can hardly criticize the present generation of
parents if they do less than we did.

Distractions are not the only enemy of cultural reading.
The amount of specialized reading that professional and
business men have to do is large and constantly increasing.
Moreover, the growth of large-scale organization means
that more and more of the well educated must entertain
superiors, inferiors, clients and buyers. The length of the
work day has not decreased for this group, while the demands on leisure time have increased. Good reading tends
to get squeezed out.

Since strong pressures are working in a contrary direction, the better educated sections of the public will have
to be more highly motivated than ever toward reading if
they are to develop and maintain a lifetime reading habit.
Where are the citizens of tomorrow to find this motivation?
A few of them will do so at home. Among our honors stu-

dents at this university, some are emulating studious parents. But these are rare in the general population. Parents who are not themselves great readers can hardly excite a love of reading in their children. Very occasionally a Scout leader or a minister or a librarian will quicken the child's interest. But their opportunities are slim indeed compared with those of another group—the teachers. From the age of six to maturity the growing boy or girl is in contact with teachers; it is chiefly with them that whatever hope there is lies.

It would be most encouraging if we could report that a large proportion of our young people come under the influence of a teacher who arouses in them intellectual enthusiasm. In grade or high school, when they are most plastic, a strong enthusiasm would presumably leave a lasting impression. Unfortunately such firing of the imagination is rare. The usual story is quite different. The first stirrings of literary passion are all too often permanently chilled by dull and uninspiring teachers. How frequently one hears the comment, "That book was spoiled for me by being required in school." One of our honors students said to me last fall that she enjoyed reading all kinds of books, but never those assigned.

Evidently the college has a great responsibility for the lifetime reading habit. The few freshmen who come with a well-developed taste for serious reading must have it reinforced, not weakened; and the great majority who have not yet developed it must, though the hour is late, be stimulated to do so. A small study by one of Dr. Janowitz' classes here at Michigan is most discouraging in this connection. The data show that students read progressively *less* on their own initiative as they go through college, mainly because extracurricular activities and social engagements

take up an increasing segment of time. If this is generally
true, we are faced with a problem indeed.

My assignment is to discuss the development of a lifetime
reading habit from the angle of the social science teacher.
Before I narrow my perspective to that degree, however,
let me make some general observations on possibilities in
the college setting.

As a sociologist I am inclined to approach a question of
this kind by reconnoitering the social terrain. Our problem
is how to generate and maintain strong motivation to read.
Such motivation may occasionally come from the impact
of a chance encounter with a great book which has whetted
lasting appetite for more. But usually there is social stimulation too. Either older persons or one's peers arouse the
interest in the first place or keep it ardent through suggestion, discussion and criticism. On or near the college campus
there are many opportunities for this sort of stimulation.
The roles of libraries, bookstores and the media of student
communication are being taken up in other papers. Still
left, however, are several other possibilities beside the classroom. There are the fraternities, sororities and dormitories.
There are the numerous student activities, some of them
with intellectual content. And there are other nonacademic
situations where students and faculty can be brought together—in political parties, on the handball court, in religious activities. I believe all these would more often serve
to deepen intellectual interest if two general strategies
were adopted in the college community. I shall label these
"giving status to the superior student," and "cultivating
the opportunities for faculty-student friendships outside
the classroom."

The strategy of giving status to the superior student
flows from two hypotheses. The first is that he is likely to
be a voracious reader. My contacts with the freshman

honors students during the last six months convince me that this is more than a plausible hypothesis. Most of these promising young persons love books and have managed to indulge their reading appetite, even in the face of a heavy schedule of extracurricular activities in high school. The second hypothesis is that, if we can somehow heighten their repute among their fellows, the process of emulation will set in. The local study referred to earlier supports this. Dr. Janowitz reports that a fraternity or other group is likely to have a high level of reading if there is an admired figure in it who acts as a "reading pioneer."

In the course of preparing this paper I bethought myself of something I wrote at the beginning of my career. It is a now yellowed, mimeographed "Report on Methods of Increasing the Intellectual Interest of Students at the University of Michigan," submitted by request in 1924. Part Three is entitled "Methods of Enhancing the Prestige Attaching to Intellectual Achievement." I trust my return to the same subject after 34 years does not indicate obsession.

The central problem is how to get the general run of undergraduates to accept the faculty's high opinion of superior students. All too often scholarship is depreciated and its devotees remain suspect. To overcome these negative attitudes it is not enough to extend privileges which the superior students themselves, or even their families, appreciate. Thus close contact with faculty members in departmental clubs, on research projects, or even in leisure pursuits may not excite envy in those of little intellectual bent. Even prizes of sets of Shakespeare or the *Encyclopedia Britannica* or election to Phi Beta Kappa may leave the average undergraduate cold. The tradition of the Honors Convocation here at Michigan is an admirable one but it is noticeable that the audience is made up largely of the parents and close friends of those being honored rather than of students generally. If, however, top students are taken on scientific expeditions, if they receive large pecuniary prizes, or are awarded a summer of travel abroad— these are distinctions that all would appreciate. Even so simple a matter as exemption from the more routine aspects of courses makes the good student somewhat glamorous and incites emulation.

One of the best ways to carry out the strategy is to admit superior students to a special honors group which possesses many advantages and opportunities, at least some of which are envied by the student body at large. Because of the connection between unusual achievement in a specialized field and subsequent employment opportunities, honors work at upperclass levels has been regarded with general respect. The University of Colorado has pioneered, and now Michigan among others is following, in establishing an honors program aimed to capture the undergraduate imagination from the start of the freshman year. Privileges that can be given are special courses or sections of courses, interdisciplinary colloquia, the bypassing of prerequisites, tutorial arrangements, special access to libraries, and a center for reading, discussion and social activities. It has even been suggested, but I doubt that it is wise, that students in an honors program be given special priorities in housing and exemptions from some college regulations.

The other side of the coin is that the superior students must be kept from becoming narrowly bookish. No matter what privileges they are given, if they appear to be "grinds," they will have no leadership value. It should be one of the major concerns of those who direct honors programs to keep or make their students well-rounded. Quite aside from its desirability for their sake, this is essential if the life of scholarship is to appeal to the rest of the under-graduates.

It may be that the Sputniks have done more to improve the status of superior students than anything we can do on the campus. The American people are being rudely awakened to the inadequacies of a fun psychology and permissive high schools. Perhaps students who are achieving on the intellectual front will become generally appreciated for a change.

My second line of nonclassroom strategy is to afford more favorable opportunities for faculty-student friendship. We are not here talking about the excellent student so much as about his ordinary fellow. Faculty members are likely in one way or another to make friends with their most interested and interesting charges. And most of the highly motivated ones have acquired the habit of serious reading anyway. But it is hard to put scholars into intimate touch with the average student, in part because the professor often finds such contacts a bore. Indirection must again be the keynote. The best hope is to find something other than matters academic or intellectual which both parties enjoy. Sports like golf, tennis, badminton, and squash-racquets afford such a meeting ground. So do those campus activities in which there is of necessity much professorial participation, like dramatics. Faculty men and women who have maintained an interest in their fraternities and sororities have a natural contact there. In many institutions professors are related to the dormitories. Where they actually live in, as at Harvard and Yale, intimacy with many students is almost guaranteed; even where they are merely counselors, close friendships sometimes develop. Finally, common religious interest may draw the two groups together. Perhaps this is more likely in a small college than in a large university. Where each church serves hundreds of students,

the activities for them are often split off into separate programs.

From the standpoint of this paper a faculty-student
friendship is an entering wedge. Once established, the force
of the mature personality comes to bear. The professor's
intellectual curiosity may be transmitted and with it the
urge to read.

As we turn to the classroom—which affords after all the
chief opportunity for stimulating students to acquire
the lifetime reading habit—we will do well not to forget
the strategies we have discussed. Anything in the conduct
of the class which makes the good student admirable in the
eyes of the rest, or which creates a sense of intimacy between professor and members of the class, is so much to the
good. This is true whether the subject is mathematics or
literature, political science or geology. I am sure that
faculty men will generally agree that it is the duty of each
of us, no matter what his field, to make some contribution
to the cause of good reading. Perhaps teachers in the humanities have the greatest opportunities, and those in the
natural sciences the least, but all can do something. My job
is to discuss the problem from the perspective of the social
sciences.

The social science classroom is a place where books and
periodicals are used as sources of information and analysis.
Some of these materials are central to the course and are
subjected to searching discussion; others are assigned as
collateral reading or are suggested as worth later and more
leisurely perusal. In short, reading is a chief method of instruction. If the classroom is to contribute to the lifetime
reading habit, what is assigned must whet the appetite for
more. But this will not occur if the material fails to satisfy
at least some of the tastes the students already possess. We
can hope to lead the student progressively and pleasurably

into new reading pastures; but in good part we must let him graze on accustomed grasses.

With the aid of members of our library staff I have skimmed a good many articles on reading habits. Unfortunately data on college students are hard to interpret. Figures on all their reading include a high proportion that is assigned, much of which may not be enjoyed; if one looks only at their nonassigned reading one gets a one-sided picture because they may like some of their assignments. I have therefore decided to use data on the books read by college graduates. Probably tastes in college would not differ greatly.

By comparing the evidence in various studies I have come to the conclusion that we will not be far off the mark if we say that 58 per cent of all books read by college graduates —paperbacks as well as hard covers—are fiction. Within the 42 per cent nonfiction their reading seems to be very evenly distributed over a number of types. My estimate is that about half of it—21 per cent of the total—is made up of four that are about equally popular: biography, religion and philosophy, including inspirational books; adventure and travel; and works on political, economic and social affairs. Another 10 per cent of the nonfiction (4 per cent of the total) consists of history, with the useful arts, the fine arts, and science each contributing somewhat less. This leaves a residuum of approximately 9 per cent of the total distributed in small categories.

If these are the tastes of our students—and I have no evidence that they are not—there are two striking facts for the social scientists to mull over. One is that the college man or woman, like everyone else, prefers fiction. The other is that social science is read very sparingly.

It is certainly not the responsibility of the social science teacher to develop or improve the student's interest in fiction or biography or travel. But these other types of reading can play a role in teaching social science more effectively at the same time that the lifetime reading habit is fostered. The student's interest in the course and his fondness for fiction, biography or travel can become mutually supportive. If these popular types of book are made apposite to the class discussion the student will enjoy the course more and his motivation to read will be strengthened. Thus *Executive Suite* may increase interest in the subject of bureaucracy at the same time that it suggests that novels are one place to look for light on economic, political and social questions.

As a sociologist I have found that there are several weaknesses in the ordinary college student's grasp of our courses which can be overcome by judicious reading of fiction. They all stem from the fact that he is a particular person brought up in a particular milieu with only a limited understanding of processes and problems with which he has not been personally in contact. Strictly speaking, the aims of the sociologist and the writer of fiction are somewhat divergent. The former is merely interested in accurate description and analysis of social situations. The latter is concerned with the development of character and the interplay among characters under varying circumstances. The intricacies of a first class writer's plot may actually blur impressions that sociologists would wish to have clearly conveyed. The novelist is fully concrete where the social scientist is in some degree abstract. Nevertheless fiction can contribute greatly to the social science class by making textbook generalizations come alive.

One glaring weakness of college students is their inability to appreciate how the other half lives. The great majority of them are from upper and middle class families. They have been kept insulated from lower class life. Novels like *The Grapes of Wrath* or the *Studs Lonigan* trilogy, or plays like *Street Scene* or *Dead End* can open their eyes. They become emotionally involved in the fortunes of the characters and are led to experience—vicariously it is true —events and relationships of which they would otherwise be ignorant.

A similar problem is to get students to feel the strength of the mores of regions different from their own. They can read about the strange ways of other sections of the country in textbooks and monographs but the knowledge remains abstract and is not inwardly felt until the differences are brought home in human terms. Fiction is unexcelled for this purpose. Several of the novels of John P. Marquand have given non-New Englanders a feeling for New England. The works of Erskine Caldwell and most of those of William Faulkner have served similarly for the Deep South. Ellen Glasgow introduces us to the élite of Virginia. Ruth Suckow and, in an earlier generation, Willa Cather make the settlers on the Great Plains come alive.

The hidden places in a modern society are not all in other classes or other regions. They may lie in the depths of organizations whose workings are obscure to the un-initiated. Undoubtedly the popularity of novels like Henry Robinson's *The Cardinal*, Cameron Hawley's *Executive Suite*, Harvey Swados' *On the Line*, Calder Willingham's *End as a Man*, and (in England) C. P. Snow's *The Masters* and *The New Men* comes from the public's ignorance of what churches, business managements, automobile facto-ries, military schools, universities and government bureauc-racies are like from the inside. The sociology teacher has powerful allies in this public curiosity about large organiza-tions and the fiction that ministers to it.

Beside curing ignorance of social processes in areas distant from one's own stamping ground, fiction can deepen the understanding of the strains and conflicts among social forces in the contemporary world. In particular, race relations have been illumined in this way. The works of Richard Wright, Bucklin Moon, and Ralph Ellison from the Negro side and Lillian Smith's *Strange Fruit* and Faulkner's *Intruder in the Dust* from the white side are outstanding. *Gentlemen's Agreement* by Laura Hobson similarly heightens one's insight into Jewish-Gentile relations in this country. Novels on the relation between capital and labor seem to have been less successful, perhaps because the social distance between the two parties makes treatment in personal terms difficult. Most of Upton Sinclair's work has been too propagandist. The novels of Louis Bromfield which dealt with this issue did so without bias but their literary quality was hardly sustained enough to carry conviction.

The strains of our civilization are often evidenced in the mobile person, either the one who changes his class or who moves from one part of the country to another. John P. Marquand's *Point of No Return* and his *Sincerely, Willis Wade* have themes of this kind. The problem of marriage across class lines is dealt with realistically in Christopher Morley's *Kitty Foyle*. Budd Schulberg's *What Makes Sammy Run* is partly concerned with social mobility but at a deeper level is a searching criticism of our whole society. For a similar criticism, but with special emphasis on the effects of science and technology, Aldous Huxley's *Brave New World* employs satire devastatingly.

Urbanism itself can be considered a problem, perhaps the greatest problem of our age. It is the epitome of all the confusion, the uprooting, the inability to organize meaningfully which we think of as the dark side of modern civilization. Blanche Housman Gelfant explores the literature of urbanism in *The American City Novel*.[2] She thinks

[2] Norman: University of Oklahoma Press, 1954.

Dreiser was the first to see "urban life as an organic whole," and express "a coherent, organized, and total vision of the city." *Sister Carrie* and *An American Tragedy* are vivid commentary on the metropolis. Perhaps the most successful of all our writers on this topic is John Dos Passos. *Manhattan Transfer* and his trilogy *U.S.A.* are, after more than two decades, surprisingly current sociological documents.

Best suited to the exposition of social change is a series of novels like *The Forsyte Saga* because of the time span thus available. For a single volume, Sherwood Anderson's *Poor White* is remarkably successful in portraying the dynamics of American urbanism in the last half of the nineteenth century.

A completely different way in which fiction can be used is to study books as causal to social change. *Uncle Tom's Cabin* is the case that immediately comes to my mind. Again, early in this century Upton Sinclair's *The Jungle* played a great role in developing public consciousness of the need for pure food laws by portraying conditions in the stockyards. And probably *The Grapes of Wrath* was similarly influential on behalf of migrant workers.

If one turns to the more psychological aspects of sociology, one finds plays like Arthur Miller's *Death of a Salesman* and novels like J. D. Salinger's *Catcher in the Rye* that deal with personal aspiration and adjustment. Farrell's *Father and Son* and *My Days of Anger* and Richard Wright's last book, *The Outsider,* are similarly concerned with the fate of human beings in a chaotic world. The plays of Eugene O'Neill explore man's inhumanity to man in many contexts.

Cultural anthropology these days is almost indistinguishable from sociology. The usual difference is that anthropologists explore exotic cultures while sociologists stay close to home. Because the material of cultural anthropology is

strange and often bizarre, the teacher has less need than
does the sociologist for help from fiction. Students are
already fascinated. Nevertheless there are works like Oliver
La Farge's *Laughing Boy* and Pearl Buck's *The Good Earth*
which sensitively picture life in cultures, such as the American Indian and the Chinese, which are not completely alien.

So far I have spoken only of fiction—novels and plays.
Obviously biography and books of travel and adventure
can supplement the ordinary social science textbook too.
Richard Wright's *Black Boy* is unforgettable autobiography. H. G. Wells' *Experiment in Autobiography* reveals
much about English civilization as well as much about its
author. Since World War I the anthropologists have been
securing biographies as a method of studying cultures. Paul
Radin's *Crashing Thunder,* Leo Simmons' *Sun Chief,* Walter Dyk's *Old Man Hat,* and C. S. Ford's *Smoke from their
Fires* afford much insight into Indian life. The sociologists
have not been so successful, though Clifford Shaw's *The
Jack Roller* is essentially a biography, and a very good one,
and Chic Conwell's *Professional Thief* is an autobiography
procured by Professor Ernest Sutherland. Biographies written in the normal course of things rarely lend themselves
to sociological use because the figures about whom they are
written tend to be unusual men and women who are not
typical of any social category. It is only for the study of
social change that such biographies may be helpful. The life
of an individual who leads a social movement or pioneers
in the development of an institution does throw light on
social process. One sees the problem of assimilating for-
eigners in great American cities and the creation of social
machinery to meet the problem in the life of Jane Addams.
In a similar way, the lives of great educators—Horace
Mann, Charles Eliot, Daniel Gilman—are sociologically instructive.

In the field of travel I will mention only one book, but one that has fascinated me. This is *Interview with India* by one of our own English faculty, John Frederick Muehl. This account of a trip by donkey through much of that subcontinent is full of the intimate glimpses of daily life that yield real understanding.

I have not mentioned historical books as likely to increase interest in social science courses because the figures do not indicate that they are very popular. I cannot refrain from calling attention, however, to Vann Woodward's *The Life and Times of Jim Crow*. To the sociology student concerned with race relations it is invaluable. Frederick Lewis Allen's *Only Yesterday* and *Since Yesterday* are also gems for those interested in the changing American society of the twenties and thirties.

Passing to the field of political science, we find that fiction is a great source of insight. Two recent monographs, *The Political Novel* by Joseph L. Blotner[3] and *The Radical Novel in the United States 1900-1954* by Walter B. Rideout[4] survey the field for us. Interestingly the two works overlap very little, for the former treats novels that keep close to the political process itself, while the latter focuses on novels about conditions which the writers hope will give rise to revolutionary action. The less propagandist of the radical novels, such as the *Studs Lonigan* trilogy of James T. Farrell mentioned above, can serve as "slice-of-life" background for students of either political science or sociology. In this category would also fall Richard Wright's *Native Son* and Nelson Algren's *Somebody in Boots, Never Come Morning* and *The Man with the Golden Arm*.

The teacher can find supplemental material in fiction for many aspects of politics. Criticism of political systems

[3] Garden City: Doubleday, 1955.
[4] Cambridge: Harvard University Press.

is perhaps the most common theme. Alan Paton's *Cry, the Beloved Country* castigates the South African régime. Koestler's *Darkness at Noon* shows the cruelties of Russian Communism. Silone's *Fontamara* is an anti-Fascist novel; Kaufman's *Heaven Pays No Dividends* is an anti-Nazi one. The dangers of native Fascism were shown in Sinclair Lewis' *It Can't Happen Here* and in three novels dealing with Huey Long's career by John Dos Passos (*Number One*), Robert Penn Warren (*All the King's Men*) and Adria Locke Langley (*A Lion in the Streets*). Totalitarianism of any variety is the butt of George Orwell's incomparable *1984*.

The most common theme in the criticism of the democratic system is political corruption. So distinguished a man as Henry Adams wrote the novel *Democracy* on this theme. Later Jack London contributed *The Iron Heel*. The Harding administration was pilloried in Samuel Adams' *Revelry*. William Manchester has recently dealt with municipal corruption in *City of Anger*.

Fiction that attempts to give insight into normal political processes has been more characteristic of England than of the United States. We have no counterpart of Benjamin Disraeli who wrote political fiction before he became prime minister. George Eliot in *Felix Holt* and Anthony Trollope in several novels concerned themselves with parliamentary life. Joyce Cary is a contemporary who has carried on this tradition. In this country the best of a small number of attempts are F. Marion Crawford's *An American Politician* and Dos Passos' *The Grand Design* (about the New Deal).

Political parties have sometimes been treated in fiction. Howard Spring's *Fame is the Spur* has the British Labor party for its subject. Silone's *Bread and Wine* is largely about Italian Communists. Dos Passos' *Adventures of a Young Man* deals with their American counterparts. So does John Steinbeck's *In Dubious Battle*. James T. Farrell has written about the Communist party in *Yet Other Waters* and *The Road Between*. Ralph Ellison's *Invisible Man* is the story of a young Negro who becomes disillusioned and leaves the party.

International affairs are the subject of several important works. E. M. Forster's *A Passage to India* is almost unique in its sensitive treatment of East and West. Joseph Conrad was fascinated by political themes. Most pertinent of his novels to contemporary events is *Under Western Eyes*. Ernest Hemingway's *For Whom the Bell Tolls*, Jean-Paul Sartre's *The Reprieve* and Koestler's *The Age of Longing* treat respectively the Spanish Civil War, the Munich crisis before World War II and the Cold War since.

The possibilities for enriching the teaching of political science by drawing on biography and travel are obvious. Of all men, politicians are most likely to write their own biographies. They have a consuming desire that posterity see their actions in the best possible light. But whether they write autobiographies or not, the lives of important political figures will be written by others. Both types are fascinating sources of knowledge and insight. Winston Churchill's great four-volume *The Second World War* and Robert Sherwood's *Roosevelt and Hopkins* are good cases in point. One of the most significant books of our times is *The God that Failed* edited by Richard Crossman. In it six outstanding writers—Arthur Koestler, Richard Wright, Louis Fischer, Ignazio Silone, Andre Gide and Stephen Spender—tell of their conversion to Communism and their ultimate disillusionment. For depth of insight into the most important political movement of our times this book stands alone.

Perhaps the books of foreign correspondents are not usually classified as adventure or travel, but we can treat

them as such. Our generation has seen a distinguished series
of such books by Vincent Sheean, William L. Shirer, Walter
Duranty and Pierre van Paassen, to mention only a few.
Surely teachers dealing with Fascism, Communism and the
Cold War might find the accounts of correspondents stimu-
lating to students.

Of all the social scientists the economists are perhaps
most handicapped in cultivating the lifetime reading habit
through the use of nontechnical works in their courses.
Their science has become so specialized in its many branches
that "human interest" material is hardly appropriate. If
assigned, it would seem too far removed from the topics of
daily discussion.

One clear exception is the field of labor. There biography
can be a most illuminating supplement. The lives of important leaders like Samuel Gompers, John L. Lewis and Walter
Reuther throw much light on economic issues and the development of the labor movement. For a realization of how
dedicated some labor sympathizers have been the *Autobiography of Mother Jones* is probably unequalled.

On the other side is the understanding of the pure capi-
talist, the perfect "economic man." Here the life of Daniel
Drew is a classic. Among books of fiction there is Frank
Norris' *The Pit*, a study of the grain exchange, and Theo-
dore Dreiser's *The Titan*.

My colleague Kenneth Boulding has suggested that
another way in which biography is useful to economists is
in showing the background of new theoretical departures.
Keynes' essay on Malthus and John R. Commons' autobiography, *Myself*, help one to understand the Malthusian population theory and institutional economics. Though not a
great theorist, Beatrice Webb's contributions to economic
policy were notable. Her autobiographical volume, *My
Apprenticeship*, shows the motivation of her work.

I hope I have not left the impression that I think large numbers of the more popular types of books should be assigned as required reading in social science courses. It is very easy to have too much of a good thing. In my own teaching I have found it more acceptable to students to give them wide choice. Often the distribution of a list of suitable books with the comment that they throw interesting light on topics discussed in the course is enough to start many reading. A further step is to require either a written report on one or two books or a class presentation of their leading ideas.

So much for the attempt to hitch social science's wagon to the star of popular taste and thus both increase interest in social science and cultivate a stronger habit of reading. There is another side to the matter however. We need to increase the reading of strictly social science literature too. This is partly a matter of taking better advantage of the attractive writings that now exist and partly a matter of making social scientists improve the quality of their output so that their books will be more acceptable, less repellent.

That ours is a dull literature is generally conceded. Our fraternity has often been held up to ridicule, and with good cause. Ten years ago Samuel T. Williamson penned a recipe for writing like a social scientist.[5] I quote two of his six rules: "Never use one word when you can use two," and "put one-syllable thoughts into polysyllabic terms." He illustrated the first by pointing to a social scientist who, instead of writing "probably" had written: "available evidence would tend to indicate that it is not unreasonable to suppose." The second was illustrated by: "The fact of rapid deterioration of musical skill when not in use converts

[5] "How to Write Like a Social Scientist," *Saturday Review of Literature*, XXX, No. 40 (Oct. 4, 1947), 17, 27-28.

the unemployed into the unemployable." He suggested that the writer meant, "Musicians out of practice can't hold jobs."

Malcolm Cowley is another who has taken us hilariously to task: "A child says 'Do it again,' a teacher says 'Repeat the exercise,' but the sociologist says 'It was determined to replicate the investigation.' . . . A sociologist never cuts anything in half or divides it in two like a layman. Instead he dichotomizes it, bifurcates it, subjects it to a process of binary fission, or restructures it in a dyadic conformation —around polar foci."[6]

Though in general deserved, these blanket condemnations are a little undiscriminating. William James was a great stylist as well as a great social psychologist. Two contemporaries in the same field, Hadley Cantril and David Riesman, are a pleasure to read. Among the older generation of sociologists Charles Horton Cooley had a quietly flowing style, Edward Alsworth Ross wrote with vigor and imagination, and William I. Thomas was always clear and precise. Among contemporaries C. Wright Mills is highly readable though hardly judicious, and there are younger men like Robert A. Nisbet and Albert K. Cohen whose work has literary merit. In Loren Eisley and Margaret Mead the anthropologists have two outstandingly able writers. Political science has also been fortunate. James Bryce, Woodrow Wilson, and Charles Beard set a high standard; but younger men like V. O. Key and Peter Odegard are following in their footsteps. Not to mention Walter Lippmann—if the fraternity will admit him as a political scientist! I cannot speak with much knowledge in the field of economics. For one, John Maynard Keynes wrote with typical British

[6] Malcom Cowley, "Sociological Habit Patterns in Linguistic Transmogrification," *The Reporter*, XV (Sept. 1956), 41-43.

polish. And, if somewhat turgid, I have always found the prose of Thorstein Veblen exciting.

Parenthetically, I should make clear that social scientists have the same right to their own vocabulary and their own technical expressions as do the natural scientists. Graduate students and even undergraduates who are majoring in a subject must expect to wade through heavy monographs. Only thus can the abstract analysis of complex data be conveyed clearly. We are here concerned, however, with the lifetime reading habit, and it is certainly not this kind of material, necessary though it is, that is conducive to that habit.

Since many of the better writers in social science belong to a former generation, we cannot expect that their works will be widely used in courses today. Some of their books, however, should be known to the better students if only for the light they can throw on the evolution of the disciplines. There are also contemporary works worthy of student acquaintance even if they are written by men without full academic respectability. Books of these two kinds might well be made the subject of more frequent professorial allusion. It is quite easy, and I believe quite effective, to toss off impromptu remarks like: "That reminds me of Veblen's conspicuous consumption. This is an idea that has been quite influential both in sociology and economics. All of you must read sometime his *The Theory of the Leisure Class*. It's available in a paperback now." Or: "Speaking of group dynamics, you might like to look at the rather severe strictures William H. Whyte, Jr. voices on the subject in *The Organization Man*. I would be interested to see whether you think them deserved."

Accessibility of books has been shown to be most important in feeding an incipient reading appetite. Though we

usually leave this problem to the librarians, teachers can be
of great help. Some will be willing to go to the perilous
length of lending their own books. Others will perhaps
bring them to class for student inspection. Better yet,
departments might get together collections to exhibit
once or twice a year. Since students can afford to buy paperbacks, these above all should be shown. Exhibit or no exhibit, a real service to students would be the distribution
of lists of books in particular fields that are available in
cheap editions.[7]

But try as we will to refer our students to the well-written social science books, we have to admit that there are few
of them. Our colleagues in the main write badly. They
clutter up their sentences with jargon and, determined to be
accurate if it kills them (and the reader), they introduce
all possibly relevant qualifications. Schooled by the dreadful
unwritten law of the Ph. D. thesis that one must never use
the word "I," they use the passive voice until it is hoarse.
In a nutshell, there is little grace in their style.

It is easier to be critical of the written output of social
scientists than to do something constructive about it. We
can hardly expect to change professorial training, habits
and tastes in a few years so that the books used in college
classrooms will be as inviting as an Ernest Hemingway
novel or a Lytton Strachey biography. There are no mil-
lennia in such matters. We will have to work away at the
problem. But to be conscious that there is a problem is
the first step. And we have some leads for positive action
that are promising.

In the first place, even though there is no really well-

---

[7] Such lists can be made up from *Paperbound Books in Print* published by R. R. Bowker Co. [A selected edition of titles suitable for
college use has been issued by the publisher since the conference. Ed.]

written textbook for the course one is giving, one can surely choose the best of a rather indifferent lot. All too often we select a textbook because the author is famous for his journal articles and research monographs. We do not ask whether for the purpose of undergraduate teaching another book by some lesser known but more literate figure may not be superior. We can at least make readability one of the principal criteria in choosing what the student is assigned.

Because textbooks are likely to be so deadly we should consider whether we can use them less. Lively research reports like the Lynds' *Middletown* and *Middletown in Transition,* Davis and Gardner's *Deep South,* Thrasher's *The Gang,* Hollingshead's *Elmtown's Youth,* and Underwood's *Catholic and Protestant* are certainly much more titillating to the undergraduate taste. I have cited titles from sociology because I am familiar with them, but there must be similar examples from other fields. Even though the teacher continues to use a text, he can spice up his course with an admixture of "human interest" materials from the research firing line.

There are not, by any stretch of the imagination, enough well-written social science books to equip our courses. Selection is not a sufficient answer. In the long run we have got to see to it that better books are written. I wish I could feel that the natural trial and error of life would bring this about, that the rare books of literary merit would survive in the struggle and the many dull ones be weeded out. I am not sanguine about this; however, I feel that those who are aware of the problem must make definite efforts. First, through exhortation and example, we must get social science authors into the habit of revising their manuscripts for style after they have perfected them from the standpoint of substance. As a preparation for this final task they could read Fowler's *The King's English,* Sir Ernest Gowers' *Plain Words: Their A B C,* or if they have not time for these, Sheridan Baker's admirable article, "Scholarly Style, or the Lack Thereof."[8] One way or another they should get it into their heads that even complex ideas can be clearly expressed if they are put in the simplest and most straightforward manner. But unless a social science author is already a star in the literary firmament like Margaret Mead he should be advised to take a further step, that of calling upon the services of a professional editor. Whatever it may cost it will be worth it in the improvement of the manuscript. What is lost in ego deflation will be more than regained at the hands of the reviewer.

Of the four suggestions I have made for cultivating the lifetime reading habit—two of them general and two of them specific to the social sciences—none is likely to bring spectacular results. Raising the status of the superior student so that his reading habits will be emulated will work very slowly; but we may hope that the diffusion of influence will be steady and broad. The fostering of faculty-student friendships should pay off dramatically for the students who become involved but the incidence will be highly selective. Increasing the amount of reading from popular types of books in social science courses should have some tendency to make these courses more enjoyable and to accustom students to reading good literature. Perhaps most effective of all, if it were to happen, would be the improvement of the quality of books written by social scientists and used as the backbone of courses.

There is one hopeful fact, however, in a rather dismal outlook. No matter how feebly the four suggestions are

[8] *AAUP Bulletin* XLII, No. 3, 464-70.

carried out, they will tend to support each other, and their effects will tend to cumulate through time. Every improvement in the intellectual climate of our colleges will make easier further improvement. Though the ball may start to roll very slowly, it should pick up momentum.

7

The Natural Scientist
and the Reading Tradition

BY WILLIAM C. STEERE

IN OPENING this working paper, I must first declare myself
on the side of the angels—I believe that the college and
university teacher has a very real responsibility to do as
much as he can to influence students to develop good reading habits that will remain with them throughout their
lives. Whether this influence can be effective, and if so, to
what extent, are questions that do not fall into the category of science, but must be considered under the heading
of art, or of magic. Real and obvious incongruities develop
when someone who has been educated to think as a scientist
attempts to evaluate a topic as nonquantitative and as
imponderable as the one assigned to me. Consequently, in
the best interests of self-defense, I should point out at once
that what I have to say here results not at all from scientific
inquiry into an important problem but, quite to the contrary, only a serious reflection on my own opinions, experiences, and prejudices.

So far as I can see, our approach to the question can be
only wholly subjective until eventually we have in hand a
substantial body of data derived from significant popula-

tions of students and alumni—and I would applaud such a study as thoroughly worthwhile, if done on a sufficiently large scale. The few studies of this sort that I have uncovered in the literature available to me and through queries of friends have little significance for one or several reasons: small samples, false assumptions, incomplete coverage of problems, and wrong interpretation of data, among others. Some excellent insights into the development of "lifetime reading habits" may be gained not from questionable statistics but from reading the better autobiographies of the past century or so. As an avocational collector and reader of biographies and autobiographies, especially of scientists, I have been impressed through the years by the tremendous impact and significance of books in the awakening and development of creative scholars.

After more than a quarter of a century at the University of Michigan both as student and as faculty member, I feel quite at home now in bringing together and analyzing some of my own experiences in influencing the "lifetime reading habits" of undergraduate students, because most of whatever influence (if any!) I may have had was exerted right here in Ann Arbor. Moreover, I have been away from large classes composed exclusively of lower classmen long enough to have gained a rather clear perspective.

In my opinion, students in the better American universities today are more literate than were my classmates of thirty years ago. This apparent improvement in no small way resulted from higher standards of admission enforced by our leading universities. Among American state universities, the University of Michigan shares with the University of California the unique privilege of admitting only those students who have demonstrated convincingly their ability to benefit from a high-level educational opportunity. The outstanding nature of the student body of these two insti-

tutions clearly contributes to their very high scholarly repu-
tations, because able scholars are attracted to them. Perhaps
today's student can't spell very well, and perhaps he has
more trouble than his counterpart of a generation ago with
grammatical constructions because of his lack of knowledge
of Latin, but he tends to be less prejudiced and less inhibited
than the students of my day, an emancipation that naturally leads to wider reading, more confident speaking, and
more articulate writing. Moreover, an increasing number
of successful "general studies" programs in American universities take as their central theme the development of
greater literateness in students. Debates on the desirability
of these programs have raged with fury among faculties,
but the obvious effectiveness of good curricula has gradually assuaged faculty antagonism. As a survivor of an earlier
educational fad that put the emphasis on free election of
courses, beyond a minimal group requirement, I am encouraged to witness the exposure of more students to
broader but firmer course requirements. To me, the basic
ideas are sound, although occasional elements of faddism
have produced detrimental results. Under any circumstances, we as educators must favor strongly those curricula
that strive for literateness in students and for the development of vigorous and independent reading habits.

I believe that the increasing availability today of good
modern and classic literature in paperback editions in
college bookstores—as well as in airports and drugstores—
is an encouraging sign of the times. Of course, the pessimist
can point out also the growth of comic books, pulp magazines, and luridly covered shockers. However, the increasingly easier availability of good literature is definitely a
strong cultural advance, since it reflects a growing demand.

In answer to the specific question, "Is the average undergraduate or college graduate today a conscious and mean-

ingful participant in that western 'lettered' culture of
which universities boast themselves the guardians and
transmitters?," I can express only reservations. Disregarding
my conviction to be elaborated later that no such thing as
an average student exists, I would give a somewhat hesitant
"yes," if we are speaking of some few leading universities,
and a definite "no" for most others. In the best universities
and colleges, our students are really conscious and meaningful—in addition to being reluctant and confused—participants. My son recently embarrassed me (both personally
and financially) by pointing out that only about half the
books on his required reading list for his course in Western
Civilization were on my own shelves. The amount and the
variety of required reading in this and in other undergraduate courses today is astonishing, even though discouraging
enough to slow readers and too often lethal to foreign
students insufficiently grounded in English. The answer to
"How and what does the entering freshman read?" is clear
and inexorable—he reads in frantic haste and with considerable insecurity exactly what has been assigned to him
to read; rarely more, rarely less. If less, he doesn't pass
the course; if more, he is an unusually able and enterprising
student. The "why" answers itself, then.

What the entering freshman was reading when, in his
innocence, he first crossed the threshold of the university,
was undoubtedly something quite different. As an Academic Counselor for many years at the University of
Michigan, and as a Freshman Adviser at Stanford, I have
had the opportunity to read hundreds of freshman applications, and those of course only of the highly selected students from the upper part of the intellectual spectrum
who were finally admitted. One of the most significant and
illuminating standard questions on the applications concerns itself with just this topic of our discussion: What

does the student read habitually, and what books has he read during the past year? A scholarly analysis and evaluation of the answers to this question by the applicants to any good university would be highly rewarding, and such an investigation would certainly produce a very significant doctoral dissertation. Of course, as one might expect, the majority of the books listed as read are selections by the Book of the Month Club or other standardized selections, serial novels in the popular magazines of large circulation, and the perennial classics assigned to high-school students. Even among these superior students who apply for admission to colleges and universities, too few display well-developed personal tastes.

The rare students who show individual and discriminating taste may have preferences that are excellent or are deplorable—or they may reflect only an avocational interest of the moment. The literary tastes of the student who in all probability will enter some field of science tend to be less well defined and somewhat more restricted, since toward the end of high school he is usually more concerned with "things" than with ideas. His "hot rod," his "ham" radio activities, his butterfly collection, his insectivorous plants, his living ants, bees, budgies, snakes, ferrets, rabbits, tropical fish, alligators, and guinea pigs, his stamp collection, as well as other and manifold interests that alarm his mother and please his father, take much of the time and energy that might otherwise be put into the development of literateness of a more classical type. Nevertheless, in defense of our potential scientist, I can testify to his surprising facility in reading and comprehending technical books and articles related to his avocation, a facility usually gained without special instruction.

The ability of the well-motivated student of science to dig into and to organize the literature of his field of interest

is undoubtedly related to his ability to design and to conduct experiments, and later, to enter the field of scientific
investigation. If any measurable difference exists between
students of natural sciences and students of humanities
and social sciences, it may be discovered in the area of reading. The student of natural science is less likely to read
the whole book he refers to than his colleagues in other
scholarly areas—he reads until he finds the specific answer
to a specific question. The graduate student in the sciences
must develop skill in finding the books he needs, and of
course his work in a large university is made easier by the
customary segregation of the books he works with into
separate departmental libraries. The concomitant danger
is that through too concentrated use of one special library,
a student may overlook important and useful books in
related fields, or the fundamental reference works in the
main library. Graduate students in humanities and in social
sciences tend to read whole books because of a more general
interest, and because of the pressures upon them. The
volume of reading by students in the nonscience disciplines,
then, tends to be perceptibly greater than in the natural
sciences.

Although an intuitive belief certainly exists—and some
implications may be read into what I have already said—
that students in the natural sciences tend to be less literate
than students in humanities and social sciences, enough
outstanding exceptions arise at once to demolish any generalization. As Dean of the Graduate Division at Stanford
University, I examine and sign hundreds of doctoral dissertations, some of them written so in the jargon of chemistry
as to be completely unintelligible to the layman, and others
written in other jargons—of sociology, of education, of
economics, of psychology, of anthropology, of music, of
symbolic logic—that are just as unintelligible. I see beauti-

fully written dissertations from the departments of English and History—and also in the natural sciences. If any generalization must be made, it will have to be based on tendencies discovered statistically instead of on absolute differences. Dissertations in the natural sciences tend to be more factual, more straightforward, and of less intrinsic literary excellence than dissertations in more classical fields. This generally inconspicuous difference between dissertations in different areas of scholarship of course reflects differences of interest and of emphasis of students in their high-school and undergraduate years, as well as differences that will also continue on into professional life. In the professional scientific journals we find occasional scientific articles of high literary quality as well as many poorly written articles—but this situation is by no means absent in nonscientific journals. To emphasize my point, these differences in literateness represent more strongly the normal spectrum of differences among men in general than they do some mysterious, innate, and absolute difference between scientists and nonscientists.

A good science teacher can contribute substantially to the improvement of the reading habits of students. In the first place, he can conduct his courses so as to arouse the curiosity of the student to such a pitch that he will start reading spontaneously. Showing students the actual book or article in which some well-known scientific discovery was first elucidated, for example, is an excellent technique for stimulating the interest of students. In the second place, the placing of books of general interest in the laboratory and classroom, where they are easily accessible, and mentioning them specifically during class discussions, will lead many students painlessly to a wider reading program than they would otherwise follow. In the third place, the assignment in science courses of brief written reports whose topics are to be chosen by the student according to his already established interests, will force the student into the library and will help him become familiar with a larger body of literature than the usual textbook and assigned reading procedure will. My own contribution to student reading habits has been to make a serious attempt in each course to find at least some one point or topic of mutual interest between each student and myself, and to encourage the student to read further into this area where he is already well motivated. It is extremely rewarding for a teacher to see some of his students "come alive" and begin to read with pleasure such informative works as *The Origin of Species, The Life of Pasteur, Flight from Reality, The Sea Around Us,* and others of this type too numerous to list here.

Teachers' attitudes are extremely important to students. The teacher who holds the full respect of his students can exert an enormous influence on them. If this teacher takes quite for granted that books are important, and if he uses them freely in his teaching procedures, his students will adopt the same point of view, without even realizing their own change in attitude. The teacher who assumes an apologetic attitude, however, soon loses his student following.

Helping graduate students to discover that the classic historical books and pamphlets of their discipline are still available from secondhand bookdealers in this country and abroad (as well as in facsimile) is always a stimulating experience for both teacher and student. Some of my doctoral candidates bought more books during their graduate-student days than they could really afford, and yet I approve the motives that led them to do so.

Much present-day teaching, even in our proudest universities, follows antediluvian procedures and patterns. I am convinced that too much of the anti-intellectualism so prevalent in America today stems from uninspiring, impersonal, and highly formalized teaching. Among the many overlooked crimes of the dull teacher is that he damns his own profession irrevocably in the eyes of his students and thereby discourages potentially good teachers from entering the academic fold. Moreover, in passive or active disappointment with education as they find it, students tend to downgrade all intellectual activity. As a consequence, anti-intellectualism arises and propagates itself in the last place we would expect or should tolerate it—in too many colleges and universities. Hoopes and Marshall[1] well expressed this problem:

> Every college campus is marked by a set of values, a milieu of its own, which is a product of the students' backgrounds, the kinds of homes and high schools from which they come, and the campus traditions which, when once established, are handed down from one student generation to the next. At many colleges this milieu is one of anti-intellectualism undergirded by excessive emphasis on intercollegiate sports, social activities, and a narrowly vocational curriculum which reduces higher education to little more than four years of the kind of training that might be obtained at a trade school far removed from the college or university environment. At the end of four years in this sort of college the student is given a diploma and is eligible for certain kinds of employment which would otherwise have been closed to him.

Even in the best universities, sensitive students tend to be apologetic about high grades, per se, unless they are able to distinguish themselves also in athletics or other student activities. The poor student envies the scholastic achievements of the able student, yet expresses his insecurity and

[1] Robert Hoopes and Hubert Marshall, *The Undergraduate in the University. A Report to the Faculty by the Executive Committee of the Stanford Study of Undergraduate Education, 1954-56* (Stanford: Stanford University Press, 1957), p. 73.

aggressions by sneering at high scholarship, with unanticipated success.

At the high-school level, anti-intellectualism seems to be expected and tolerated, as an inevitable attitude of healthy young animals "going through a phase." Certainly, there is nothing new about it, as we can ascertain from the gruesome accounts by many American and British authors of conditions and attitudes in preparatory schools a century ago—it occurs on a larger scale now and in a somewhat different form, in that the antipathy of the student tends now to be directed against the more rigorous and demanding teacher of science rather than the Latin master of another era.

When I was a student, the popular image of the scientist represented a pathologically absent-minded but essentially kindly person, invariably engaged in research designed for the eventual benefit of humanity. Cartoons identified the scientist by one or several standard "props": a white coat, a butterfly net, a test tube or retort, an ophthalmoscope, or a stethoscope. Only the white coat remains—the Atomic Age has produced a revolution in this general stereotype of a scientist, of which Morris offers the following analysis:[2]

The low estate of both the scientist and the teacher of science has become alarmingly evident in recent years. The scientific worker is increasingly regarded as an odd kind of person who works on material which is not only politically secret but technologically so erudite that no ordinary person can comprehend it. With this stereotype in mind, the youngster who is planning a career finds it difficult to visualize himself in an occupation that he does not know anything about. And when he confronts scientists of his acquaintance, his high-school science teacher for instance, he may run into other confusions that characterize

[2] Van Cleve Morris, "Training of a Scientist," *Scientific Monthly*, LXXXV (1957), 126-29.

our puzzling social system. I refer to the fact that the teacher of science, being a teacher, unfortunately inhabits the lower socio-economic echelons of society and too infrequently stands as the symbol of excitement and adventure for which a youngster in high school is looking. In view of these conditions, many people turn away from science, despite the generous rewards that are now being offered by industry.

In a recent analysis of samplings of the attitudes of high-school students, Mead and Métraux[3] discovered that although their state of mind toward science in general was favorable—"without science, we would still be living in caves; science is responsible for progress, is necessary for the defense of the country, is responsible for preserving more lives and for improving the health and comfort of the population"—their attitude toward personal contact with science, as a career choice or involving the choice of a husband, proves to be overwhelmingly negative. This study by a distinguished social anthropologist is a "must" for thoughtful high-school and college teachers, especially for the illuminating, thought-provoking and often shocking quotations from the anonymous essays written by the students. The students' stereotype of "the scientist" obviously arises from horror movies, television programs, comic books, and science fiction, and not from reading books about science or from direct contact with scientists.

The image of the scholar in the mind of the general public also suffers from more than a bit of fuzziness. Many of us here recall, some of us perhaps more painfully than others, the loose talk about "those professors in Washington," and the "Brains Trust" during the early days of the New Deal. Much more recently, we have seen the popular adoption of the term "egg-head" as an opprobrious epi-

    [3] Margaret Mead and Rhoda Métraux, "Image of the Scientist Among High-School Students," Science, CXXVI (1957), 384-90.

thet applied to intellectuals. We have also witnessed the spectacle of an intelligent presidential candidate urged by his supporters to tone down the intellectual level of his campaign speeches to avoid antagonizing the voters. In this connection, I will quote here some amusing remarks made by Professor Isaac Asimov,[4] also a popular science fiction writer, on the role of spectacles in movies and television as a symbol of a developed intellect:

No, the glasses are not literally glasses. They are merely a symbol, a symbol of intelligence. The audience is taught two things: (a) Evidence of extensive education is a social hindrance and causes unhappiness; (b) Formal education is unnecessary, can be minimized at will, and the resulting limited intellectual development leads to happiness.

In a recent AP release from Hollywood (December 3, 1957), Bob Thomas informs scientists of still worse things to come. Post-Sputnik Hollywood is now eager to make its mission in the national emergency the glamorizing of the American scientist—to "make him appear dashing and important, so kids will want to be like him"! The means proposed for this gilding of the lily are too preposterous and too revolting even for a brief review here.

Thoughtful scholars in the natural and physical sciences have become increasingly concerned over the rapidly worsening problem of communication between scientists and nonscientists, whether it be in the teaching of science to students or in informing the general public. The biased public attitudes toward scientists and science and the inaccurate popular image already discussed emphasize the urgent need for improved means of "putting across" to the public what science *really* is and what scientists *really*

[4] Isaac Asimov, "The By-product of Science Fiction," *American Institute of Biological Sciences Bulletin,* VII (1957), 25-27.

do, as well as how they think and work. Horror films, science fiction, comic books and television combine to create a wholly fictitious impression of the scientist in the public mind, and now Hollywood threatens to glamorize him! On the other hand, we must confess that with rare and outstanding exceptions, the busy scientist makes little or no attempt to interpret himself correctly to the public. Moreover, he feels, perhaps with false pride, that it would be beneath his dignity to glamorize himself, his work, or his field. In fact, more often than not, he tends to work and to write for his colleagues, as if the public did not even exist. How, then, can a scientist expect to be understood properly for what he is? Dael Wolfle, a distinguished psychologist, has stated the problem so brilliantly that I shall succumb to the temptation of quoting him at some length:[5]

The intelligent cooperation of scientists and nonscientists in arriving at answers is made difficult by the progress of science itself. For as science progresses, other men find it more and more difficult to appreciate what science is about and to understand the scientists' language, problems, and intentions. As scientists have moved farther and farther from processes and problems that are open to the inspection of other men, they have dealt more and more in abstractions, have developed specialized vocabularies and a technical jargon, and frequently have concluded that their subject matter is too esoteric for general understanding. In truth, it is difficult for the nonscientist to know what modern science is about. When the scientist speaks of megaton bombs, of distances a billion and more light years away, of space that is negatively curved, the nonscientist looks puzzled. Even if he recognizes the individual words, the magnitudes are beyond his comprehension, and he lacks a framework of experience and understanding into which to fit such strange concepts.

[5] Dael Wolfle, "Science and Public Understanding," *Science*, CXXV (1957), 179-82.

The absence of understanding leads to confusion and to a public attitude toward scientists that is muddled instead of being clear and coherent. On the one hand, a considerable amount of anti-intellectualism exists. The scientist is frequently an object of suspicion and mistrust. His loyalty is more likely to be questioned than is that of other men. He is considered strange, unusual, not altogether honest, and sometimes antisocial. The teacher is a "square," and rigorous intellectual scholarship is out of date. These disquieting attitudes show up in many forms and places. On the other hand, however, the public is not opposed to science; it welcomes and enjoys those fruits of science that it can assimilate. There is no serious opposition to radar, television, antibiotics, or electronic computers, and we know that the individual who perfects a cure for cancer will be a public hero. Thus, while the fruits of science and scholarship are honored, the scientist is not. This is what I mean by saying that popular attitudes are muddled.

Wolfle's wonderfully prophetic remarks have been borne out by the sudden trend toward science and scientists since the appearance of Sputnik I and II. The press, the radio, and other media of communication now reproach roundly all responsible individuals and groups, from the President down, for our suddenly exposed relative lack of know-how—in a country that has revered know-how above all else.

One problem in the communication of science that might not be generally suspected is the poor communication between scientists themselves, even among those in the same field. Fortunately, this problem is receiving serious attention, and some remedial measures have already been taken. Nevertheless, the increasing volume of scientific publication raises progressively complex and perplexing questions, and since some data relating to them may be of interest to the group of scholars at this conference, it seems

highly appropriate to quote a thought-provoking paragraph from an editorial by W. R. Duryee:[6]

A harsh critic might say that the most unscientific thing about
modern science is how it does business. He might point out that
we write more and more articles, books, reviews, speeches, and,
yes, editorials. Yet we insist on using a system, centuries old, of
publishing bulky papers with charts, tables and illustrations and
expensively pushing these into the already overcrowded libraries
of the world. Our large scientific meetings have tended to
become a series of hurried papers, run off in simultaneous batches.
It is extremely difficult to escape the conclusion that there are
just too many words in our libraries, too many articles, too many
journals, too many books, and too little organization of our
ideas. Approximately 40,000 technical and scientific journals
are published throughout the world. Of this number, over
20,000 are in the field of biology. In the United States the
Library of Congress takes over half of this world's total in
biology (approximately 12,000) while most of the other large
libraries subscribe to about 2,000 per year. *Biological Abstracts*
uses some material from about 2,000 journals but is able to do
a complete coverage of only 200. When it is realized that an
average biologist can read only about 4 or 5 journals carefully
and skim the titles of say 20 or 30 more, we might well ask the
question: Is science defeating its own purposes?

This conference is timely indeed. The dedication of this
new University of Michigan Undergraduate Library marks
several forward steps in a too deliberate trend in this country toward the reduction of formality in teaching and the
concomitant placing of greater responsibility on the student himself for acquiring his own education—a trend
that must increase rapidly in tempo if American colleges
and universities are to deal adequately with the doubled

[6] William R. Duryee, "Better Communications by 1960," *American
Institute of Biological Sciences Bulletin*, IV (1954), 3.

enrollments promised us for 1970, of more than six million college students.

The President's Committee on Education Beyond the
High School, in its "Second Report to the President" (p.
31), has summarized this point cogently, as follows:

> It is imperative that we learn how to teach more people more
> effectively. The Committee particularly urges increasing em-
> phasis on the development of educational methods which place
> larger responsibility for learning on the student himself. This
> could actually improve the quality of education at the same
> time it helped to relieve the teacher shortage.

To me, the concept of the Undergraduate Library, and
the Undergraduate Library itself, present major advances
in the development of educational methods so urgently
recommended by the President's Committee. Such a special
facility furnishes a favorable and even persuasive milieu for
the intellectual growth of the undergraduate, since he
thereby becomes a participant and not just a nuisance to
graduate students and faculty, who in their turn are perhaps an equal or greater nuisance to him. This new library
is for him, and he belongs, as is shown by the unanticipated
and immediate acceptance of it by the students, who have
already moved into it in overwhelming numbers. The psychological importance of this library in giving status to
undergraduates is one of its most significant features. The
informality, the reduction of hustle and bustle, and the
removal of the need to stand in line at the book delivery
desk all give the student a much greater sense of confidence
and of security than the coldly impersonal treatment one
usually receives in any great general library, with its very
natural emphasis on scholarly research.

Most important and most essential, of course, is the con-
frontation of the student with the books themselves. The

sense of discovery in the mind of a college undergraduate
who is turned loose in the stacks of a library to browse in
comfort and leisure is very important to him. I still remember with pleasure my own naïve "discovery" of the
Natural Science Library here at the University of Michigan
over thirty years ago. Parenthetically, my discovery of the
bookstores, with their shelves of new and of secondhand
books was also a never-to-be-forgotten experience. While
a graduate student at the University of Pennsylvania, I
"discovered" Leary's bookstore in downtown Philadelphia,
one of the highlights of my graduate student career. Helping and encouraging students to learn to browse and to
develop personal tastes in reading must be among the responsibilities of a university teacher, in my opinion.

The arbitrary assignment by a professor of readings in
"the Book," which the student obtains by filling out a request slip and then standing in line until the library assistant finds it, or reports back that it is missing or already
charged out, is a terribly negative experience for an intelligent student, and reduces rather than increases his interest in the course involved. I speak feelingly from my
own experience as an undergraduate student. If, on the
other hand, he is given permission and encouragement to
look on the shelves himself, with perhaps some wise suggestions about titles and authors if he is inexperienced, his
interest, his knowledge, and his independence will all grow
perceptibly. An important event in my career as an undergraduate student was the attainment of a pass to the stacks
of the General Library of the University of Michigan,
through the kindly and forceful efforts on my behalf of a
great teacher and scholar, Harley H. Bartlett. The permanent influence on my own thinking and reading habits as a
result of this special privilege led me quite naturally to
plead for passes for my own qualified students. Now that

this new library has been designed especially for them, undergraduate students will no longer need special privilege or influence to attain that which should be their normal right—the free access to new ideas.

Stanford University recently underwent the throes of developing plans for an Undergraduate Library, not in any casual imitation of Harvard, Cornell and Michigan, but as the result of the same educational forces that eventually brought the necessary facilities to those great universities. Some of the ideas arising from our endemic study are so well phrased that they merit quotation here. First, I shall quote from Robert Hoopes:[7]

The road to discipline and knowledge and wisdom is and has always been the traditional and difficult way of learning. Part of the business of motivating the undergraduate is to make him aware of the nature of that road. We do all we can by improving course content and arrangement, by urging teachers to do the best job they can in the classroom—all that we can do in short to put the student on the road. Once on it, excited by the prospect of intellectual adventure and discovery, where shall he go?

He must go to the crystallized record of the civilization and culture that he has inherited. He must go to books, and they will serve him as a guide, a solace, and a reward. Without them the journey of the mind remains aimless and arid.

Of books there are many at Stanford. The Library's million and a quarter volumes make it one of the major research centers of the United States. Yet in its very magnitude and the diversity of interests represented in the university community which it serves, it is for undergraduates at best puzzling, often inconvenient and not infrequently a completely discouraging barrier between them and their books.

Here, then, is the need for the undergraduate library, and

[7] Robert Hoopes, "Undergraduate Study and the Library," *Appreciation* (Stanford University Libraries), III (1), (1955), 2-3.

with its coming the opportunity will arise for that free communication between the books and the undergraduates that is
so necessary for the success of our project.

A further series of wise and pertinent remarks on this
topic, made semianonymously by David Heron,[8] apply so
well to the subject of this conference that I wish I could
have written them myself. Because of their obvious appro-
priateness here, then, I take the liberty of quoting them *in
extenso:*

The ability to read intelligently and critically is perhaps the
most tangible and valuable endowment of a liberal education.
It is a voluntary and satisfying process—even an end in itself:
the satisfaction of that peculiar appetite for ideas which is the
creative and rational force of a democratic society.

It is an ability which can be developed only through practice
—an acquired habit which all too many university graduates
escape in spite of the most inspired instruction. University
libraries bear their full share of blame for this failure: they are
first, and are forced to be, research institutions, and their very
size and complexity is a handicap to undergraduate reading.

The evolution of American university libraries has followed a
pattern in which the needs of undergraduates have been subordinated to the needs of faculty and graduate students. University
libraries are at least accessories to the practice of assigning mere
fragments of books, often out of their full context, as mandatory
reading for undergraduate courses. Even these scraps of intellectual nourishment are doled out through reserve book rooms, and
must generally be gulped without tasting from the bare boards
of a crowded study hall.

University libraries have been forced in recent years to recognize the growing barrier which has arisen, aggravated by increases in enrollment and the growth of their reserve collections,
between undergraduate students and the books they should be

[8] D. W. H., "The Stanford Undergraduate Library," *Appreciation*
(Stanford University Libraries), III (1), (1955) 4-7.

learning to read and know. The problem has been most acute in the social sciences and humanities, whose literature constitutes the major part of any university library, and whose disciplines are so interdependent that they cannot be readily set aside in the more adequate facilities which the sciences and professions have achieved in their special libraries.

The ideal way for an undergraduate to read in the humanities or social sciences would be to buy his own books: the alternatives are most often the slim rations of reserve book reading and the ordeal of waiting upon the deliberate and mysterious rites of the loan desk. But students cannot buy all their own books, and ways must be found of making it less difficult for them to use the library.

The establishment of an undergraduate library, whose design, furnishing, services, and special facilities are purposefully devoted to this encouragement of reading, is an essential adjunct to the changes which Stanford is effecting in the conduct of undergraduate education. Two of the three broad questions which the Stanford Study of Undergraduate Education is considering—namely, the effectiveness of undergraduate teaching and the intellectual motivation of undergraduate students— have inevitably involved consideration of library services. Clearly a new and dynamic undergraduate library must play an important role in this evolutionary process. . . .

The special facilities should be subordinate, however, to the books and the reading of them and to the creation of a stimulating library atmosphere. It is not as easy to make students want to read today as it was before the advent of the cathode ray, the commercial, the digest, and the multipurpose capsule.

Their four years in the University are for Stanford students their best and often their last chance to acquire the habit of reading. Giving them an adequate place in which to develop this habit is an opportunity of the greatest importance in the program of undergraduate education.

The relatively recent (November 21, 1957) report of a special committee established at Stanford University to develop plans for an Undergraduate Library pointed out, quite in line with David Heron's remarks just quoted that "It will be used primarily by students in courses in humanities and the social sciences." It is further concluded that "Its facilities will certainly be of great value to students in the natural sciences as well, but it is recognized that they will inevitably do much of their library work in the specialized collections maintained by various science departments."

The implication that science students should not be interested in the opportunities offered by this new facility— or should not be considered in the same way as other students during the planning stages—I find more than a bit shocking, and as a member of the committee, I registered a dissenting vote against this opinion. Although few quantitative data exist, at least in published form, on the relative use of the library by students in the different major disciplines, it is perhaps true that students in the various areas of natural sciences do not read, and do not have to read, quite as large a volume as do students in humanities and social sciences. It is reasonably clear, at least in qualitative terms, that students' interests in areas of science tend to be engrossed in *doing*, rather than *reading*, during their formative years in high school and college. However, like most generalizations, this one is undoubtedly more noteworthy for its exceptions than for its over-all reliability.

One of the best refutations of the slighting implication that science does not require the same degree of literateness as other fields is to be found in the reception of the inspiring Traveling High-School Science Library Program of the American Association for the Advancement of Science. With financial support from the National Science Foundation and under the able direction of Hilary J. Deason, the AAAS has organized a traveling library, in multiples of 300, of over 200 books dealing with the general and the broad aspects of science, from anthropology to zoology.[9]

These libraries circulate in self-contained box-shelves among small and underprivileged high schools with the motive of bringing science to students in out-of-the-way districts. These students might otherwise be greatly delayed in becoming acquainted with the concepts and the literature of science, because of the all too frequent prejudice against science teaching in such high schools as too expensive. The books circulated to these underprivileged high schools were recommended by professional scientists and educators and were then subjected to scrupulous screening for readability not only by experienced teachers of recognized ability but also by bright high-school students. Parenthetically, it can be added here that most of the books are of equal interest and are as challenging to college students and to intelligent adult nonscientists, as they are to high-school students. I would recommend warmly that these carefully selected books, a list of which is available from the American Association for the Advancement of Science in Washington, D.C., also be acquired by university and municipal libraries.

A most significant endorsement for the AAAS traveling science library is its unexpectedly favorable treatment in a review by, of all people, a teacher of English,[10] who contrasted it with a selection of 365 recommended supplementary readings—the "Combined Book Exhibit"—in a publication of the National Council of Teachers.

I return now to the "Second Report to the President" and its recognition of the urgent need for college and university students to accept more responsibility for their own education. If taken seriously by educators and its full

[9] Hilary J. Deason, *Science*, CXXII (1955), 1173-76; CXXIV (1956), 1013-20; CXXVI (1957), 740-43.

[10] Joseph Gallant, "Literature, Science, and the Manpower Crisis," *Science*, CXXV (1957), 787.

potential realized, this idea can bring about a very good improvement in education.

John Masefield displayed a remarkably pragmatic and illustrative bit of folk wisdom in the following lines:

> Sitting still and wishing
> Makes no person great,
> The good Lord sends the fishing
> But you must dig the bait.

Honors courses and other forms of independent reading, study, and actual research should be developed or reinforced in every college and university. At Stanford, honors courses are available to its juniors and seniors in biology, psychology, and other areas of science, to afford highly able students an opportunity to work directly with some one faculty member or graduate student. Many liberal arts colleges expect every senior to produce a senior thesis or to take a comprehensive examination, in the normal course of events, as the result of independent work. The number of students who decide to become scholars—in contrast to those who decide to enter graduate work in one of the various professional schools—appears to be directly proportional to the opportunity given them, or thrust upon them, to do independent reading, thinking and study.

One of the most successful devices with which I am acquainted is the assignment of outstanding juniors and seniors as assistants to graduate students, as is done in the Department of Psychology at Stanford. The personal relationship between an undergraduate and a graduate student is naturally much more informal than between the student and his professor. Nonetheless, the graduate student in turn has a major professor who advises him and who can help the undergraduate, too, when necessary. The undergraduate is either paid on an hourly basis for his assistance to the graduate student, or receives some credit toward graduation if he registers for a research participation project. The graduate student, of course, receives at no cost to him an additional pair of hands and the benefit of new and open-minded ideas. Several seniors have already published short papers as the result of this stimulation of their talents for individual and original thinking, and through their introduction to the ideas and the literature of a field at a time in their career when too many students are reading only textbooks. The potential benefits of this sort of program to able students are enormous.

The importance of books to students must not and cannot be underestimated. My own naïve discovery of the library and of bookstores is probably a typical example. Every biographical or autobiographical study of intelligent people, whether in humanities, social sciences or in natural sciences, emphasizes the influence of a relatively small number of books—sometimes only one—at a formative stage, and their impact on the whole life and development of the individual. Charles Darwin, for example, gave much credit to his boyhood reading of Lyell's *Principles* for his intuitive recognition of evolution after his inspired realization of the effects of natural selection upon the survival of the fittest, as well as the effects of the removal of competition. The discovery of some one book that suddenly develops real meaning to the reader, and that may almost immediately revolutionize his thought, often heralds the beginning of a scholarly career.

An illuminating case history is given by G. S. Ford[11] concerning the influence of a teacher upon his reading habits and upon his development as a scholar:

[11] G. S. Ford, "Teacher and Taught," *AAUP Bulletin*, XLI (1955), 476-88.

But somehow, some way, she put in my hands a little book by the Reverend John Todd called *Todd's Student Manual,* written in the first half of the nineteenth century. I have met only one person who ever heard of the Reverend John Todd, and that was because the author was a great-uncle of his. The book, which he did not know, prescribed rules for study and student conduct that would have turned Loyola, the founder of the Jesuits, green with envy by their preciseness and exacting character. I mastered it except for certain Latin quotations. By the context I surmised that they described youthful sins that he did not think it nice to discuss in English. I adhered to it till even my limited world of knowledge made impossible the prescribed daily, weekly, and monthly reviews of all that had gone before. And while speaking of these two village teachers, let me not forget a study I saw somewhere on influential teachers, which reported that a substantial number of the persons questioned mentioned the encouragement given them by a high school teacher—especially, encouragement to go on to college.

The next name in my list was the same double play of teacher to book to student. The old president of the little institution I first attended gave some of us the opportunity to read with him a book he had discovered. It was Bryce's *American Commonwealth.* No one today can picture what a revelation that book was to a lad in his teens or to any thoughtful American citizen in 1890. For me it was the first revelation of how a scholar works. It had footnotes. All my other texts were self-contained and seemed the products of one superior intellect that knew or had discovered all there was to know in history or literature or zoology.

Once students develop a reading habit, it usually becomes a real lifetime habit. The addiction of students—and of adults—to working their way through a series of writings by the same author, whether a serial article or novel in a popular magazine or a series of "sequels" in book form, is well known by parents and teachers. Much advantage could be taken of this human attribute of following the course of least resistance by putting scholarly materials in serial form, to lead interested students to ever-increasing levels of intellectual achievement, as well as to bridge subjects. Graded reading series, one book leading to the next, are seriously needed at the college level in every field. Our present practice of publishing college texts in a highly competitive manner is certainly in accord with our system of free enterprise. However, somewhat fuller communication among textbook manufacturers and some arrangement for the grading of texts before publication would enhance rather than reduce sales.

One of the important factors in a student's background that influences his attitudes toward reading and toward independent work in general is, of course, whether or not he has been exposed to books at home and has been encouraged to read freely and widely. Economics are not involved here, as there seems to be little correlation between the economic status of the family and the intellectual motivation of the child. Students from the most solvent families may be the least literate, whereas students from poor economic backgrounds may enter college eager for education and take very naturally to independent reading. In fact, the eagerness for education of economically underprivileged youth seems to be an old American tradition, as is emphasized in so many biographies. In my opinion, here is still one more important question that needs serious inquiry. We can conclude with certainty that intellectual force in a family is more significant than financial solvency in inspiring children towards scholarship and a scholarly career. However, the relatively underprivileged economic and social status of the teacher in America at the moment does not bode well for increasing the popular acceptance of intellectual ideas and activities.

My point in stressing the importance of good teaching

and the disastrous effects of bad teaching may be too obvious: the inspiring teacher arouses and stimulates the interest of students in the subject; with his interest stirred, the student wishes to know more about the subject, and so proceeds very naturally to independent reading. Consequently, the relationship between an exciting teacher and the reading habits of students is most direct.

Like Tristam Shandy, I have wandered far and wide in attaining my central theme and have made many side excursions into perhaps too many diverse and yet relevant fields while setting the scene for it. In the first place, my delay was more or less conscious, because I am totally ignorant about and completely unable to define "the student." I recognize "a student" and "students," but, so far as I am concerned, "the student," or worse, "the average student," does not exist except as a datum in statistical studies. Students are individuals who vary in every conceivable manner from each other.

Averages can be established for height, age, weight, I.Q., economic status, number of siblings and for dozens of other ponderables, but I defy anyone, even our Eniac computer, to discover positive correlations between these variables to such an extent that an "average student" emerges, or even can be seen dimly. Quite to the contrary, successful teaching requires a real sensitivity on the part of the teacher to the great range of variation in the motivation, family background, previous school training, and interests of the students in his discussion groups. Probably no institution in the country attracts a more cosmopolitan, diverse and complex student body than the University of Michigan. It draws from all economic, social and racial groups within the state, from highly industrialized areas, from submarginal agricultural regions, from mining communities, from lake-faring families, and from numerous other groups.

From the East Coast come students who for economic or other reasons do not enter the Ivy League schools. From the South, from the West, and from all over the world come students who do not find suitable educational opportunity conveniently at hand. One finds, as a consequence, every degree of sophistication among Michigan students.

Of my nineteen years on the faculty of the University of Michigan, the first eight or nine were devoted almost exclusively to teaching a large elementary course, elected largely by freshmen. This meant two sections a semester, four sections a year, year after year—but I liked it, even though it meant sixteen hours of student contact each week, without respite. All the students in all the sections, approximately 350, were corralled twice a week into a general lecture that was sometimes correlated with the recitation or laboratory work, but just as often was quite unrelated. The casual co-existence of these lectures, tacked on as they were to an otherwise very homogeneous course, mystified the students as much as it did the instructors, although I had not yet come to the realization that universities tend to retain useless appendages, just as do organisms, explainable through history and tradition, but still difficult to extirpate. I still recall with facility the violent contrast between the warm and close-knit group spirit of the discussion and laboratory sections, where I came to know the students very well as individuals, and the passive or rebellious attitude of the students toward the lectures. I bring in this nostalgic reference to illustrate the importance of taking a good, new and hard look at the structure and aims of courses, as well as how they are taught—something too rarely done in colleges and universities.

I believe that the teacher of natural sciences has certain advantages over the teacher of humanities and of social sciences, although many of them may be more apparent than

real. In the first place, six hours a week in the laboratory
with a group of twenty to twenty-five students enables
the teacher to know them rather well. By the same token, the
friendly relationship engendered by close association in the
laboratory between the teacher and the students, as well as
between the students themselves, carries over a more informal and relaxed attitude to the discussion sections that
enables students to ask questions and give information that
might embarrass them in a more formal context. Referring
back to my outburst about "the student" versus the fearful
complexity of individual students and the teacher's need
to know something about the backgrounds of the members
of his classes: at the first meeting of each semester, I asked
the students to write a paragraph about themselves. Occasionally, if the rapport of this first meeting seemed unusually good, I asked the students also to present their
statements orally, which as luncheon clubs discovered long
ago is a most effective method of breaking the ice within a
group. These written paragraphs are extremely enlightening, much more so than the student can possibly realize,
since in addition to the specific items he is asked to cover,
as age, home town, preparatory school, interests, etc., he
unknowingly reveals much more, as for example his ability
to select what is significant and what should be emphasized,
his use of English, the extent of his vocabulary, and his
spelling—and of even greater interest to the teacher, something of what kind of person he is.

The second advantage of the teacher in natural sciences
is that these fields are probably easier to teach, and obviously
the examinations are easier to rate. The timeworn anecdote
of the student who received a low grade on an essay that
had brought an "A" to his fraternity brother the preceding
year reflects a permissible spread of value judgments in non-

scientific fields. Although one teacher of chemistry may grade more severely than another, the grading within any class will be consistent, because personal opinions and values will be subordinated to the subject matter itself. The concepts and hypotheses that have arisen from the body of knowledge we now call the natural sciences are based in large part on something that can be weighed and/or measured, whether it be an elephant or an atom. The highly quantitative nature of natural sciences, as well as the high degree of predictability made possible through the experimental approach, distinguishes the natural sciences from the humanities and, to a lesser degree, from the social sciences. In geology, botany, zoology, chemistry, and in many areas of physics, the student can "get his hands on" something—he can see it, manipulate it, demonstrate it, and thereby understand it more easily than he can some abstract concept in mathematics or symbolic logic, no matter how elegant it may be. Unfortunately, perhaps because of these very advantages and because of demands on their time for productive research, inferior teachers seem to appear in disproportionate numbers in the natural sciences. These uninspired teachers emphasize the body of knowledge itself rather than the concepts and the ideas; they alienate student interest by too much measurement, too much weighing, too much description, and too many facts to be committed to memory, instead of utilizing these same data constructively as a means by which the student is guided to that point where he can rediscover for himself, with excitement, the idea, the concept, or the correlation.

As I look back to my freshman year and to subsequent undergraduate years, I can't understand what now exhausted resource enabled me to overcome frustration and impatience in order to continue regular attendance in some

of my undergraduate classes. I agree wholeheartedly with
G. S. Ford's wise advice:[12]

> . . . it is the student's privilege, I might say his duty, to walk
> out when a lecturer walks in and says in word or manner, "Well,
> what can I bore you with today?"

While reading Ford's remarks, I suddenly recalled walking out in the middle of an incredibly dull lecture (given
by a scholar of outstanding prestige!) on the spur of the
moment and dropping the course officially in the same
moment. Too many teachers feel, unfortunately for the
students, that they have a vested right to give poor lectures,
again supporting Ford's thesis.

One of my colleagues at Michigan, may God rest his soul,
was a reasonably successful teacher for small advanced
classes, but an absolute and spectacular failure as a lecturer
in the large elementary course—to which, by that curious
logic by which universities run themselves, he was assigned.
A durable campus legend indicates that substantial numbers
of students walked out of his lectures, and that when he
used lantern slides, the auditorium was usually completely
empty by the time the lights came on again! To illustrate
that the professor was as lacking in good judgment as he
was in oratorical skill, the legend goes on to say that, in-
furiated by the shrinkage of student attendance, he finally
complained to the Dean that students wouldn't stay in his
lectures. Then, as now, professorial tenure was a mixed
blessing!

I hold the unpopular belief that even our better universities take too scant an interest in, and concern themselves
too little with the level at which courses are taught, largely
because of the strong inhibiting force of departmental au-
tonomy. The administrations of most universities would be

[12] G. S. Ford, "Teacher and Taught," *AAUP Bulletin*, XLI (1955),
476-88.

frankly shocked if they realized the number of courses taught wholly from a single text, without required outside readings or required written reports. As a student, I found this type of course—and teacher—by far the most uninspiring of all. The only manner in which a course can be made even more stultifying is for the professor himself to have written the text, and to repeat it word for word in his lectures. Quite seriously, overdependence on a text by teacher or student does a great deal of harm. It gives the student a wholly misleading idea of the scope and nature of the field; it gives him the false impression that all to be known is known. He is thereby deprived of the intellectual excitement of entering the wonderful world of unsolved problems, and is thereby robbed of an opportunity to find the pleasure of discovering books and of reading them.

Why don't more teachers take advantage of the inherent human curiosity and interest in what is new? A really successful teacher appeals to the same motives that impel the student (and the teacher) to read mystery novels, "whodunits," and science fiction, by stressing the new, the unsolved, and the exciting—and yet without loss of dignity or intellectual level. The development of enthusiasm and of a sense of participation by students indicates best the measure of effective teaching. The uninspiring teacher, on the other hand, produces in his captive audience an increasingly passive attitude toward the subject and a completely negative attitude toward himself. Student evaluation of professors was inaugurated at the University of Michigan a year or so before my move to Stanford. Yet, with only a brief experience, I was impressed by the discrimination and penetration of student comments. Although many of the faculty feared that in general the good students would be calm and the poor students vociferously critical, I believe that these fears reflected in large part the insecurity of those who did not wish to be identified by students as poor teachers. A serious and full-scale evaluation of this program of student rating of professors will be enormously illuminating and might be helpful eventually in leading us to a fuller understanding of student-teacher interaction.

The great teacher, or even the successful and effective teacher, resists definition. Reduced to simplest terms, he contributes most by making important and exciting to the student something that previously did not stir him. One of the significant elements of this process may be that in some way, either subtly or forthrightly, he is able to relate the topic under discussion to the experience of the students. The bringing to life of an abstract concept by relating it clearly to what the students already know or feel, can be a work of art on the part of the teacher and a never-to-be-forgotten experience for a student. The dull teacher may be so imbued with his subject that he is never even aware of the keen sense of disappointment and the inevitable boredom of his students, who might have enjoyed knowing something about his subject, under happier circumstances.

Harry Fuller, himself a great teacher, has skillfully summarized the attributes of a good teacher, as follows:[13]

That college and university facultymen vary enormously in those qualities which constitute excellence in teaching—patience, sympathetic understanding of young people, enthusiasm for one's field of learning, the transplanting of that enthusiasm into students, a sense of humor, breadth of background, experience, and interests, and almost ecclessiastical zeal to touch and enter and nurture young, impressionable minds—is obvious to all who have taught or studied in our collegiate institutions. Similarly discernible are those traits which at their least toxic level make of teaching a dull and neutral experience, at their worst a dead and

[13] Harry J. Fuller, "College Teaching; Its Present Status and Improvement," *American Institute of Biological Science Bulletin* III (1953), 20-22.

corrosive one—lack of interest in students as human individuals, impatience, narrowness of interests and of background, the mistaken use of sarcasm and cynicism as educational devices, inelasticity of classroom procedures, intellectual isolationism, a humorless approach to teaching.

One of the most unforgettable anecdotes I heard while teaching at the University of Michigan concerns the naïve freshman writing a theme on the assigned topic of the responsibilities of teachers. "Every student," wrote the freshman, "has some small spark of genius, even though it may be a very small one. It is the duty of the professor to water this spark." The humor of this anecdote lies superficially in the student's mixed metaphor, but much more surely in the uncomfortable and somewhat bitter recognition of the unintentional correctness of the student's statement. Poor teachers do extinguish the small spark of genius, even though larger sparks tend to nourish themselves and to thrive on conflict and on challenge.

One of the most serious problems in American education, in my opinion, is the striving for conformity and the almost automatic pinching back of areas in which individuality and creativity in intellectual pursuits should be developed and encouraged. If some of the latent creative energy and inventiveness that students display in their extracurricular activities, and that too often get them into trouble, could be harnessed and brought in as a new force in education, we could really develop a "new look" in university teaching. The tremendous capabilities of gifted youth constitute a grossly neglected resource in this country, thanks to the demands of numbers on our school systems, and to the current tendency towards conformity and "lock-step" procedures in primary and secondary schools.

The development in this country of special facilities for the recognition and encouragement of gifted and genius-level children is urgently necessary as well as long overdue. My vehemence results in part from the enormous influence at Stanford of the late Lewis Terman, and his magnificent studies of gifted children, and later, of their progeny. Moreover, I am also influenced by even a casual reflection on historical cases of genius, and will quote briefly from a stimulating inquiry into "the nature and nurture of genius" by S. L. Pressey:[14]

Handel played on the clavichord when but an infant and was composing by the age of 11. Haydn played and composed at the age of 6. Mozart played the harpsichord at 3, was composing at 4, and was on a tour at 6. Chopin played in public at the age of 8; Liszt, at 11; Verdi, at 10; Schubert, at 12; and Rossini, at 14. Mendelssohn was playing publicly and also composing by the age of 9, as was Debussy at 11, Dvorak at 12, and Berlioz at 14. Wagner conducted one of his own compositions in public when he was 17.

John Stuart Mill began the study of Greek at 3. By the age of 8 he had read Xenophon, Herodotus, and Plato and had begun to study geometry and algebra. At 12 he began logic, reading Aristotle in the original. The next year he began the study of political economy; at 16 he was publishing controversial articles in that field. When he was 6 years old, John Ruskin wrote verse. Macaulay compiled a "universal history" at the age of 7. Published poems of William Blake, Thomas Chatterton, and Alexander Pope go back to their 12th years; poems of Robert Burns go back to his 14th year, and of Milton to his 15th year. Pascal wrote a treatise on acoustics when he was 12. Galileo made his famous observations of the swinging cathedral lamp when he was 17. Perkins discovered the first synthetic dye when he was 18. Farnsworth, at 15, "evolved an electronic means of sending pictures through the air." Recently, 11-year-old Italian Severino Guidi, 10-year-old Turkish Hasan Kaptan, and 11-year-old French Thierry Vaubourgoin have been mentioned as precocious

[14] Sidney L. Pressey, "Concerning the Nature and Nurture of Genius," *Scientific Monthly*, LXXXI (1955), 123-29.

painters. Norbert Wiener has written his sensitive account of his own precocity: college entrance at 11, Harvard doctorate at 18. However, as compared with music and athletics, precocity seems more rare in art, literature, and science, and especially so in this country. Why?

Pressey proceeds by answering his own question, elucidating the primary problems of too frequent lack within the family of encouragement of intellectually gifted small children, the mass education of children without reference to special ability, an indifference to the needs of gifted children and the lack of individualized guidance and instruction for excellence. In this country, out of the many fields recognized, only music and athletics do give an opportunity for rapid development of precocity through individual attention and encouragement. When one thinks of the individual attention and encouragement given in other countries to children who are gifted, especially in the direction of mathematics and physics, he suddenly realizes all the more poignantly what extensive resources of leadership we are neglecting to develop.

In conclusion, I will reiterate my major premise that a teacher does have a serious responsibility to help college students in the development and improvement of permanent reading habits. Each teacher may have a different method and each student may develop a different area of interest. However, it is safe to predict that the dedicated teachers and the progressively highly selected student bodies of our leading universities, supported by growing public awareness of the value of intellectual activities, will interact in such a manner that greater literateness and sounder reading habits will result.

8

The Broad and Narrow Paths

A FORUM ON THE FUNCTION OF THE CLASSROOM TEACHER
IN THE DEVELOPMENT OF READING INTEREST

IN THEIR DISCUSSION of the reading problem as seen from the classroom, the conferees devoted most of their attention to the problem as a whole, rather than to the separate problems raised by the individual papers. Nevertheless, some remarks of the highest interest and relevance were made in reference to particular papers.

The conferees in general found themselves agreeably provoked by the distinction Professor Brower made between the "slow reading" course he feels freshmen really need to enable them to experience the literary quality of literature and the "extensive reading of great ideas" or "great books" course they so often get today as their introduction to the "humanities." Mr. Brower agreed, though, with Provost Gross that the intellectual advantages of the close reading method of teaching were by no means confined to the development of literary perception in a narrow sense. Rather, as Mr. Gross put it, such training should make the student sensitive to language as a tool and be carried over from the basic course to other courses in literature, philosophy, etc. Mr. Brower pointed out that it was usually his practice to introduce into the second part of his course some history or other texts not literary in the narrowest sense. They had to be chosen carefully but could add a dimension to the student's perception.

There was considerable feeling that Professor Brower's suggestions were entirely admirable but not practical in any but the smallest classes. Mr. Brower insisted, though, that with assistance in handling the written exercises, he had taught this sort of course to groups of up to two hundred students. He had also found it possible to elicit and control successful student discussion in larger groups, though he admitted that this required careful advance planning by the instructor. Naturally, in the smaller group, a tighter control over the whole class was possible than in a larger group.

Several members of the conference were impressed by the chronological informality suggested by Professor Brower's program. Mr. Haydn, speaking from his own experience, felt that the conventional formal chronological presentation of literature failed to bridge the chasm of alienation between the student and the main literary tradition. It was all very well to get to Faulkner in the senior year, but what about the student who never took an English course after his freshman year? Wouldn't it be easier to connect literature to the interests arising out of the student's own life if one started with Faulkner and moved backwards in time? He remembered the tremendous impact that an unconventional freshman English teacher had had upon him and his classmates. Taking advantage of the flexibility permitted by the organization of the course, the instructor assigned novels of Galsworthy, Willa Cather, even Louis Bromfield and others then fashionable. Not only did this instructor at the end of the year have the most devoted body of readers one could hope to find, but it was Mr. Haydn's clear impression that this particular group of students through their senior year kept reading much more than did their average classmate. Mr. Guinzburg whole-heartedly endorsed Mr. Haydn's idea and suggested that the chronologically reversed method of presentation might well prove to be the best normal method of teaching. He hoped that full-scale formal studies would be made of this question.

Professor Brower was not so absolutely sure about inverse chronology, but it did seem to him that if one wanted to connect the student with his reading one ought very much to start from where the student was. He had often thought that it was very unkind and cruel to take the average American freshman and plunge him suddenly into the *Iliad*, Dante, Goethe, etc. Rather one could approach Homer from the evidence of Grant's memoirs on what a battle was like; or from the *Red Badge of Courage* or Park-man—Parkman is our Homer, his our heroic literature. Let the student meet the heroic in some environment he recog-nizes; then one might get him to go and read Homer more meaningfully. Mr. Brower had himself taught Homer for fourteen years in Greek, but disliked the superstitious re-striction of great to Homer, Dante, Goethe, and a very few others.

In his extended comments, Professor Goldberg found himself in embarrassing agreement with virtually every-thing that Professor Brower had proposed. At the same time, he felt that there was something to be said on the other side. The kind of course advocated by Dr. Brower is, he felt, a reaction against a very loose, sloppy and senti-mental type of enthusiasm that used to be prevalent, at least in the days when he was a student. He had fully recognized the need, during the past several decades, for correctives such as those advocated by Mr. Brower. Never-theless, he felt that there was a place for what might be called gross feeding as well as for the carefully planned and regulated balanced diet prepared for students in systematic courses. He would plead for the role of zest as well as that of taste in reading. He liked to think of the terrific enthusiasm with which a Hazlitt responded to literature. In dealing with the individual student in particular, we must take into account their highly individual and not always "refined" enjoyment in reading. He was prepared to encourage this enthusiasm even if it didn't function at the highest level of perception and to feed it with readings not always perhaps of the highest level.

At the same time, Professor Goldberg felt that these nascent enthusiasms in students were frequently blocked by mental inhibitions that confined reading narrowly to certain types of materials and to certain ends. He wanted to get students released from the barriers that inhibit their readings, so that they would want to read and would dare to read in response to the total needs of their whole growing and developing personalities, and not simply in response to the cognitive demands of the mind, or the desire for the fine aesthetic experience, the emotive, the imagined. The reading which, in our present confused social and cultural situation, will be able to suggest to students the wide range and rich resources of a reading in fact feeding the full inner needs of the growing personality, may not be systematic reading at all.

Professor Goldberg was reminded of Gilbert Murray's essay on *Literature as Revelation* in which Murray spoke of those authors that seem just suddenly to open whole vistas for us, vistas of imagination driving towards future fulfillment. In this same connection, he recalled the illustration from Coleridge used so effectively by Mr. Brower. It was the Reverend James Bowyer that was cited by Coleridge and by Professor Brower as the upholder of that kind

of close reading and that kind of close writing that is the
goal of Professor Brower's course. But, after all, who is it
in fact that remembers this school experience if not Coleridge? And while he pays great tribute to his classical
master, while he indeed continued loyal to what might be
termed the more restricted virtues represented by the kind
of schooling he himself got, Coleridge is nevertheless historically identified with that great movement freshly
affirming a more expansive sum of human feelings.

Professor Brower found himself in complete agreement
with Mr. Goldberg's remarks. He had always thought of
himself as a pupil of Coleridge. When asked by Mr. Buck
if, generally speaking, it was his thesis that it was better
for the student to work intensively on a few selected titles
rather than have a wide range of free reading as a way to
start the lifetime habit, Mr. Brower replied that he preferred not to accept those two positions as alternatives. It
was very important to have the experience of close reading
as a basis for future reading and as a standard of what the
finest reading is. Nevertheless, he believed very much in
extensive reading too, and was genuinely pleased merely to
see a student with a book in his hand. If a student read
voraciously, he didn't look too carefully at the titles.

Voracious reading, however, was not an end in itself,
Professor Loewenberg pointed out. Nor was it the exclusive
goal of education. Though Professor Brower's teacher of
humanities could rejoice to see a student read extensively,
still he had to be concerned with how the student read. All
conscientious teachers had a similar concern with why the
student read. A student concerned with significant questions could derive meaningful knowledge and understanding from the most unlikely, even unacademic sources.

In his extended remarks on Professor Angell's paper with
which he found himself in substantial agreement, Profes-

sor Loewenberg confessed that it was easier to endorse Professor Angell's prescriptions for wider undergraduate reading than it was to accept all the assumptions underlying the ends for which they were proposed. The methods suggested for closer faculty-student exchange, for including in social science reading assignments examples of vibrant creative literature, and for re-establishing the status of scholarship were all valid and desirable. However, the validity of these hypotheses was also related to premises other than those implied. Professor Loewenberg did not believe that one could accept without definition the suggestion carried by the adjective "significant" qualifying "books." Nor did he believe that we could automatically equate "lettered" culture with books, or culture with Western, or, for this purpose, the values of the past with the values of the present. Specifically, learning is composed of items other than books that people, including undergraduates, are impelled to read because of the joys and satisfactions derived from reading. The statistics of library book circulation, of pulp used for bookprint, of books purchased are indices of a deeper problem: the indifference of our culture to the humanism of science and to the science of art. Put another way, it is an indifference to sustained analysis, to contemplation, to the savor of creativity.

The problem of the reading of books is the problem of the cultural status of scholarship. And the problem of scholarship is the separation of learning from the actualities of living. The poverty of reading in or out of class caused Professor Loewenberg less anguish than did the routine class or the routine student, the class without a vital purpose, the student without a continuing quest. The answer to this dilemma can only lie in the virility of our education, its meaningfulness, its relevance to the issues of life. It

lies ultimately, therefore, in the quality of teaching. If the
present system is to be creatively altered, it is the teacher
who by his work will alter it. When this occurs, not only
reading habits but writing habits, not only attitudes
toward the language of print but towards the language of
nature, will change with it. It will alter the unspoken language of living and awaken the unarticulated language
of unfulfilled human possibilities. Then responses to the
idiom of scholarship will echo the inner voice of man and
begin to reflect the esperanto of human needs.

Were this the current fact, which it is not, teachers of
science would be less eager to endorse uncritically every
suggestion which comes out of desperation. They would be
somewhat less willing to hitch the wagon of learning to a
rocket. Nuclear physicists may help defend the frontiers
of the free world, they will never save the world for
freedom. Chemistry and mathematics at ten, cultivated
without awareness of humanistic purpose, is more likely to
produce trained incompetence than wisdom. If, to cite another example, educators were truly identified with the
values they profess, they would not advocate pushing out
the walls of buildings and erecting new ones in order to
accommodate the oncoming deluge. They would cooperate
in breaking down the barriers separating thought in order
to discover novel and creative solutions. You can lead a
student to a creative teacher and you can make them both
think. But you cannot pour the young into a cultural mold
and get anything else but uniformity.

Questions of this order, Professor Loewenberg emphasized, when presented to students may begin with the
newspaper as well as with the so-called hundred best books.
Considered as reading matter, he had no disdain for the
Congressional Record, the *Bedford Bugle,* or the decennial
census. He believed that the study of the issues evoked by

these printed sources led to Plato's cave, to Aristotle's golden mean, to Spinoza's ethics. They led as well to Kafka, to Stendhal, and to Tolstoy. He was not at all concerned that they did not all lead to the same place or that everybody was not led to all of them.

The problem which confronts us, Professor Loewenberg concluded, is the nature of our culture. The problem of education is teaching. Teachers are not only the custodians of cultural traditions; they are also obligated to evaluate them. The functions of teaching include criticism, assessment and judgment. Through these processes the teacher helps students to decide when they can and should say "no" to their culture. If we would have them say "no" to hidden contemporary vulgarity persuaders, to the slick paper cult, to slick ideas, we must first help them in learning to understand their heritage and to evaluate their contemporary situation. Reading and writing and arithmetic are not acquired by penciled symbols alone. They are nurtured by the human spirit which feeds them and by the human values which are thus fed.

Professor Angell in reply observed that the core of Mr. Loewenberg's critique seemed to be that all courses, whether social science, natural science or humanities, ought at bottom to be philosophy courses. Social scientists in particular ought to confront students with the problem of values, etc. As individuals, Professor Angell felt, many social scientists did have such an effect upon students, not perhaps so much by their formal presentation of course material as by their asides, their passing comments on life, etc. At the same time, he emphasized that the great bulk of social scientists did not feel that the raising of value questions was part of their job and did not in fact do it at all systematically.

Dean Odegaard noted that the use of materials other

than imaginative literature, the use of reading matter like newspapers, the *Congressional Record*, etc., was a common and valuable technique in historical teaching. Professor Angell replied in answer to other queries in this same area that, though he had not regarded history as part of his assignment, he felt most emphatically that the development of historical interest was a most sure and lasting stimulant to an active lifetime reading habit. In this same connection, Mr. Heckscher observed that since historians have on the whole written more great books that are works of art in themselves than have writers in the other social sciences, history serves as a rather broad bridge from aesthetic to technical reading.

This same distinction between general and technical reading underlay the remarks of Professor Bates on Dean Steere's paper. At bottom, Mr. Bates pointed out, scientists in our universities today tend to be concerned almost exclusively with the education of scientists. This is unfortunate since future scientists compose at best five percent of undergraduate enrollment. Professor Bates and his coadjutors at Michigan recognized the obligation of the science departments to contribute to the general education of the student and were trying to work out ways of fulfilling this obligation. In his personal effort, Mr. Bates tried to bridge the gap between science and the nonscientist by the use of trade books in his science classes. This had not met with complete approval. He had the impression that many of his professional colleagues felt that a book that deals with a scientific subject in a light and easy way is somehow not scholarly, somehow bad, somehow interdicted and not to be done. It also seemed to him that in contemporary usage "scholarly" had become equated with "dull." Yet Mr. Bates in many years' use of trade books had found his practice pedagogically sound. When he had on occasion gone back to textbooks, he had found his worst fears substantiated.

Consequently, Professor Bates was a little unhappy in going through the papers of this conference to find an undergraduate library mentioned as something very important for the humanities and social sciences but somehow not for the natural sciences. Natural sciences as much as social sciences depend in the long run on the written word. Thus an understanding of science is bound up with books as much as that of any other area; and to further this understanding the science teacher as much as any other is obliged to help develop reading interest.

In his own undergraduate course, Professor Bates had had as a conscious and stated objective the hope that the student after graduation will be tempted to buy a scientific paperback at the newsstand at an airport instead of Mickey Spillane. He has not found success immediate and overwhelming. He is still forced to assign readings and to threaten specific exam questions to make sure readings are read. But the effort continues. The new undergraduate library with facilities in it for scientific browsing should help. For ultimately, he concluded, the distinction between science and the humanities was false. Science to him was only one of the humanities.

Dean Steere observed that at Stanford too, in planning for an undergraduate library, it was generally assumed that the needs of science students would be met elsewhere in the departmental libraries, etc. He as the scientist on the committee was the lone demurrer. Scientific works carefully selected, as Hilary Deason and the American Association for the Advancement of Science had done for high schools, had a most integral place in an undergraduate, even in a browsing library.

In addition to the discussion of the several papers, considerable attention was given at the second session and in
subsequent correspondence to the general character of college teaching today. Conferee after conferee returned to a
remark originally made by Dean Asheim: that the practices
and goals of the individual classroom teacher are frequently
at variance with the declared objectives of his institution.
While the institution may speak of training the whole
mind, of developing the student's powers of original thinking and analysis, reflection, imagination, sensitivity, feeling, as well as aesthetic appreciation and understanding,
of encouraging students to see problems as they exist in life
and in nature outside the defining limits of individual disciplines—with all of which no one could possibly disagree
—individual instructors in their separate courses organize
their instruction to present a narrowly defined body of
knowledge or system of analysis with little relevance to
other courses, to the student's over-all intellectual training
or to the avowed goals of the institution.

Mr. Lacy noted that this problem was generally met in
its most acute form in the large lecture course, particularly
in the introductory or survey course. All the research reported at the first session found that more reading took
place in small discussion courses than in large lecture
courses. Yet the pressure of increasing numbers would
suggest that larger not smaller classes can be predicted for
the immediate future.

Mr. Canfield suggested that one thing wrong with formal
lecture courses was that they were frequently too good.
That is, they were so well organized and so comprehensive
that the student with a good set of lecture notes felt that
he needn't do the reading carefully if at all. Thus the very
virtues of the lecturer tended to discourage reading. He
had in mind the freshman introductory history course he

had taken at Harvard (which he suspected was increasingly typical) in which anyone could get a C with a good set of notes from the excellent lectures. Though there was a lot of reading from textbooks and from a very interesting outside reading list, it was not an integral part of the course for many students. He thought that much more reading and much more learning would result in the long run if the teacher, instead of giving a formally organized lecture, would simply say to his class, "Next week I am going to talk about four or five books that you are going to read; I am not going to give you facts, but am going to comment on the ideas and problems arising out of those facts which you can get for yourselves from the reading."

Professor Angell agreed that the method suggested by Mr. Canfield was infinitely superior to the cut and dried lecture, but observed that such extensive reading was not physically possible in large courses in large universities unless some special facility were available like the Michigan Undergraduate Library. Mr. Canfield replied that even where there was plenty of study space and an adequate number of copies of each title, students would not be encouraged to do the assigned reading or more if the structure of the lectures and exams, etc. encouraged them to think they could get away with less.

Dean Steere agreed with Mr. Canfield but felt that the form of the individual lecture must vary with the individual instructor and the instructional situation. He personally felt that his whole function on the lecture platform was simply to keep his students interested and/or amused for an hour in the fashion of a good magazine article.

Professor Brower admitted that there may be dangers in the too well-organized lecture which may just stop thought, but he rather cringed at the notion of simple entertainment. Students compose themselves into an audience far too easily, and there is nothing more fun than a ham. Nevertheless, he thought that one could give a lecture containing sustained analysis systematically organized and still maintain active interest in a classroom. Of course, "systematic organization" could be interpreted most broadly, one lecturer's sense of "system" being entirely unlike that of another teaching substantially the same material.

Dean Odegaard noted that conventional systems of organization and presentation may not be as educationally necessary as they are sometimes thought to be. Various committees at Michigan have been studying the organization of both lecture and laboratory instruction in the sciences. In an experimental geology course, instead of presenting a neatly organized version of the accepted classification systems, the instructors simply dumped a pile of rocks down in front of the students and asked them to classify the specimens. Knowing nothing of the canonized way of classifying in geology, the students proceeded to work out their own system of classification, making observations along the way interesting enough to merit an article in a professional journal.

Closely allied with the formality of the lecture were the equally stifling formalities of textbook reading and objective examinations. Mrs. Knapp pointed out that one was commonly made the excuse for the other. Large courses required easily accessible textbook reading and easily graded examinations, etc., while mechanical examinations could more readily test factual textbook material than they could the more diverse insights gained from wide reading. She felt, though, that these tended to be conventional rationalizations of existing practices rather than true reasons. Where faculty members chose to exert themselves, interestingly varied readings could be worked out even for large classes and examinations devised to test even such diverse readings.

Professor Heyns observed that many of the most conscientious university teachers today are not fully convinced about the primary place of reading in the learning process. One of the committees now at work at the University of Michigan on an honors program for advanced students has for some time had before it proposals for summer off-campus credit reading courses. The committee has handled the proposals very gingerly, unable to come to a decision despite strong advocacy in some quarters because in the eyes of many, "reading really isn't a substitute for a course." It is difficult to answer such objections when in fact answers have yet to be worked out to such fundamental policy questions as the place of the book, the classroom, the laboratory, etc. in the educational process.

The educational process, however, is not something confined to the months and years the student spends on campus. It has started long before and should continue long after. Mrs. Smith was particularly concerned about the success of the precollege learning process in teaching the student how to read effectively. Much more could still be done in giving entering freshmen reading speed and comprehension tests. Though this might be considered "old hat" at some institutions and be regarded as unnecessary at others accepting only superior students, there were still hundreds of other institutions which still had not tried but which could most usefully take advantage of these new examining techniques. The examinations themselves were of little use unless followed by corrective training for the retarded or inefficient reader. She would like to see colleges giving such examinations to incoming freshmen follow them up with comparative examinations for seniors. The amount of improvement might prove highly revelatory.

But what about after graduation? The theme of the conference was after all "the undergraduate and the *lifetime*
reading interest." Conferee after conferee had suspected
that this was the most crucial area of all but few seemed
sure exactly how it should be attacked. Even before reading
Dean Asheim's statistics, most had feared that the reading
habits of college graduates were in the aggregate deplorable
(however superior they might be to those of noncollege
graduates). Most had a vague but strong feeling that the
colleges could somehow and should definitely do consider-
ably more than they are doing to mold lifetime reading
interest.

Mr. Lacy in a subsequent communication sought to
focus attention on this problem and to clarify it. To him it
seemed that the real problem which we must face is what
can be done at the university to create an alumnus with a
continuing and active intellectual curiosity, and with skills
and habits that enable him to satisfy that curiosity by wide
and active reading in his adult life. The teacher can come
to grips with this problem on at least three levels.

First of all, the teacher must develop a sincere awareness
of and concern for the student's lifetime intellectual career.
The immediate concern of any instructor is naturally to
teach the student a specific sector of knowledge as such
may exist at the time of instruction. However, does the
university not fail in its responsibility to the student if
instructors do not look beyond this immediate responsibility
to a more general concern for the postcollege intellectual
engagement of the student in the subject? This concern
should be particularly immediate to teachers of basic survey courses. The instructor in a survey course in science
ought to have a real concern for developing his students'
ability to comprehend and follow the developments in
science that will occur in their postcollege days. Do those

teaching the general course in economics always remember that, as producer, consumer, manager, and citizen, their students will be dealing with changing economic problems during later life, and that equipping them to comprehend and adapt their thinking to such changing problems should be an important responsibility of the course? It is equally obvious that a professor of literature or the arts ought to feel a real sense of responsibility for turning out a student whose adult life will be enriched by a continuing interest in and ability to appreciate the literary and artistic developments of his own times. Since general survey courses are commonly taught by numerous staff operating within programs and syllabi developed by departmental or university planners, it would not be impossible for responsible officials concerned with the on-going aspects of pedagogy to see that such aspects are reflected in the philosophy and practice of basic courses.

Secondly, the teacher must be continuously aware of the coming obsolescence of the body of knowledge he is teaching and strive to convey this awareness to the student along with an understanding of the need to keep fresh any knowledge that would remain real knowledge. Has not one of the great causes of failure in public economic policy been the fact that the economic understanding of those in authority, public or business, has usually been that of their college years so that our society has generally been governed by a body of economic knowledge and theory roughly thirty years out of date? Perhaps the tendency to think of economic truth as an immutable body of laws was the peculiar weakness of economists of the first quarter of this century, but one wonders if even today's economists, who are so aware of the inadequacies of the economics of a generation ago, are equally aware of the presumption of fallacy and obsolescence in their own economics and, if so, if they

effectively convey to their students an understanding of
knowledge as a "flow" or continuing quest which the student touches only at particular points in time. Is not this
basic philosophic concept especially important in college
teaching today when the content of scholarly disciplines,
like so much of our culture, is in a state of particularly
rapid change? This of course is equally apropos in literature and the arts. Even courses in contemporary literature
seem to bog down somewhere around Dreiser and Shaw. Is
it not the rare professor of literature who can convey to
his students the anticipation of the new generations of
achievement, literary, musical, artistic, that will be un-
folded during their lifetimes along with the understanding
that a lively and appreciative experience of that unfolding
can be one of the most rewarding aspects of their lives?

Thirdly, Mr. Lacy stressed, these need not remain pious
desiderata. There are a number of practical steps open to
a teacher thinking of his students as lifelong self-educators.
In survey courses, one might make it a regular practice to
acquaint students with the principal contemporary reviews
and to encourage their regular use of them. In the natural
and social sciences a few lectures in survey courses might
be set aside to stimulate in the students an interest in postcollege reading by acquainting them with some of the
literature that might help a layman follow the field and
by suggesting ways in which they can keep posted on such
books as they appear.

Mrs. Smith suggested that universities themselves might
be much more active in the area of "further education."
College libraries might cooperate with alumni magazines in
compiling and publishing regular lists of books in various
fields. These lists need not be confined to popular works of
general interest. Some of the lists at least should be fairly
technical to apprise graduates of important new material

in their particular fields. In some instances, even more specialized lists might be mailed directly by schools or departments to appropriate groups of graduates. Where local libraries and other organizations are trying to form discussion groups in special fields, colleges and universities might co-operate by furnishing lists of alumni in the vicinity with appropriate specialties. At class reunion time, one or more of the special sessions at the "alumni institutes" that are now becoming so common might be devoted to the important current literature in fields of interest to the alumni.

It was quite clear from the more general discussion at the second session that there was something of a division between the greater part of the teachers and the greater part of the nonteachers at the conference. The latter quite evidently felt that the former were not doing all they might to develop lifetime readers. Implicit in much of the discussion was the fundamental problem of educational priorities. Mrs. Knapp summed up the sense of the critics. She would like college professors to think of all college students as being students for the rest of their lives. Though they might never be scholars in the narrow sense, they did possess germs of intellectual curiosity that could be nurtured and stimulated. At all undergraduate levels, teachers should be less concerned with imparting knowledge in a given subject and more concerned with developing the bit of intellectual curiosity in every student. And at every turn, instructors must think less about the narrow function of the book in their particular courses and more about the broader function of the book in the life of the student. Fundamentally, the book must be made to appear the means by which the student lifetime self-educator satisfies his intellectual curiosity.

PART III:
The Problem Outside the Classroom

9

The Role of the Campus Bookstore
and Campus Media of Communication

BY HAROLD K. GUINZBURG

THE TOPIC of this conference seems to be based on three propositions: that reading books, or at least some books, is a good thing, that Americans are backward in this regard, and that the colleges and universities of the country ought to be able to do something to improve the situation. None of us would be participating in this discussion if we did not share these views. The first of them expresses a conviction which does not call for argument here. The second is supported by many studies but still leaves ground for a good deal more examination. The third is the one to which we are asked to address ourselves today. I find it difficult to observe strictly my own assigned portion of this topic for it seems to me that most of what can be done effectively in a college community depends largely on the atmosphere of the institution as a whole, created by its facilities, its faculty, its standards, the type of students it attracts, and the tone set by its administration.

In spite of these qualifications I do believe that much could be accomplished on most of the nation's campuses outside the classroom and the library. At the top of my

list, second in importance only to the presence of a first
class library, I would put the presence of a first class bookstore. Because it is of such importance and because I think
few realize how deficient most of our colleges and universities (and for that matter, most of the cities of the
United States) are in this respect, I shall try in this paper
to give a rough picture of the status of the general bookstore in the country as a whole and in the college communities in particular. It seems to me to shed some additional
light on the reasons for the lack of adequate book reading
habits among adult Americans.

To what extent do Americans read books, what kinds do
they buy, and how do they get them? I will not repeat the
familiar comparisons with conditions in other countries,
such as those made by Dr. Gallup, but I cannot refrain
from using one set of figures which seems to me especially
startling. Americans currently spend more money on *repairs* to their radio and television sets than they do on all
kinds of books.

We have fairly reliable information on the dollar
amounts of book purchases from publishers, by certain
rather arbitrarily described categories. Omitting textbooks
entirely, one careful estimate for 1956 breaks down as
follows:[1]

[1] Figures prepared by Robert W. Frase, Associate Managing Director
and Economist, American Book Publishers Council, based on 1956
Annual Survey of the General Book Publishing Industry by Stanley
B. Hunt Associates and 1954 Census of Manufactures (U.S. Department of Commerce). It should be noted that they represent publishers'
receipts, not consumers' expenditure—i.e. the wholesale rather than the
retail cost. In the types of publishing listed here in which sales are
ordinarily made direct from publisher to consumer, the retail figures
would be about the same as the wholesale; in the rest, they would be
higher, but this does not materially affect their usefulness for our
purpose here. It should also be noted that there is no direct correlation
between the dollar figures and the number of books sold. Encyclopedia
sales frequently represent multivolume sets costing hundreds of dollars
while newsstand type paper books seldom go over fifty cents at retail.

Adult Trade Books	$60.4 millions
Juvenile Books ($1.00 and over retail)	33.7
Juvenile Books (under $1.00 retail)	18.4
Bibles, Testaments, & Hymnals	24.8
Other Religious Books	15.3
Hard-bound Reprint Books	7.8
Paper-bound Books, Newsstand Type	46.5
Other Paper-bound Books	5.1
Book Club Books	98.1
University Press Books (except textbooks)	4.8
Business, Technical, Scientific, Law and Medical Books (except textbooks)	87.5
Other Books	37.2
Encyclopedias	190.8
Total	$630.4

Let us see what these figures represent in terms of serious books of a general nature going through bookstores to the American consumer. Book Club books, Encyclopedias, and, to a large extent, Business, Technical, Scientific, Law, and Medical books almost always go directly from the publisher to the final user without benefit of any intermediary. Few are sold through bookstores. Bibles and Religious Books are to a large extent sold through special outlets. Children's Books, a category that has shown a healthy growth, involve rather different problems. Of the higher-priced books in this classification, the schools and libraries are the principal purchasers. Of the inexpensive ones, a great deal of the sale goes through a variety of outlets other than bookstores. The Newsstand Type of Paper-bound Book, as its name implies, is also sold largely in outlets other than bookstores. Aside from the Book Club item, that reduces the categories of books that concern us here to the headings of Adult Trade Books, Hard-bound Reprints, Other Paper-bound

Books, and University Press Books. And in these categories
as in all the others, the figures include not only individual
sales, but also sales to libraries and institutions and sales for
export.

It can be seen, then, that the amount of business that
goes through bookstores is only a small portion of the dollar
volume for retail book sales of all kinds. If we were to
eliminate all but those titles that might be considered of
general cultural interest, we would be making another big
cut in the total. A great many of the books listed in the
general book categories are written to give practical information of one sort or another. For example, at the very
top of the lists of hard-bound best-sellers over the years are
a number of cookbooks. Many other excellent and useful
books, such as those on child care, gardening, how to make
home repairs, etc., are also brought out every year and have
large circulation. Thus, when someone tells one of Gallup's
interviewers that he has read a book during the past month,
he is more likely to have been trying to save money through
a copy of that popular annual, *Your Income Tax*, than to
have curled up with, say, Plato's *Republic*. It would be extremely helpful if the interviewer could carry the question
a step farther sometime and find out what book he was
reading and where he acquired it.

A difficulty of attempting any analysis of kinds of reading is that there is no satisfactory standard for deciding
what a book of serious cultural value is. Even within
the general trade book classification, who is to say which
ones are of cultural value? No two people would draw
their lines at the same spot. It is almost as hard to decide
arbitrarily what sort of retail establishment deserves the
name of bookstore. My own guess is that those places that
could properly be called bookstores (or book departments
in department stores) do not sell annually more than about

150 million dollars' worth of books at retail and that of this total a great proportion do not come within the classifications that we normally think of when we discuss the state of book reading in America.

A breakdown of kinds of reading and sources of supply is relevant because there are many people within the book trade itself who have looked at the statistics that show growth either of dollar volume or of the numbers of books distributed and talk with enthusiasm of the great increase of reading in the United States. To a large extent they are right. The consumption of books has grown enormously. It has been of a rather special kind, however, being predominantly represented by the steady spread of sales by book clubs, low-priced reprints, and encyclopedias. I do not mean to suggest that the distributors of such books have not made a great contribution in supplying the nation with their wares, but their special methods of distribution are not applicable to all kinds of books and therefore do not solve all our problems.

Today, the book clubs as a group are selling a greater number of hardbound books to their subscribers than the publishers are through all of the retail bookstores of the country. The publishers of paperbacks are in turn distributing more copies of their output than both of the above groups put together. (Note, however, that the monies earned by authors, in the aggregate, from trade sales still far outweigh the monies received by them from book club distribution and paperback reprints combined.) Although in terms of book use this increase is an impressive accomplishment, it is well to remember that any one of our most popular weekly magazines circulates more copies by itself in a year than the total of all the publishers of newsstand type books do together. The low-priced paperback publishers point with pride, and with a great deal of

justification, to the multitude of excellent titles they have
made available both to existing book readers and to a large
part of the population that presumably never went in for
book buying before. It still remains true, however, that if
you examine the best-seller compilations, you will see how
many of the greatest sellers in this field run to certain special types. Except for Dr. Spock's famous baby book,
Mickey Spillane, Erle Stanley Gardner, and Erskine Caldwell sweep all before them among contemporary writers.
In the list of all-time best-sellers no less than 37 titles by
Erle Stanley Gardner, many of whose books have given me
much pleasure, appear near the top of the compilation.
And it is significant that *Peyton Place,* after a fabulous
career in hard covers, became the second largest-selling
novel in the history of American publishing within a few
months after its appearance as a paperback.

It is useful, I think, to investigate why the great growth
in paperbacks, encyclopedias, and books issued by clubs has
taken place while bookstore distribution has lagged so badly.
The answer, it seems to me, is that in each case the publishers and distributors in these fields have used acceptable,
proved American methods of large-scale selling. The clubs
and the paperbacks particularly have aimed at giving
excellent value and achieving mass distribution. One
important element in cutting their costs, frequently overlooked, has been to reduce sharply both the absolute amount
per copy and the percentage paid to the author compared
to what he normally receives on original hardbound editions. For example, on a 35 cent paperback the author
receives from .70 cents to 1.05 cents per copy when he
might have been getting as much as 60 cents per copy on
a $4.00 novel. In both cases there is a strong bargain appeal.
In both cases the book is made easily accessible, in one by
using the post offices of the nation and in the other by

using more than 100,000 outlets to tempt the casual passerby to purchase. The great growth of encyclopedia distribution has come about as a result of other methods. Encyclopedia publishers send skillful salesmen to potential
customers' doors with a well-learned sales talk and the
now familiar American lure of easy monthly payments.
A most recent merchandising development is the selling
of books through supermarkets. The volume of this business, which is rapidly growing, is not included in the
figures above. Here again, some of the methods just mentioned—accessibility, low price or a form of installment
selling—are used to attract the shopper. There is a certain
miscellaneous volume of selling by mail order that does
not quite fit in any of the above categories but that also
sheds interesting light on how and why people are induced
to buy books. It is best exemplified perhaps by the activities
of *Life* magazine which has produced a number of impressive volumes made up of material which first appeared in
that periodical. These books are sold first by the magazine
itself, through its own advertising pages and to its own
mailing lists, at prepublication bargain rates, and then at
somewhat higher prices to the general public. The mail
order sales have run about ten to one as against the retail
store sales.

It can be reasonably asked whether we care what the
method of sale is so long as books get sold. What of it if the
bookstore loses its importance in the distributive scheme of
things?

It makes, I think, an enormous difference. There still
remain great numbers of titles published every year that
do not lend themselves to any of the newer forms of distribution and must rely on the retail store. When someone walks into a bookstore he may be looking for any one
of 100,000 different titles. The mass market distributors

must be selective, must on the whole seek out what will achieve wide popularity, while one of the principal values of book publishing has been traditionally that it is so diverse, that it is the outlet for the new writer, for the man with new ideas, for the unconventional, and for the author who is addressing only a relatively small section of the population. The problem of these authors and of serious publishers is increasingly that the new and the special books are unable to get any substantial audience.

Bookstores themselves for the most part find it more and more difficult to stock much other than standard reference works, self-help books, best-sellers and inexpensive books. We increase the difficulty for them by the number of excellent books that are now produced in low-priced editions. No one can be critical of the taste of readers in or out of college who decide that they prefer Homer, Cervantes or Shakespeare, Melville, Conrad or D. H. Lawrence, in an inexpensive edition, to this month's interesting new book in a more expensive format, but, if too few people buy this month's interesting new book, it will eventually cease to exist and the whole stream of continuing literary culture will be threatened. Authors, like other people, want their families to eat, and they want to believe they are reaching an audience, and if book writing is too unrewarding in achieving these ends, they are bound to turn to something else, except in those cases where the book is a specialized by-product of some other occupation, such as teaching, and wide circulation is not even hoped for.

Publishers, too, except for the university presses, are living in a competitive economic world, and they simply have to limit the percentage of titles on which experience tells them to expect that they will take a loss. Nor can we expect the general public to understand the factors that make new books seem so expensive in comparison to the cheap reprints: the higher prevailing royalty rates, the initial costs of selecting and editing, the heavy investment in type and plates, and the big expense of launching a new title—all of which are reduced or eliminated for the re-printer.

Because I believe that the contemporary quality book is such a special problem, because it seems logical that it should find some substantial support in the college and university communities, and because I think that the book-store as well as the library is such a key part of this process, I undertook to make for this meeting my own small sam-pling of what had happened in a cross-section of college communities to a representative group of current books. For this purpose, I sent questionnaires to all the listed col-leges and universities in Massachusetts and Michigan, asking them for information about the circulation of certain titles in their libraries and asking them to get, if they could, the sale of those same titles in their local bookstores. Rather than pick the titles myself, I arbitrarily took those books published during the first quarter of 1957 that had been nominated for this year's National Book Awards. The list is:

Letter from a Distant Land by Philip Booth
The Lion and the Throne by Catherine Drinker Bowen
Days of the Phoenix by Van Wyck Brooks
The Wapshot Chronicle by John Cheever
The Town by William Faulkner
The Day the Money Stopped by Brendan Gill
Poets in a Landscape by Gilbert Highet
Memories of a Catholic Girlhood by Mary McCarthy
The Assistant by Bernard Malamud
The Crisis of the Old Order by Arthur M. Schlesinger, Jr.
As France Goes by David Schoenbrun
The Rain and the Fire and the Will of God by Donald Wetzel

These books on average were successful although no outstanding best-seller appears among them. They are, for
the most part, by authors with distinguished names, they
were widely and, generally, favorably reviewed. The results
of this little survey, although showing a wide variation of
experience, are on the whole disheartening indeed.

A large percentage of the institutions took the trouble
to answer. In some places, where libraries have books on
open shelves, they were unable to supply circulation figures. In some cases, where the institution was in a large
city, it was impossible to pin down any meaningful figure
as to bookstore sales. Eliminating those reports and taking
only the ones from locations where fairly accurate information was available, we are able to get at least some sort of
picture.

The number of institutions polled in Michigan was
twenty-two, of whom sixteen replied; in Massachusetts it
was thirty-one, of whom eighteen replied. In Massachusetts
there were six communities (one of which has two colleges)
with trade bookstores, excluding Boston but counting
Cambridge, where of course there are many bookstores. In
Michigan there were just three communities reporting trade
bookstores, excluding Detroit but counting Ann Arbor,
where, again, there are several bookstores. The number of
libraries giving stock or circulation figures, as noted earlier,
was smaller: seventeen in Massachusetts, and sixteen in
Michigan. The number of bookstores giving sales figures
was smaller still; in Massachusetts reports came in from
thirteen stores in seven communities outside Boston, and
in Michigan from eight stores in three communities outside
Detroit.

These limitations on the coverage of the survey obviously
require us to treat with caution any statistical results. I
present them without any claim to authority. Nor is this

the place to present all the possible details. The questionnaires themselves are available for anyone who would like
to see them. It is my hope that some group with proper
resources may be stimulated to make a far more thorough
study along similar but expanded lines. The figures, however, do indicate at least a range of experience and a range
of possibilities. Given these cautions, then, what do we
find?

Of the twelve titles selected for the survey, the eighteen
Massachusetts libraries, representing enrollments of 59,000,
had an average number of 7.2 copies in their collections; the
average for the sixteen Michigan libraries representing enrollments of 83,500 was 7.6. The total circulation of the
twelve titles taken together was 403 for Massachusetts and
for Michigan it was 320, but this clearly on the low side
because the Lamont Library at Harvard does not keep circulation records, and in some other cases the circulation
figures are not complete. Wayne State University could
not supply figures other than for volumes on hand but for
this calculation they have been arbitrarily included as
having the same circulation as the average of the other
Michigan institutions.

In Massachusetts, not counting Boston, reports from ten
institutions with enrollments of 14,675 showed no trade
bookstores in the community or no copies of any of the
listed titles on hand. In Michigan, not counting Detroit,
ten institutions with enrollments of 45,659 reported no
trade bookstores in the community or no copies of any of
the listed titles on hand. The bookstore sales for Massachusetts showed that ten stores had sold 363 copies of the
twelve books combined, or an average of 36.3 copies per
store. These results would have been far better for Massachusetts were it not that the Harvard Co-op which undoubtedly sells more trade books than any other college

store in the country could provide no information about
the number of copies of these books that they had sold.
The Wellesley bookstore also reported good sales for many
of these books but provided no figures and therefore has
not been included. In one case, where a book was used in
a course, the quantity sold has been eliminated. In Michigan,
six stores had sold a total of 300 books or an average of
50 per store. Here again, Detroit was not included.

If therefore we are looking for the average use in these
institutions for single titles, we find that each was bought
or borrowed by 116 students out of a combined total audience of 142,500. However, no sales are included in this for
the 28,000 students at Wayne State University in Detroit
or Northeastern University in Boston, nor are allowances
made for the other gaps in information previously noted.

There are two additional important factors that must
be taken into account, one of which would undoubtedly
improve the showing and the other of which would clearly
make it worse. Students particularly in or near the metro-
politan centers of both states undoubtedly bought some of
the books at stores not covered by the replies. Some of the
books thus bought were possibly read by roommates, or
even borrowed, never to be returned, by friends across the
way. Other students, as suggested before, read some of
these books in library browsing rooms or in reserve collections where no circulation records are kept; one student at
one college, which shall be nameless here, liked one of the
books so well that he stole it from the library, thus render-
ing further circulation figures unavailable (the library had
not bought another copy by the time the questionnaire was
returned). Presumably some students, particularly in small
towns with no stores, get some books elsewhere—from
home, from book clubs, from large city stores.

On the other hand, all of the figures used for potential

readers were based only on the student enrollment of the institutions. No allowance has been made for the fact that members of the faculty or the administration, husbands or wives of married students, or any member of the community in which the institution is located, might have bought, let alone borrowed, a book. I have no way of judging how big a factor this may be, but from some booksellers in college towns whom I have queried, I get estimates that possibly fifteen to twenty per cent of their business comes from outside the college community. In addition, Massachusetts must be far above the national average because of the nature of many of the institutions located in that state. Incidentally, at least two of the authors on the list teach in Massachusetts colleges and therefore undoubtedly had a wider local circulation than would otherwise be the case. Ann Arbor is obviously also in the class of the unusually good book town and university.

Let us narrow the range of inquiry by looking at the state of Michigan, which has something over 3 per cent of the total college and university population of the country, and, eliminating Detroit as impossible to analyze fairly, let us examine the results from Ann Arbor and from the rest of the state. Let us narrow the study further and, to make the results as favorable as possible, see what happened to two of the titles by particularly distinguished authors which were most widely noticed and which sold better than most: *The Town* by William Faulkner and *The Crisis of the Old Order* by Arthur M. Schlesinger, Jr.

The Michigan colleges and universities outside of Ann Arbor and Detroit which answered the questionnaire have a combined enrollment of approximately 46,000. Their libraries reported that they had in stock a total of nine copies of *The Town* which had circulated, through last November 30, nineteen times. They had in stock eight

copies of *The Crisis of the Old Order,* which had circulated
eight times. There was no report of a single bookstore sale
of either title. However, one store in a small city couldn't
give sales figures, but reported that it had both these books
in stock. Let's be generous and assume that it sold two
copies of each.

The combined coverage for library copies circulated and
copies sold, then, for students not in Ann Arbor or Detroit,
was one for approximately 2,190 students for *The Town,*
and one for every 4,600 students for *The Crisis of the Old
Order.* By comparison, coverage in Ann Arbor only was
one in every 241 students for *The Town* and one in every
384 for *The Crisis of the Old Order.*

One obvious element in the wide difference of readership
rates between Ann Arbor and the rest of the state is that
Ann Arbor has trade bookstores and the other places do
not. That this is keenly felt by the other institutions is
demonstrated by the large number of replies from librarians
that in effect said "our bookstore carries no trade books"
or "our bookstores handle only textbooks and some paperbacks." In fact, the reports on sales of the twelve titles
in the survey (eliminating the small store mentioned
above) show that of 300 sales 299 were made in Ann Arbor.

Throughout the country one finds these sharp discrepan-
cies in book availability and use. Nothing is more startling,
to people who have not examined the situation before, than
to discover how many towns all across the country, college
or otherwise, do not have a single outlet that can be called
a trade bookstore. Even among the college towns, it adds
up to a depressing desert with occasional oases. The older,
high-standard private colleges which show up well no doubt
attract bright students, many of whom are not pinched for
money, often coming from schools and homes where good
reading habits have already been established. It is natural,

perhaps, that they are more likely than the average to buy nonrequired books. But this hardly explains why some colleges in small towns with enrollments of only one or two thousand should support, as some do, an excellent trade bookstore while some state universities with 20,000 or so in attendance do not. In the generally gloomy national picture there are enough bright spots to prove that given the will, and a really good bookseller, an effective job can be done. The cheerful examples are by no means limited to the Ivy League. In the northwest, for instance, Reed College with a student population of under 700 has an outstandingly good store.

Another encouraging fact is that wherever stores or libraries are improved, enlarged, or made more attractive, book use goes up. It can be confidently predicted that this new undergraduate library here at Michigan will produce such a result. But this kind of experience is not confined to campuses. It is equally true when new facilities are made available or old ones renovated in other communities. Even in well-served Manhattan we have seen this happen. When the old-established Scribner bookstore not long ago installed better lights, spruced up its premises and made them more inviting to the passerby, the increase in its volume of business was astonishing. When a new modern branch of the New York Public Library, attractive inside and out, was built not much more than half a mile from either the main building or from existing branches, it at once was used to capacity. Most significantly, more than three-quarters of its users had never before had a library card. Even at Harvard, already the best served university as to libraries and bookstores, a new undergraduate library and an expanded and rearranged college store caused a marked spurt in sales and borrowings. Another valuable case history comes from the experience of the Harvard Co-op in installing a trade department in the Massachusetts Institute of Technology bookstore, previously handling only texts. The students theoretically absorbed in scientific specialization at the institution, located only a short distance from the existing stores of Cambridge and Boston, proceeded to make it an immediate success. In fact, the returns from that bookstore on my questionnaire on current reading were among the highest in proportion to enrollment of those from any polled.

Thus, I repeat my conviction that one specific thing a college or university can do outside the classroom and the library to help change the nonintellectual atmosphere too often found on the average campus is to see that a first-class bookstore is accessible to it.

There are of course numerous other things that are of importance as well. All of them, I think, depend to a large degree on a concerted effort on the part of the college authorities, the president, the administrators, the faculty, to try to alter the existing climate in which books other than texts seem to have so low a priority in the minds of the students and too often in the minds of the faculty as well. If we could change the academic attitude that regards nonrequired book reading as no more than a pleasant but unessential adjunct to education, we should have taken a major step.

When you talk to people about books they seldom say that they don't like them. They say either that they have no time for books or that they can't afford to buy them. What these statements in fact usually mean is that they prefer, as do most of their associates, to spend their time and their money on other things. Individuals usually mirror the tastes and standards of the group of which they are a part. In a simpler time, when there were fewer studies of behavior patterns and "motivation research" was an unknown phrase, this was called "keeping up with the Joneses." Americans today have unprecedented wealth and leisure. For the most part they have not formed the habit of spending much of either on book reading. On the Washington scene where, in spite of the influence of pressure groups, the preferences of the majority of our people are likely eventually to be reflected, we have seen in recent years how difficult it has been to get appropriations for school construction, for library extension activities in rural areas, or for other educational purposes, while a gigantic federal road building program was speedily and enthusiastically passed. Possibly the present uncomfortable state of the world will bring about some beneficial changes in attitudes. At the moment, words like professor, intellectual, or even egghead are no longer used much as derogatory epithets. If the Russians have suddenly managed, however inadvertently, to give us a wider respect for learning, we are greatly in their debt, but not if our citizens and our authorities are spurred only to make greater efforts in developing "useful" scientists rather than a better, more broadly educated population on all fronts.

The neglected economic position of our teachers at all levels is beginning all too belatedly to receive wide public attention. Most of them are overworked and underpaid and for them reading outside their own fields and particularly buying books for their own libraries is likely to be a serious matter. Teachers also frequently get books free, or at a substantial discount; at least, those books related to the subjects they are teaching. But it seems to me that the members of the faculty ought to be in a position to set a good reading example to their pupils. Possibly some small but dramatic stimulus should be provided to help them do so. If a college decided to give every teacher some stated credit at a local bookseller for the purchase of miscellaneous books that interested him, this might serve such a purpose. Businesses buy trade journals and books related to their own activities as necessary tools for their senior employees, treating this as a legitimate business expense. Why shouldn't a college consider that an essential part of the teacher's equipment is to be able to own some books that interest him and make provision accordingly?

Along the lines of the teachers' role in creating an atmosphere favorable to intellectual pursuits, nothing could be more valuable, I think, than to abandon the present almost obsessive idea that the student can't be expected to buy more than a trifling number of books. Even in the field of required reading the practice seems to be spreading of adopting the lowest priced edition, regardless of its quality, and even of selecting the texts that are to be used in courses on the basis of what they will cost the student. Of course there are many students to whom any expenditure is important, but haven't the colleges themselves been spreading the damaging notion that books are an unnecessary luxury? On the contrary, students might well be encouraged to think of their college years as the time to begin, however modestly, the formation of their own private libraries. I am told that in many of the large state universities up to two-thirds of the students own and operate their own automobiles. One can look at pictures of the great stadiums all over the country full of undergraduates for football games during each autumn season and realize that one such game with its attendant social activities often takes more of their funds than they spend in a year for books. But I have yet to see an argument for deemphasizing football based on the thought that the student spectators "can't afford it."

We should of course continue to build up library facilities so that the student for whom even a few extra dollars is a real hardship can get most of the reading he needs without payment. But few are quite that close to a bare subsistence level. At least merchants of commodities other than books seem to think that the college market is better than that, and that it is in fact highly attractive. An article in late 1956 in the magazine *Sales Management* takes a look at the college population and says in large type: "The purchasing power is sizable. But beyond immediate sales, business is interested in Joe and Betty Coed as style-setters and as customers likely to become centers of influence in the social and business world after graduation." It describes at length the elaborate methods used by many companies to cultivate the market, including all the promotion stunts that are familiar to American business. Among a number of other examples it refers to the great success of many of the popular magazines in developing this field. As a conspicuous instance, it says that *Playboy*, which sells for fifty cents a copy, has over 200,000 regular readers among college and university students. *Mademoiselle* and *Seventeen* are mentioned as other somewhat specialized periodicals that have done particularly well. More than 200 national advertisers are said to use college newspapers regularly. Two paragraphs from the article are worth quoting:

Though its size is impressive, the college market has other attractions. Its members have higher than average buying power. They influence the buying habits of others: of their families, of high school students who imitate them, of noncollege young people, who look to the campus for style leadership. They start fads and fashions: Moccasin-type shoes, gaily colored vests, hatlessness, sweater wardrobes, mix-and-match outfits. Their future, as a market, is of interest to the business community. They are the leaders, the high earners, of coming years.

And again, later on:

Students buy food, shelter and clothing, of course. But they also buy books, records, fountain pens, typewriters, college jewelry and other 'tools' and appurtenances of their current station in life, plus whatever it takes to conform to current campus customs. Example: stuffed animal toys, now a 'must' for many a college girl. They travel to reach the campus, go home for holidays, go visiting on week ends.

It seems to me that the key words in this paragraph are "they also buy . . . whatever it takes to conform to current campus customs." The customs and the habits of students are what we are concerned with.

Let us return to the question of the bookstore and its feeble state on the campuses. There are in this country about 1,900 institutions listed as colleges and universities. Some, of course, are quite small. One thousand or more have enrollments in excess of 500 and there are almost that many stores that belong to the well-organized National Association of College Stores. Of this number, many carry paperbacks as well as textbooks, but only a small proportion can be said to have anything like adequate trade book departments. You, here in Ann Arbor, may not realize how fortunate and unusual you are. Possibly because of the standards of your university, possibly for other reasons, you have a half-dozen bookstores and your community rates as one of the best book towns in the country. On any publisher's list of principal retail accounts, which would include only a few hundred stores, most of yours would be found. To emphasize how untypical this is, I can point out in line with the findings given before that, except for those in Ann Arbor and Detroit, it would be hard to name more than one or two establishments in the whole state of Michigan that could properly be called general bookstores.

The National Association of College Stores, a group that began humbly when most of its original members were little more than textbook depositories in basements, is today a flourishing group of businesses covering most of the principal colleges and universities whose members do a volume well in excess of $100,000,000 a year. They have an impressive trade paper and they hold an annual convention where about 200 exhibitors take booths to display their wares. The energetic general manager of the organization believes that they serve "the fastest growing market in America." He, too, tells businessmen that "College graduates will be the style, opinion, and business leaders of tomorrow." And he also points out that "Numerous style trends, such as bobby sox and saddle shoes, skirts and sweaters, pipe smoking men and women, and the Ivy League look, start on the college campus." He has shown a lively and intelligent interest in the development of trade book outlets among his constituents. In fact, a running debate has been going on for a long time within the pages of their magazine between those college store operators who are convinced that part of their job, and a potentially profitable part, is to carry general trade books and the majority of the store managers who still show no interest in doing so. The paperbacks have made a difference since their introduction and have been changing the complexion of many of these outlets. The stores are more and more going in for self-service departments for both texts and paperbacks which they believe both cut expenses and increase sales. The pity in this, from the point of view of one who has known good personal bookstores, is that it tends to eliminate the role of the able bookseller as a guide and counselor to students, and even often to faculty members, and as one who could play a major role in interesting young people in books that they might not be inclined to pick up for themselves.

There are reasons why the retail book business has not

been an especially attractive one. It is not easy and the
profits are not high. It requires direction that combines
solid business skill with the sort of knowledge and interest
that only a first-class bookman can have, but it does not
require great capital. Why should not those colleges that
now are not properly served feel that the establishment of
an adequate bookstore is their responsibility? Possibly this
would mean some form of subsidy but probably no more
than providing premises and a small amount of capital,
possibly as a loan, to help the store get started. The library
building in which this conference is being held, I am told,
cost over three million dollars for the structure alone, to
which must be added the cost of books and equipment and
the continuing operating expenses. For one per cent of the
amount of the building cost, a college that has no going
bookstore would be able to provide the capital needs for
starting one, which would probably then require no further support.

I do not wish to advise college authorities as to how this
should be done. Whether stores should be privately or institutionally owned, for instance, is a matter for them to
decide. But it seems to me that, whatever the method of
accomplishing it, the administration of a college should be
as determined to have a good, readily-accessible bookstore
with a first-class bookseller running it, as it is to have high
standards in any part of its academic curriculum or staff.
Many universities have in recent years established their own
presses, and in the aggregate they make a singularly useful
contribution, particularly in the field of the scholarly book
that might not otherwise be published. But no similar concern seems to have been shown for the distribution of
books. One of the great weaknesses within the serious book
world is that while much energy and philanthropic support
is forthcoming to get important works written and printed,

little or no attention is paid to getting them into the hands of the people who might benefit from them.

Other campus activities that might enhance the prestige of the book and encourage the formation of good reading habits do not require much space, for most of them are self-evident enough in theory, however difficult they may be to make practically effective. Most college newspapers and college radio stations could usefully give more space or time to book reviews, as well as more attention to events connected with other cultural affairs. The more intellectual members of the student body will no doubt rely for guidance on criticism and reviews in leading newspapers or magazines. The point is not that we can expect the local efforts to sell many additional books by themselves but that we can hope that they will contribute to making current reading seem newsworthy and important. The college authorities should do whatever is in their power to promote a high regard in the undergraduate world for those students who are on the paper, or on the literary magazine where one exists, to help make them "big names" on the campus. Outside lecturers distinguished in the world of letters could be induced to pay visits more than is usually done. When such a visit occurs the occasion should be made as noteworthy as possible.

To treat the book as something to be prized and cherished is an intangible contribution that the college community can well make. Books can be used effectively as prizes on many occasions—as are Harvard's famous "Deturs" for scholastic standing. In some places, prizes have been established for the best library formed by an undergraduate while he is in residence. But how many rooms are equipped with an amount of shelving that would suggest that students would naturally want to begin forming the nucleus of a personal, permanent book collection?

Similar competition might be stimulated for the best library in fraternity or sorority houses, especially where they are used as residences.

A much more far-reaching possibility, however, exists in the awarding of scholarship funds with some portion of them allocated specifically for book buying. To do this would be an emphatic way of making it clear that part of the essential educational process is assumed to be the acquisition and use of both required and nonrequired volumes.

One device that might be helpful would be to prepare a simple booklet to be given to all freshmen on entering a college, describing the book resources of the institution. Many of these young people come from nonbookish backgrounds and are probably quite unhabituated to using library facilities. The opening up of these useful treasuries should provide the student with one of the great experiences of college. If this can be combined with an invitation from the bookstore—where one exists—to learn the pleasant pastime of browsing among the new books, even more will be accomplished. Nor is there any reason why the good influences should end when the student leaves college. The Alumni bulletin should be encouraged to report on books in its pages, as some do already, especially books by alumni and faculty members. This can be turned to practical advantage, if there is a local bookstore, by reminding the widely-scattered readers, wherever they may be, that the college bookstore can supply them.

Currently there is probably more widespread concern in the United States over the state of education than there has ever been in the past. Innumerable groups are appalled by the prospect of handling the added numbers of young people who will be knocking at the doors of the colleges in the next decade or so. The members of the President's Committee on Education Beyond the High School are among those who believe we must plan for approximately a doubled college and university population in the next dozen years. They also believe that in that period it is imperative that the salaries of teachers should be at least doubled. This as well as the obvious requirements of huge new outlays for building and equipment present a staggering prospect. Most thoughtful people who have examined it feel that new methods of instruction will have to be found and that among these it will be essential that the student himself should take greater initiative about his own broad learning, rather than merely relying on attending lectures and going through the required texts. It may be significant that in the great English universities they speak of "reading" a subject, where we in America are more likely to speak of "taking" a course or "sitting in" or "listening in" on it.

In the summary report of the President's Committee, there are two remarks having to do with "increasing the effectiveness and productiveness of the teacher" which bear on the topic we have been discussing. One of them says: "Among the promising approaches being explored are: (1) Giving students more responsibility for their own education through greater reliance on independent study and less on daily instruction from teachers"; the other, under the general recommendations, urges "that there be vigorous and objective exploration and application by faculties and administrators of methods of increasing the effectiveness and productiveness of the teacher, including electronic devices such as television, (and) instructional procedures which place on the student more responsibility for self-education . . ." Although there are divided opinions about the possibility of television becoming a significant educational element, most educators, I think, still believe that the principal tool for the foreseeable future is certain

to be the book. If that is so and if the general picture that
is currently being painted of the problems ahead in higher
education is anything like accurate, we simply must find
ways of developing greater book use. Particularly, we must
change the prevailing attitude that relies on lectures and
on texts to one that presupposes that the student will be an
independent and competent reader. In stark economic
terms alone, a greater reliance on the wide use of books
would be the quickest, the least expensive, and the most
effective way of heightening the intellectual level of the
colleges and universities and of accelerating and improving
the broad educational process. At the same time, a program
based on such an approach would be bound to have a profound effect on the formation of lifetime reading habits.

10

Book-Buying as a Way of Life

SOME QUESTIONS RAISED BY MR. GUINZBURG'S PAPER

MR. MARSHALL as a bookseller in a college town was asked to comment extensively upon the publisher's view of the college bookselling situation as presented by Mr. Guinzburg. Mr. Marshall reported that his own experience amply corroborated Mr. Guinzburg's representation of the American bookselling situation—a desert with occasional oases. If anything, he found Mr. Guinzburg a bit too gentle; the actual situation was probably a trifle worse than represented. He felt most strongly that any institution with the least hope of developing lifetime reading interest in its students must have in its vicinity an alive, viable bookselling facility offering a wide variety of scholarly books and general books of significant intellectual and artistic quality. This was too rarely the case. It was all too easy for those in positions of responsibility to say "How horrible" and blame the general cultural morass that failed to supply and support more and better bookstores. The situation, though, was not hopeless. Something could be done about it, though an intensive propaganda campaign was probably needed.

Booksellers did not always have the best public relations or the most understanding public. Students on all campuses seemed to regard the local booksellers as a bunch of greedy, grouchy people deriving enormous profits from a pretty effortless business. Mr. Marshall felt that this attitude was part of the general feeling of resentment that unconsciously boiled up in students as they found themselves shuttled about in the registration rush at the beginning of every term. The last stage in this interminable queuing and "processing" was the jam at the bookstores where students lined up once more to buy their assigned reading and where booksellers were forced for two or three days to struggle with a tide several times their optimum capacity, gathering upon themselves all the students' pent up resentment in the process. Despite the students' myths, the financial rewards of bookselling were hardly magnificent, at best no more than those of teaching (hardly a lofty standard), rather worse when the absence of sabbaticals and fellowships was considered. In particular, it was the most creative parts of bookselling (in the scholarly and artistic sense) that were the least profitable. Yet, although it offered but dubious financial rewards, bookselling required a considerable degree of business acumen in an age when small business generally has been having tough going, plus a passionate missionary zeal and that elusive body of skills, the art of bookmanship.

People with this peculiar package of skills and interests, though not common, did exist and frequently went into bookselling. One of the great tragedies of the present situation, however, is that many of them, after becoming senior clerks or assistant managers, were lost to the trade. There was no lifetime career as an assistant in the book business. The most interested bookseller could hardly ever make it worth while for an intelligent and professionally competent person to stay on in a subordinate position. Yet, if the trade was to grow and more oases were to be opened up in the desert, the trade must continuously recruit more and more bright young people with the necessary business sense and missionary zeal. These people could be found, recruited and trained, but to keep them in the trade, there must be opportunities for them to go on and open their own shops.

Mr. Marshall agreed with Mr. Guinzburg that by the standards of many other trades the amount of capital needed to open a bookstore was incredibly small. Yet it could be fantastically large to a young person trying to accumulate his capital out of his savings as an employee in a bookstore. It must be emphasized that it was impossible for bookstores to go to commercial lending institutions for financial assistance. In an ordinary commercial situation, major booksellers could not go to a bank and borrow a few thousand dollars on ninety day or comparable terms. Mr. Marshall had himself worked for a famous American bookseller for two and a half years, during which time his employer had financed his payroll on a week-to-week basis. It would therefore be futile for the universities, publishers or other interested parties to imagine that commercial lending institutions were going to help solve the bookstore problem in America today.

Therefore, if a college or university wanted to have the bookselling facilities its educational function required, it would probably have to take some sort of initiative itself. Mr. Marshall was, however, much less sanguine than Mr. Guinzburg at the prospect of institutions opening more of their own bookstores. Most institutional stores were notoriously poor in the creative end of bookselling. Perhaps because of a subsidy, perhaps because of the economics of the situation, they confined their activities to textbook distribution and the sale of everything but books. He was prepared to admit, though, that there might be special situations in poor or very small towns where the only possi-

bility of getting a general trade book outlet would be in an
institutionally financed and operated store. Nevertheless,
he felt that one of the reasons why Ann Arbor was a good
book town was that it did not have an institutionally run
store. (More fundamental, of course, for his own success
in the general book trade was the most amazing and unex-
pected response from the local academic and intellectual
community.)

The key to the situation, as Mr. Marshall saw it, was
finance and credit. Since the creative parts of the trade
were so relatively unprofitable and since there was such
great difficulty in getting normal commercial credit to
initiate and expand the creative bookstore, colleges and
universities, desirous of getting the right sort of bookstore
established in their vicinity, might consider lending money
or guaranteeing the lending of money to individual entre-
preneurs of bookmanlike promise.

For the rest, there was much that the publishers could
do to help put down a few more oases in the desert. Their
own interest was, after all, that most immediately associated
with bookselling. On the one hand, there was room for a
considerable public relations campaign to make the public
and college administrators bookstore conscious. With sufficient interest established it should not be difficult to add
trade book departments to existing textbook outlets and to
get university administrations to see to it that their campuses were properly served with bookselling facilities. On
the other hand, an organization like the American Book
Publishers Council might set up a standing committee on
the location, personnel problems and financial needs of
bookstores in America. Such a committee could work with
college and university administrations that desired to improve bookselling facilities in their vicinities. Such institutions could be offered specific advice on the type of shop

needed, the capital necessary to get such a facility started, as well as the names of persons available as managers or owner-operators. Such a service need not involve publishers in any great new expenditure since it could depend for its information on the large number of publishers' field representatives, salesmen, travelling editors, etc. who were usually quite well informed about local selling conditions, needs and opportunities and who had in many cases spotted young men now apprentice-clerking in existing stores who would like to go into business for themselves but who had reached a blind wall in their lack of working capital.

Finally, in addition to the above rather cost-free services, Mr. Marshall was prepared to recommend that publishers consider going further into areas that might cost them something more, at least initially. They might, for example, raise a fund in the trade by a general assessment (of perhaps only a fraction of what each house spends annually on exhibiting at trade conventions) to be entrusted to a non-profit corporation for lending at low interest and on long terms to persons starting or expanding bookstores. In addition, individual houses might experiment with different ways of putting books on long-term consignment into those campus outlets where investigation suggested opportunities for expanded service and sales.

In short, both educational institutions and publishers, as the parties most directly affected by present inadequate bookselling facilities on American college campuses, must assume some direct responsibility for amending this situation.

Mr. Canfield agreed with Mr. Marshall that publishing should help in this area and that ways and means should be most carefully and energetically explored. He thought that something might also be done in the direction of scholarships or subsidies to aid the professional training of young

men who wanted to be booksellers. Though Mr. Guinzburg
had pointed out the truly distressing proportions of the
cultural void existing at the many institutions that had
nothing but textbook outlets, he thought that in one sense
the situation was encouraging. Compared to the total sums
spent on education in this country, the sums needed to
start even a large number of bookstores were relatively
insignificant. On any given campus, the cost of setting up
such an outlet would be trifling compared to the total
campus budget. The key to the situation then was public
relations. He hoped that all present at the meeting would
cooperate in bringing this matter before the attention of
college presidents on a national scale.

In a reply to a query from Mr. Hamlin, Mr. Lacy explained that college presidents and others desiring information on bookstore financial problems could obtain a considerable amount of information both from the American
Book Publishers Council[1] and the American Booksellers
Association.[2]

Mr. Guinzburg asked the librarians present if there had
been any significant discussion in their profession, particularly among librarians at state institutions, about encouraging local booksellers by buying library books from them.
He noted that some private institutions subsidized a local
bookstore outright. He wondered if this might not more
easily be done at a public institution by routing a certain
proportion of library business locally. Mr. Ellsworth replied
that most state university librarians felt so pressed for
funds that they looked for the jobber with the longest discount and shut their eyes to the needs of the local man.
Mr. Wagman added that a number of state institutions
were obliged by law to do their purchasing through the

[1] 24 West 40th Street, New York 18, New York.
[2] 175 Fifth Avenue, New York 10, New York.

state purchasing agency or under its regulations. This usually made it mandatory to accept the longest discount. Occasionally exemptions were allowed for obtaining certain classes of books from wholesalers, but it usually was not possible to direct any business to a local retailer.

Professor Angell observed that he had recently learned from the executive of a publishing house how large the returns to publishers from book clubs could be. He wondered if publishers had ever considered tackling the problem of the dying bookstore by putting some of their returns from book clubs back into bookstores as seed capital. Mr. Guinzburg pointed out in reply that all publishers were already using the returns from book clubs and so forth to subsidize in effect their less profitable undertakings. If it were not for the occasional and unpredictable book club jackpot, publishers would not be able to publish a great proportion of the books they now do. In effect, almost any quality publishing house is now subsidizing a great proportion of its output by returns from a few successes. Fifty per cent of the year's publishing program can be expected to show a loss. In fact, statistics show that trade publishers now are losing a substantial amount of money annually on what might be considered their regular business. With the exception of one or two trade houses, it is only the subsidiary income from clubs, etc. that puts the company in the black.

Mr. Heckscher wondered if this weren't making the best of a bad situation. If there were no book clubs, wouldn't the money that now went into book clubs go instead into regular bookstores and thus help maintain a stronger, more viable general book distributing system. Mr. Guinzburg replied that, even if Mr. Heckscher's assumption were verifiable and true, it was too late to do much about it. If book clubs had never come into existence, maybe the distributing situation would be better now. However, no one in the book business today could afford to refuse to sell books to the clubs in order to help the bookstores.

Provost Gross thought that the discussion was missing at least one important point. It was just a pipe dream to talk about building more bookstores on campuses and expect students to flock to them when book prices were what they were. There was a very definite price resistance to hard cover books, yet the success of paperbacks proved how flexible the demand for books was. Mr. Canfield agreed perfectly but did not see that there was anything publishers could do in the present economic situation to reduce publishing costs. Mr. Lacy pointed out, though, that in terms of the general price level, it could be said that the real price of books was less today than it had been thirty years ago, to which Mr. Gross replied that one was dealing with students who came from families that had not been buying books thirty years ago. One was trying to introduce such young people to new wants, not simply nurturing inherited tastes.

Mr. Marshall felt that paperbacks could and were creating such new wants. In the bookstores, at least, they were a distinct commercial success. They had vanquished price resistance magnificently. Viewing the general trend over the past four years during which paperbacks were coming in, he felt sure that his good customers among the students were now spending much more for books than did their predecessors six or seven years ago. Thus experience had vanquished the booksellers' premature lament of four years ago: "How are you going to make a living selling thirty-five cent or seventy-five cent works?"

Mr. Heckscher noted that paperbacks should add considerable flexibility to curriculum-planning since students could be asked to buy a half dozen or so paperbacks for the price of one conventional textbook. The instructor should thus have much greater leeway in planning his course and suggesting outside readings. Mr. Canfield agreed that there was a paperback revolution in progress, but it had, by and large, not reached the classroom yet. The best information available indicated that from two to four per cent (varying with different parts of the country) of educational sales (books required for student purchase) were paperbacks. Mr. Marshall felt that though these figures might be true for the country as a whole, at institutions like Columbia, Michigan, Princeton, Yale and Harvard, where there were booksellers who kept wide stocks of paperbacks and displayed them effectively and where faculty were paperback conscious, paperbacks must account for a much higher percentage of educational sales. Insofar as the above named institutions were innovating pace setters, one could expect the paperback percentage of educational sales to rise generally.

Mr. Goldberg observed that among the difficulties in the spread of this new teaching practice were the distribution of many paperbacks through newsdealers and the failure of many booksellers to be paperback conscious. In addition, the tradition of personal contact in textbook-selling kept many more conservative faculty people in the older, more accustomed channels. There was, however, tremendous interest in paperbacks as a teaching device as Mr. Deason was able to report from his own experience. The American Association for the Advancement of Science as an experiment had printed an unannotated list of some two hundred scientific titles available in paperback. It was intended for high school teachers. As a flyer they published six thousand copies to start with which were gone within sixty days. Some eighteen thousand copies had since been distributed. Not only high schools but colleges had sent in orders for several hundred copies for distribution to students in class.

He agreed with Mr. Goldberg that the principal barriers to greater use of paperbacks were distribution problems and a general ignorance of what was available in paperback.[3]

The paperback book, Mr. Guinzburg reminded the conference, presented many technical problems that were not generally understood. He was in the paperback business and very much interested in it. His firm was experimenting with further applications of the idea. He was thus in no sense hostile to proposals for the substitution of paperbacks for many other forms of the printed book in class and general use. Nevertheless, as important as it was, he thought its potential was being enormously exaggerated.

If one looked at the bulk of the so-called quality paperbacks on the market (he was not referring to the mass market paperbacks in the thirty-five cent to fifty cent category), one would notice that a great number of them were noncopyright books, many standard works that the publisher knew would go on selling over the years because they had already been selling regularly for years past. They were frequently books that were going out of print, or out-of-print books reproduced photographically. The publisher could therefore afford to receive much less per copy than he would receive from a hard-cover book.

Therefore, before one allowed oneself to look forward too complacently to the time when it would be possible to have all student reading in this format, one must remember the special additional problems that would arise when one attempted to publish in paperback something that had not already proved itself and paid for itself in hard covers. The paperback must then bear all the ordinary editorial expenses and the initial expenses of composing,

[3] The R. R. Bowker Company (62 West 45th Street, New York 36, N.Y.) in addition to its general catalog, *Paperbound Books*, also publishes a shorter *Paperbound Books: College Edition* listing 1900 titles suitable for college classroom use.

platemaking, etc. plus substantial fees to the author at least equivalent to what he would have expected to get from a hard-cover edition. In addition, one would have to contend with the very large, well-established existing interest of textbook publishers and authors of textbooks, particularly those that had been widely used and highly remunerative.

Experimentation was still going on, but one must be very cautious about predicting how many and what kind of titles were going to come out in paperback in the future. Up to now the paperbacks had to a considerable extent been living off the past. His own firm had a well-known series of literary reprints and collections that appeared originally in hard covers and then in paperback. Most were noncopyright books. If the firm had had to pay royalties, there was not a single title that they could have afforded to issue in paperback unless it had previously been published in hard covers. If the plates hadn't been paid for and sitting in a warehouse ready for reprinting with no new editorial or mechanical investment, the firm couldn't possibly have issued those titles in paperback at anything like the price at which they were issued. When one talked of new titles in paperback, Mr. Guinzburg concluded, one was dealing with a completely different set of economic conditions.

For all practical purposes, Mr. Canfield observed, publishers today did not issue in paperback either new titles or older works that still enjoyed a very substantial sale in hard cover. Under such a test, one could never hope to find all one's reading needs in paperback.

The over-all situation seemed to Mr. Buck to be both sad and confusing. He wondered whether from the publishers' standpoint the trend seemed to be getting better or worse. Mr. Canfield felt that market trends were irregular and mixed, though he was inclined to be more optimistic than Mr. Guinzburg. He would agree that, when compared to the great increase in the country's wealth and population, particularly college and college graduate population, the sales of quality books had declined in a relative sense in the past thirty years. From the experience of his own firm, Mr. Canfield noted that the difficult titles to sell today were volumes of poetry or essays. On the other hand, the quality novel and historical works sold a great deal better today than they did in the 'twenties,—perhaps twice as many copies. The situation was not hopeless.

Mr. Lacy observed that book sales as a whole had increased remarkably. They were now six or seven times what they had been not so many years ago. This increase, however, had taken place almost wholly in book club and inexpensive edition sales. Bookstore trade sales had remained relatively stagnant. Yet total sales had increased per capita and in proportion to the increase in total national income.

There was one facet of the bookselling situation, though, Mr. Vosper pointed out, that was not immediately connected with publishing. He referred to second-hand bookstores, traditionally so integral and important a part of the college or university scene. How many young people had developed the book-buying habit at the inexpensive used bookstores that used to be so common about college campuses! Now they seemed to be declining much more rapidly than new bookstores and are much more scarce—although, Mr. Marshall observed, they required much less capital. Used bookstores too, Mr. Vosper felt, were a legitimate object of university concern and help.

In another area, that of the "offbeat" book, the interests of publishers, booksellers, librarians and teachers were much more closely linked. Getting people to buy and/or read bestsellers and other obvious titles, Professor Gjelsness pointed out, was no great problem. Such works were widely advertised in various media as well as by word of mouth and librarians and booksellers frequently found themselves inundated by requests without any extraordinary effort on their part. Getting people to read the less obvious "quality" titles was a much more difficult problem, particularly when attention was frequently captured by the publicity of the more obvious titles. Librarians were particularly concerned about this problem of broadening reader interest.

In the previous session, some attention had been given to ways in which universities could help stimulate—and broaden—reading interest among graduates through select reading lists distributed either directly or through alumni magazines. Mr. Guinzburg noted that such efforts could be linked to the encouragement of college bookstores. This had been tried successfully at Princeton. Alumni living in areas not readily served by a first-class bookstore were reminded that all the titles on the lists circulated through the alumni magazine were quickly available by mail from the Princeton bookstore. In this way alumni reading interest and alumni financial support for the college bookstore could be developed together.

An even more obvious way, Professor Bates remarked, of breaking the grip of the obvious book on the average reader's attention was the *book review*. He was rather disheartened by the present reviewing situation. Dean Steere agreed that one of the great obstacles to decentralizing reading interest was the paucity of book reviews in newspapers. Only a few of the major papers carried daily reviews, though most carried reviews in their Sunday editions. Part of this lack could no doubt be ascribed to the indifference of those educated persons with some leisure who could but who did not co-operate by submitting reviews to their local papers. The greater part of the blame, though, he suspected lay with the papers themselves, and wondered if more influence or even pressure could not be brought to bear upon the press to make them review consciously.

Mr. Harwell agreed with Dean Steere's suggestion that academic people bore some proportion of the responsibility for the review situation. They were of all groups the most dilatory in preparing reviews. The reviews in scholarly quarterlies came out months and years after a book had appeared. As a result, the influential book-review digests had to be based upon "quickie" reviews by much less competent people writing in the newspapers.

Mr. Canfield noted that the lack of reviews complained of by Dean Steere was by no means confined to the commercial press. He was appalled by the almost total absence of reviews and news about books in student campus newspapers. An occasional list of new books received at the library was no substitute. It was astounding that the students who ran campus newspapers had not yet discovered any news value in books.

One ought not be too hard on newspaper editors, Mr. Heckscher felt. He had once edited a small newspaper with a book column. It was not a very good column for it depended on the books sent out for review by only two or three publishers. He thought that if local bookstores, instead of relying on publishers to send out review copies, would co-operate with local newspapers, far more local reviewing would be done.

Mr. Guinzburg agreed that the reviewing situation was bad but felt that it was just one part of a general situation that could not be significantly improved until the total configuration was improved. The interrelatedness of the total problem reminded him of Walt Whitman's "Great poets need great audiences." If there were more readers, there would be more bookstores; if there were more bookstores in a locality, publishers would be encouraged to advertise more there; with more publishers' advertisements, local editors would feel encouraged and obliged to publish more reviews; with more reviews one would perhaps have more readers; and so it went. One had to attack the cycle as a whole; one could not hope to solve the problem by attacking one point on it. He did not know whether reviewing is now better or worse than it was thirty years ago; he did know that the public paid less attention to it.

11

The University Library and the
Lifetime Reader

BY RALPH E. ELLSWORTH

IT MUST be admitted, if we can accept the findings of the
Gallup polls and the communications researchers, that
the college graduate as an adult citizen does not retain the
book reading habit we like to think he once possessed in
school and college. We know that on a per capita basis
fewer American adults with a college education read books
than do English or French college grads, and very probably
they read fewer books too.

But beyond these crude facts we know very little about
why people do or do not read, in and out of college. It is
certainly fashionable today—especially in the post-Sputnik
days—to lament over the poor backgrounds and learning
behavior of the college graduate, but I strongly suspect that
if we could make a valid historical comparison between the
ability of college students to extract information from
print today with that of college students fifty years ago,
we might be amazed by the capability of our youngsters.
From where I stand (and I see a good deal every day I am
in the library), it is obvious that college students are so
much more sophisticated in this skill than were their predecessors, that they can't be measured on the same scale. I am

not claiming that their knowledge of the masterpieces of literature is so extensive, or that they know how to spell, or to write clearly or beautifully, or use literary allusions in their compositions, or even that they read as many unassigned books while they are in college as did their grandfather when he was there. What I am claiming is that they are far better equipped to handle the literature of knowledge than was their grandfather.

I am prepared to defend the argument that their adult reading behavior is at fault, if it is, more because of the influence of our culture than because of weaknesses in our schools and colleges, or even in the individual. And I am not inclined to be very critical of the behavior.

Fifty years ago it was assumed that the American college educated a limited few students for an intellectual life— which carried with it a commitment to read. Because those graduates were intellectuals, they were automatically readers. But today, in the large universities this is no longer true. The intellectual training for the few is still there, but onto it has been grafted a wide variety of special training programs, for large numbers of students, that do not pretend to be intellectual and that do not carry a serious reading commitment that would develop substantial reading habits that would be expected to carry over into adult life. Except for the vocational reading graduates of such programs would indulge in (the dentist, for example, would probably keep up on his professional literature), or the prestige reading one's social relationships force, it is unreasonable to expect them to be serious readers, for the simple reason that there never was any strong intellectual appetite created when they were in college.

No one, surely, thinks that reading behavior can ever rise higher in the individual than his motivation.

To return now to the argument that influences present

in adult society probably account for much of the drop off in the reading of college graduates, no one is much concerned about the reading habits of Teller, Von Braun, Fermi, or Bahr, or even Oppenheimer, or their counterparts in Russia. The accumulated knowledge displayed on TV quiz programs by such persons as Nadler or Van Doren is, of course, greatly admired by the American public, but not so much as is the ability of little Robert Strom to think with the tools of science. The public knows that when he grows up he and his kind will take us to the moon, will find a cure for cancer, a cheap way of utilizing sea water, and a safe way of disposing of atomic waste.

Knowledge—scientific knowledge—is power—manna to our society, and if you think youth will forego acting like a scientist in favor of acting like a 19th century English gentleman, in terms of reading, you are walking with your head in the clouds.

And this, parenthetically, is the storm center of our worst fears. Science as it is today—not what it may be 100 years from now—cannot be applied to the solution of the toughest and most critical problems we face. If only we could be sure of Russia's intentions, and if they could be sure of ours, we could view the problem of getting into outer space as important and interesting, but not critical. We might be able to persuade the Robert Stroms to engage in fundamental research in the behavioral sciences so that we might find out how to teach man to live happily with other men and with himself—the *big* problem for 20th century man. Isn't it rather strange that on this problem we have advanced no further than the concepts expressed in the eighth chapter of the *Little Flowers* of St. Francis of Assisi?

Before we pass judgment on the reading habits of college students, we perhaps ought to consider a statement made

by Dr. Margaret Mead in 1951 before an American Library
Association convention.[1]

> We have come to realize that each generation in this country
> is sufficiently different from each other generation so that they
> are unknown to each other, and that you can't any longer find
> out what it is to be a teen-ager by remembering what it was like
> to have been one. . . .
> The young people of today can live comfortably in a world
> we never knew if only we will let them be free to do so. They
> must form themselves. That is the whole meaning of an age that
> is changing so rapidly. Each group must work out its own salva-
> tion. . . .

The fact that today the student union, not the library,
is the heart of the university campus may be indicative of
the fact that students rely on their own group, not on
books, as carriers of the advice of other generations, for
help in evaluating their problems.

Most university librarians today would agree that prior
to World War II most American college and university
libraries were doing a perfectly terrible job of encouraging
a friendly feeling for books and of helping students form
good reading habits. We need not flog this dead horse un-
mercifully, but we should enumerate the kinds of mistakes
we were making. Perhaps the best way to do this is to look
at ourselves through the eyes of a foreign visitor—Dr.
Wilhelm Munthe, Director of Libraries, Oslo University:

> The library on the Inside. A chance visitor to the library will
> perhaps get the opposite impression (that students don't use the
> library). Due to the large enrollment at colleges, he will as a rule
> find the reading room teeming with students in action. But he
> will be surprised to note what a small percentage really seem to
> be absorbed in their work. Most of them seem to take their read-
> ing as an assigned task. Their attention follows everyone coming

[1] *A.L.A. Bulletin,* XLV (1951), No. 8.

in or going out. The library has become the center of the campus in a sense that was not intended. It has become the one great meeting place on the campus. Here some come with their 'dates', others looking for 'dates', and still others just to visit. There is nothing left of anything like a studious atmosphere. The students have become 'poised with that air of expectancy one sees in a railway waiting room.'[2]

As you read these words, your thoughts must turn to the library of your alma mater. The image fits, doesn't it? The reason these libraries discouraged good reading habits was that they made few concessions to the idea that each reader was one person with individual needs of a physical nature. They provided just one kind of facility and that was it. They lacked graciousness in physical characteristics and in services.

At this point I wish to make clear that I am under no illusions about the potential influence of the library—as a building, a staff service and a collection—on the reading habits of students. In the vast majority of students, it is the intensity of their motivation—caused by many things, such as native ability, inclination and individuality, home background, the teacher and the classroom, the status of reading among the student group, and so forth—that determines what and how much the students will read. But most students will be influenced a little by the library and a few will be influenced tremendously. The nature of the ratio varies from individual to individual and from campus to campus.

There are now so many wonderful new library buildings on college and university campuses that we librarians tend to forget that there still are many old buildings operating on 19th century principles. What was wrong with these build-

[2] W. Munthe, *American Librarianship from a European Angle.* Chicago, 1939, 103.

ings? Why have they handicapped the development of good reading habits in students?

Their faults are legion. They herded hundreds of students together in large reading rooms and thereby prevented the feeling of seclusion students like when they read. They separated students from the books. They could not provide small conference and discussion rooms adjacent to the reading rooms. They strait-jacketed the kind of service librarians could give and this affected the kind of relationship students and librarians could have. They provided no places where students and faculty could meet in an easy, natural relationship near books. They were cold and formal and lacking in gracefulness. They were gray in color and tone. They lacked the kind of human scale twentieth century students like.

The University of Michigan's new Undergraduate Library avoids all of these faults. Let us start with the mood or tone of the building. It is certainly not cold or institutional; it seems to convey the idea that reading within will be pleasant and comfortable. Contrast it with the great reading hall of the main library where hundreds of readers must sit at rows of tables, jammed together. Dr. Munthe might have had it in mind when he wrote the statement I quoted. There is no escape for the individual who wants to be by himself or who feels overwhelmed by the crowd. There are no reading room carrells, no places to smoke or talk—or to be an individual. You are reader number 12 at table 4.

But in the new library, everything seems to be arranged for *you* as an individual. Instead of just one kind of hard-seated, badly designed wooden reading chair, there are several types as well as davenports. When one wants to read a current magazine for pleasure at home does he go to the dining room table to do so? Of course not. He chooses a

lounge chair, or a sofa. But when the student is doing close
reading and taking notes, he must have table space—free
from the distraction of other readers, if necessary. Students
today do not like to read in big reading rooms; they want
individual secluded space. Thus, the right kind of furniture
can encourage the student to think he can spend long hours
of comfortable studying. In the Michigan Library the coffee
bar will be greatly appreciated, especially during the eve-
nings when students form the habit of studying from seven
until twelve, as many will do.

This building recognizes, too, that there are times when
students need to study in small groups and for this purpose
provides many small rooms of several sizes. These will prove
to be a source of difficulty when group study becomes bois-
terous and when the rooms become so popular that student
groups try to monopolize them, and pretty soon you find
yourself trying, without much success, to outsmart them.
But, what a wonderful battle to lose! At the University
of Iowa, the student library committee finally asked us to
make students sign up in advance for these rooms, which
we gladly did. On the basis of what I now know, the next
library I plan will have 80 per cent of the reading space
in the form of reading room carrells and group study rooms
and only 20 per cent in ordinary reading room tables.

Likewise, the planners of the building were wise to recognize that the book is no sacred object, but that it is merely
an artifact—a communication carrier—and that there are
other communication carriers—phonograph records, films
(both moving and still), and pictorial art. It assumes that
the concept of reading today must cover all these carriers.
There seems to be no sentimental attitude toward the book
as the only, or even the best carrier. This is not to say,
however, that the book as an art form is not worthy of
consideration. But since most of the books that are designed

to be beautiful contain texts that are not relevant to the normal use of college students, one can do little more than display the beautiful books and hope that some day all publishers will employ fine artists in book design and that the least textbook will be beautiful to look at as well as useful to read.

Note that smoking is permitted in this library, and that it is open until midnight. One Big Ten university library stays open until 2:00 a.m. every night of the week, but Saturday.

At this point, one may admire this kind of a library building, but still ask what this has to do with the development of sound and lasting reading habits. There are two reasons for claiming that the results are positive. First, this building enables students to learn how to use all the learning media in conjunction with one another, and this should encourage a balanced use of the book, the TV, and the movie. Secondly, we have lots of evidence on what buildings of this kind do to the reading habits of students. The testimony from such institutions as Rutgers, Western Reserve, Harvard, Iowa, Georgia, and Georgia Tech, Michigan State University, Central Michigan College, Florida State University, Oklahoma State University, and Washington State College, to name only a few, is that student reading increases and that students appear to enjoy the studying they do in these buildings. We can be certain that providing this kind of reading setting does make a difference and that the difference is worthwhile.

That part of library service which could influence reading habits would be the nature and personality of the library staff. Everyone knows that the stereotype of a librarian is a fussy old maid, a battle-axe with a pencil in her hair and with a passionate concern for library rules and details. This stereotype does not fit the kind of librarians one finds today, and it certainly does not fit Mrs. Keniston and her staff. I do not wish to embarrass her with unwarranted flattery, but I do wish to explain why she, and librarians like her, can have an important influence on student attitudes toward reading. In the first place, she knows the University community, and many of the faculty, so well that she will be able to talk to them understandingly about their teaching methods that seem to result in good reading practices among the students, as well as those that do not. The librarian, by virtue of her presence at the time the student attempts to get information out of books, sees a side of the student the professor does not. Much good can result when the librarian and professor can compare notes. With a Mrs. Keniston this will be possible. In the second place, she has raised a family of boys and she has a mother's understanding, as well as a librarian's understanding of college-age readers. I consider these qualities to be priceless because I know that students crave this kind of counsel, and I know there are so few librarians capable of giving it.

Of course, there have been many good librarians who started out with banners flying, but who lost their momentum because of the working conditions universities usually impose on librarians. On the one hand, administrators and faculties expect librarians to be well-read bookmen and wise reading counsellors, but on the other, they do everything they can think of to keep them from being either. Let us take a hard look at this because it has a bearing on our problem.

Librarians are usually expected to be on duty forty hours per week, whereas the faculty are in class from eight to twelve hours per week. The librarian can examine but not read books during the day, and her work is physically exhausting. She is expected to work eleven months a year, with time off for Christmas Day, New Year's, and the

Fourth of July. Apparently, her reading, living, and everything else must be done at night. This is impossible. Librarians should be on duty a full forty-hour week, but half of this time should be spent, out of sight, reading. And she should work a nine-month year, with a carefully planned summer reading program as well as the normal time for recreation and travel.

Unless librarians can have four to six hours of free time for reading each day, they cannot know books well enough to be competent reading counsellors.

But this is only the beginning of the administrative mistakes we have been making. In many universities the head librarian has little real control over the working conditions of his staff. The real control rests with the director of personnel—one of those strange new mutations spawned out of the alleged science of personnel psychology and fathered by strange mechanistic conceptions of human nature that might be appropriate in Soviet Russia, but not in our republic. They may have applicability to work on the assembly belt, but not to intellectual work where the media consist of people in relationships on an individual basis. What do they do that is so wrong? First, they assume that a library staff is a series of jobs, not a group of people. They draw up a list of specific duties to be performed in each job. They then measure out the exact amount of education and training one must have to carry out these duties. (To be overeducated is wasteful.) Next, they lay out a salary scale so that each person is paid the same amount as others whose work is equally complex or difficult, with annual increments of increase that will be given more or less automatically unless you rob a bank or rape your neighbor's wife. Once you're on the treadmill you can play it safe, and you know exactly what your salary will be in five years. What a bureaucracy! Where is the kudos for excellence?

Will this kind of attitude towards librarians give us librarians who will exert great efforts to be learned and bookmen, the kind of librarians the faculty want and the students need? The questions answer themselves.

If anyone made a deliberate effort to do so, no better system could be devised to defeat the purpose universities have in mind for librarianship, because this system violates the basic principle that in intellectual matters you allow the individual free rein, you do not tell him when or how to work, and you judge him not by the time he puts in or the ordinary performance of his duties, but by the extraordinary results he produces. Each man is different and is a law unto himself. You must make the system fit him rather than make him fit the system.

If we want librarians to live up to their opportunities as reading counsellors to students, we must cast aside this method of "managing" them. Even a Mrs. Keniston, if she had to work under these conditions, would soon exhibit a passionate concern for library rules, not for boys and girls and books.

If universities want librarians to be bookmen and to be effective as reading counsellors, they should first of all be willing to define this work as a kind of teaching. Not the same kind that the professor does in the classroom, but teaching nevertheless. They should do this so that the librarian will know what is expected of her and so that her work will be oriented in this direction. This does not mean that librarians should be called professors (unless they profess) but it does mean that they should belong to the "teaching" staff—not in some other nonteaching category. Secondly, they should provide the kind of working conditions I have described so that librarians will know the contents of books. And, third, they should pay librarians enough so they can afford to get married, live in suitable quarters, own a Volkswagen, a hi-fi set, and a good record collection, and be able to throw an occasional cocktail party. It also means that librarians should be able to qualify in terms of education, quality of mind, and personality. Our traditional concept of "trained librarian" isn't enough.

One can cite examples of librarians exerting the kind of reading counselling service I have been describing. The work of Mr. Alexander Laing at Dartmouth is one and the library at Stephens College is another. Both examples have some elements in common: the librarians have some tangible link with the instructional staff and program of their college; they have the kind of working conditions and library setting I have described; and the administration has a clear idea of what they expect the librarians to do. The results in both cases are impressive, but one cannot prove that they lead to reading habits that will last. One can only hope.

It is easy to see why, in the past, library service has failed to exert the kind of influence on student reading habits we have all wanted. I have already explained why the librarians inevitably lost their ability to live up to expectations. You can see now why the immense, barren, and formal reading rooms offered no testimony to the idea that reading could be as fun and exciting for students at work as it could be in their home living rooms. And library service, compartmentalized into units that bore no relationship to student reading needs, such as reference, reserve, stacks, circulation desks, and rare books rooms, and maintained in these forms simply because of inertia or bad buildings, was resented by students and faculty alike.

To be sure, our professional literature is studded with gadgeteering ideas for stimulating student reading. There have been attempts to give prizes for book collecting, to place popular books in dormitory rooms, to pass out pocket books, to sell books in the library, etc., and one may assume that these devices have had some influence, but they are at best quite marginal.[3]

Finally, we should consider the third element—the book collection. We do know, in the first place, that the open shelf plan is a great boon to students who like to study, as you can plainly see in this library. This plan relieves the library staff of much wasted effort and permits them to spend their time with students who want help on difficult bibliographic problems. The students' attention can now be caught by the attractive binding, the clearly stated title, and by the presence in one place of all the types of materials he needs. No longer is he chased from one end of a building to another as he pursues information in carriers that differ only in physical form and format.

In the second place, the collection is selected for its relevance to the needs of a given kind of student—the undergraduate. To be sure, next door can be found the research collection, and there are no barriers between the two buildings.

It seems to me that we cannot look to the book collection as the place toward which we should point the finger of blame for the past failure of libraries to do all they could to

---

[3] The library professional literature contains many descriptions of specific attempts to stimulate book reading through displays, prizes for book collecting, radio and TV book reviewing, etc. A few selected references are: J. A. Bond, "Freshman Reading Program in Junior College," *Junior College Journal* XI (1940), 22-25; D. W. Heron, "The Public Relations of Academic Libraries," *College and Research Libraries*, XVI (1955), 145-47; E. A. Hunter, "Reading Centers at Wellesley," *Publishers' Weekly*, CXXXVII (1940), 1484-87; Guy L. Lyle, "College Libraries Encourage Reading," *Journal of Higher Education* XII (1941), 191-97; L. C. Powell, "Alchemy of Books," *A.L.A. Bulletin* XLVI (1952), 266-72; B. A. Robie, "Declare Your Assets," *Library Journal* LXXXI (1956), 2514-15; L. H. Smith and G. E. McCauley, "Exhibits and Displays in the Junior College Library," *Junior College Journal* LV (1955), 354-56; R. J. Wills, "Bulletin Board Displays in the University Library," *Wilson Library Bulletin*, XXIX (1955), 540-44.

encourage lasting reading habits, because the book collections have, in the larger institutions, been adequate and interesting. The manner in which they have been serviced is another matter.

If those of us who have been in charge of college and university libraries have failed in the last decade or so in encouraging good reading, it is my judgment that we have failed not so much in the way we have run our libraries, but rather in our ineffectiveness in raising the storm signals whenever we saw university practices in the area of teaching that were producing in the students reading patterns that were bad. Permit me to illustrate what I mean by pointing out some of these practices.

First, many university courses are taught through a combination of formal class lectures and specific reading assignments in fairly rigid textbooks. Perhaps courses taught in this manner are not supposed to produce readers, and they certainly don't. A more serious result is that they don't require any real mental "brain stretching" on the part of the student. The thinking has been done by the professor and the author of the textbook. Oscar Handlin comments on this situation in the December 1957 issue of the *Atlantic Monthly* with the same caution. The student is allowed no contact with source material and he does not learn what it means to evaluate sources and to draw conclusions from them. He merely learns facts and principles others have developed from facts. If this method were used in introductory courses only, the situation would not be so bad, but this is not the case. This method does not teach students to develop judgment or taste in books. It is a most serious enemy of books and reading. Book publishers make money from publishing textbooks, of course, but do they realize that the money they make from publishing textbooks may be the principal reason the readers of these texts have no desire to purchase the other nontextbooks the same publishers print? I hear many weasel words of defense on this point from publishers, but I think they're going to have to realize they can't eat their cake and have it too.

Reliance on the crutches of class lectures or on textbooks is the worst possible kind of preparation for adult reading in the U. S. today. Everyone is bombarded with one-sided direct pressure statements in the form of magazines, radio and TV programs, house and trade journals, pamphleteering, etc., and there is no one professor around to tell one what the correct line is. He who has not formed the habit of evaluating sources is quite likely to be at the mercy of the special pleader.

Deans and other administrators seem to be anxious to improve the quality of college teaching, but it is my observation that they usually place the kudos on the professors who do the best lecturing, which usually means the ones who organize and present the material so well the students have to do no or very little reading. The stultifying effects of this on the student has not seemed to worry professors because they don't really know very much about the reading behavior of students, and they care less. Neither do most of them think very much about the effect of their methods on the preparation of the good citizen.

It is only in the honors programs, limited to only a few students, that you find undergraduates placed in a learning situation where they are forced to develop judgment and taste in the handling of the literature of knowledge.

In short, we librarians should have been shouting loudly that there was something wrong with teaching methods and with the point of view of professors. I know what professors think of this charge. They say that their main concern is research and that their advancement depends on publication and that they would have no time for research if they used inductive methods of teaching undergraduates.

They would also say that our libraries couldn't hold up their end of such a procedure. They may be right, but that doesn't lessen the damage done to students.

Second, do you realize that in the big universities the writing of term papers or any other kind of writing is almost a thing of the past for undergraduates? Traditionally, it has been the term paper that has driven the student into the books on an extensive scale. Faculty have given up the term paper requirements because they no longer have time to read them and because they can't spend the effort that would be required to detect plagiarism and other forms of student laziness. Thus far, I have seen no substitute for the term paper for motivation of book reading.

Third, we should have been screaming to the high heavens about the devastating effects the so-called objective, true-false examinations are having on student reading and on writing. You will say that I am again flogging a dead horse, but I deny that the horse is dead.

If you will work in the reading rooms, where reserve books are being read, you will find that students have definite ideas about how to study for these examinations. Their ideas may be wrong, but they have them anyway. They think it is better practically to memorize a small amount of reading than it is to read widely and comparatively. They think it is better to do their reading just before the exam on the assumption that the exams are a test of memory anyway.

Everyone agrees that grading essay exams is a very subjective business and that the objective examinations are impartial. We also know that the latter can be graded on machines, thus saving faculty time. But, if it is true that, with all their virtues these examinations measure the least important part of learning and actually stultify the important parts, of what use is the impartiality or the faculty time thus saved?

Fourth, let's be honest about it, a large per cent of the courses a state university offers have very little intellectual challenge in them and, therefore, little that would cause students to want to read now or in the future. There isn't any reason to think that students who fill up their program with such courses will ever have the desire, much less the habit, of reading. Many people, both within and without the university, are dissatisfied with the number of intellectually barren courses that are offered, but I see little evidence that anyone is going to do anything about this. There are too many vested interests in the form of Heads of Departments and Deans who know that large enrollments in their areas determine salary levels, number of graduate assistants, and other forms of cheap labor that free the senior men for research. And, of course, one way of keeping the enrollment high is to increase the course offerings. The top brass in a university seem to be unable to think of any good arguments to use in wringing the water out of the curriculum—just as they seem to be unable to control intercollegiate athletics. Maybe Sputnik will be their best weapon.

Fifth, one of the worst obstacles to good reading is the faculty itself. As I watch the way in which they make their reading assignments, protect themselves from spending time with students so they can do their own research, use teaching methods that kill whatever natural desire for learning their students bring from high school, refuse to find out what college students are really like, refuse to set a good example by being good readers outside their own specialty, and refuse to believe that students can learn on their own outside the classroom, I cannot escape the conclusion that you cannot expect good results when you teach undergraduates with a faculty whose primary interest is research.

12

The Library as Home and Classroom

SOME REFLECTIONS PROVOKED BY
MR. ELLSWORTH'S OFFERING

MR. VOSPER as a librarian found himself in the most heart-felt agreement with Mr. Ellsworth's most enlightening and imaginative two main points. On the first, he himself was convinced that the most enthusiastic university librarian working in the most attractive and well-designed building could have little effect on the average undergraduate unless faculty wisely and enthusiastically propelled students into the library and into the use of books. It was only the rare student who would enter the library on his own and flourish there. For such a student education might, in Dylan Thomas' phrase, in fact consist of the opportunity for "free and wide reading with my eyes hanging out." The great bulk of students, however, must be propelled, and on this score faculty were doing a very poor job. On every side, librarians wishing to develop reading among under-graduates found in their faculties inertia, doubt and mal-practice. The faculty members gathered at the conference were all on the side of the angels and therefore atypical. The great majority of college teachers were still all too content to depend on textbooks and rote teaching. Mr. Vosper recently visited a small liberal arts college where he conducted an informal poll. The faculty were polite and replied with pious sentiments suitable to the occasion. On questioning the students, however, from freshmen to seniors, he was told by members of all classes that they had and were taking from four to six courses a year in which only textbook reading was required. He could not discover that such training was producing very many lifetime readers among those students. He agreed with Mr. Ellsworth that librarians must speak up, but noted that the teacher who let a librarian tell him how to teach was a rare creature.

Mr. Vosper would like to see some studies made of faculty reading habits. He was extremely discouraged by the experimental survey he took at this same liberal arts college. He could only say that a faculty that didn't read—even professionally—was hardly likely to develop lifetime reading interest among its students.

He would like to see more practical experiments or pilot projects attempted along the lines suggested by Mrs. Knapp's work: how can curriculum and library use be more closely integrated; how can librarians work more closely with both faculty and students? Such experiments should take place at average institutions rather than at élite institutions where one knew in advance that the results would be good.

Although Mr. Ellsworth felt that today's college student was much more adept than his predecessor of a generation or two ago at getting information from printed sources, Mr. Vosper felt that the average institution could still pay much more attention and devote much more time to the specific training of students in the use of the library, of abstracts and indices and of all the apparatus for finding books and getting information out of them. Too often this important introductory work was either perfunctorily handled as part of freshman orientation or left to one regular class or another where it might or might not be comprehensively handled.

Mr. Vosper thought that Mr. Ellsworth would agree that he had been a bit cavalier in that part of his paper in which he spoke of gadgeteering ideas for promoting reading, such as prizes for book collecting, and so forth. The important thing, Mr. Vosper stressed, was maintaining on the campus the over-all climate in which a regard for reading might develop widely; in this a lot of little things like book prizes and book talks all had their place. If the center of the campus was now the Union and not the library, their distinctness could be blurred. Something of the Union had been brought into the new Michigan Undergraduate Library in its little refreshment room. Many a union nowadays had much of the library in it with browsing rooms, book talks and book displays. Advancing in small steps on many fronts, we could strive to create the climate in which the library became the effective center of the campus.

Dean Steere agreed with both Mr. Ellsworth and Mr. Vosper that there was relatively little librarians could do to develop reading on campuses where classroom teachers did not co-operate. After extensive experience at both public and private institutions, he felt that the general level of teaching in American universities (and not excluding the liberal arts faculties) was fantastically horrible. Deans would be completely scandalized if they knew how some of their faculty taught.

Dean Odegaard felt, however, that it was all too easy to expect too much from the college teacher. Twenty-seven per cent of college students today came from families of unskilled workers with, by and large, no books on their shelves. To expect everyone of these individuals to go from a bookless society to a bookish society in one generation was to ask for a very great deal. If we expected this, we were not

accomplishing it. Thus to say that a man had a college degree today was not to say that he had acquired a literary
education. Persons moving from an uneducated background
towards an educated career most frequently went from
factory work to an engineering job. Engineering education
as it had existed in this country during the past fifty years
had not been a very bookish education. Only at latter stages
of education or social evolution did the tendency to move
into occupations requiring a more bookish training become
manifest. It was nevertheless encouraging to notice the
over-all trend in the composition of college enrollment.
Studies of enrollment patterns at the University of Michigan made by Professor Roger Heyns showed that within
the literary college it had been the "bookish" departments
which had been gaining enrollment most noticeably in the
past ten years.

Professor Heyns was disappointed that so much of the
discussion of the ability of faculty to influence reading
patterns had stopped at the level of the common cliché.
For example, the notion that an emphasis on research was
a major aspect of the style of life of a professor was an aging
fiction. There were of course great variations from university to university in the emphasis on research; within
universities the importance of research as a path to advancement and promotion varied greatly from department to
department. Every college and university in the country
was keenly aware of the importance of undergraduate
teaching and over the years had promoted many people
whose primary virtue was their ability to teach. Thus a
simple emphasis or de-emphasis of research was hardly the
crux of the question. Universities had a problem in achieving a balance among the many services they were expected
to render and which they expected their faculties to perform. A university might at some particular time empha-

size one service more than another. Nevertheless, Mr. Heyns
did not think that major pedagogical techniques were in
any substantial way governed by an overwhelming pressure
for research. Few faculty members used textbooks when
they could avoid them. No one used them in small seminars
or advanced courses. Faculty members (accused themselves
of spending too much time in the library, at research, etc.)
were hardly oblivious to the values of independent library
work for their students. Nevertheless, one must remember
that every college professor met in his class students who
had been conditioned by a very substantial experience of
the educational process. One could start out using the inductive method of teaching with green freshmen, stressing
free library research, etc., but, if they were not prepared
for such work, one might have to go a long way before
getting good results. Thus, the textbook-lecture type of
teaching was partly an effort to reach the student at the
level of his actual learning skills. From there, one moved
gradually to the inductive method as the student developed
the appropriate new skills.

Mr. Ellsworth was in substantial if not complete agreement with Professor Heyns. He confessed that he might
have been wrong in singling out research as a guilty factor,
but was not convinced that there was very much promotion on the basis of teaching. Mrs. Knapp suggested that,
where, as was too often the case, the college teacher felt too
pushed by research or administrative responsibilities to devote the necessary time to inductive teaching, the librarian
might help by doing a more creative job of bibliographical
assistance. This kind of assistance—rather than advice on
how to teach one's course—would be most graciously accepted by the faculty from the library. A good librarian
should be able to suggest ways of tying in all kinds of read-

ing to a course so as to stimulate students to read widely in connection with that course.

Mr. Wagman reported that Mrs. Keniston, in her capacity as head of the new Undergraduate Library at Michigan, was experimentally attending the lectures of several cooperating professors in order to get a feeling for their courses and hoping thereby to be able to determine how the library might be tied in more closely with the work of the several courses. The faculty members participating in this experiment had been most enthusiastic and were beginning to think anew of ways in which they might use the library in their teaching.

Mr. Wagman also called the meeting's attention to the library's relationship to the impending wave of mounting enrollments and faculty shortages. He was heartened to read in the report of the President's Committee the suggestion that faculty shortages might in part be met by adopting methods of instruction which made students more responsible for independent study and less dependent upon classroom hours. The library would of course be central in any program for making students do more work on their own.

Some of the more constructive opportunities now open to librarians were summed up by Mrs. Keniston. As one who had had considerable experience at the libraries of small and large institutions, she felt there was much that the individual librarian could do to make the college library an easier place for the student to develop a lifetime reading interest. Like Mr. Vosper, she attached great importance to proper instruction and training in the use of the library. This could be done much more effectively and systematically in a small college than in a large one. In a large state university, the librarian simply didn't have staff enough to know how or where to begin. Nevertheless, she and her staff in the new Michigan Undergraduate Library were working on the problem and were determined to do something about it—though they realized that the procedures they were devising would have to be of the mass service variety.

Mrs. Keniston also reminded the conference that the librarian's relations with the faculty had to be handled much more delicately than might have been assumed from the previous discussion. She regarded college and university faculties as one of the last strongholds of individualism in this country and thought they were to be commended for it. This meant that the library could not and should not conceive of its role as dictating to the faculty. The library could only suggest and offer assistance and work with the professor on the professor's terms. Over a period of time, however, the offer of service, the sympathetic understanding of what the professor was trying to do in his course, etc. should build up a bond of mutual understanding between faculty and library. By co-operating fully with the professors interested in co-operating with the library, and not antagonizing the rest, the library could help create on the campus an atmosphere in which even the least library-conscious members of the faculty would begin to feel that their students should be getting more library experience. Such suggestions were not as specific as some people would like, but Mrs. Keniston felt that highly specific programs pushed before the right atmosphere of faculty-library co-operation had been developed would smack of library dictation and would provoke antagonism rather than co-operation in the faculty.

RETROSPECT AND PROSPECT:
The Continuing Problem

Retrospect and Prospect:
The Continuing Problem

BY LESTER ASHEIM

FROM A CONFERENCE in which so many provocative ideas have found expression, each participant undoubtedly takes away with him his own private list of highlights, which reflect his particular interests and prejudices. This concluding chapter should not be seen, therefore, as a reliable general summary which could serve as a digest-substitute for the preceding papers. It is nothing more than one man's reaction to the ideas to which two days of the conference exposed him; if it reveals anything, it is probably the author rather than the conference. But for what it is worth, here is what stayed most tenaciously with this writer as he reviewed the contributions of the conference to his own thinking about the problems of the college student and the lifetime reading interest.

What strikes one first in this conference is the great complexity of what seems on the surface to be a simple concept: the concept of reading itself. Several speakers sought for a restrictive definition, pointing out that when we concern ourselves with the problem of the lifetime reading habit we are concerned, not with just any kind of reading, but reading of "high quality and lasting significance" (Angell), reading which "brings the whole soul of man into activity" (Brower), reading which demands "sustained analysis, contemplation, and the savor of creativity" (Loewenberg).

Even the definition of a book was limited, as in Mr. Heck-scher's statement that "not everything is necessarily a book which appears between hard covers [and] there are . . . a whole series of productions in prose which, however serviceable, do not belong in the honorable company of books." Thus to acknowledge, as most of the conferees did, that a vast amount of printed material is available to the average educated man of today and often even perused by him; or to concede, as a few of the conferees did, that graduates of today's schools are probably better able than young people ever were in the past to grasp the dictionary meaning of printed symbols at a reasonable rate of speed, is not to dismiss the central problem of the conference. The real question is: Are our colleges establishing in their students a lasting interest in ideas; are they fostering a continuing desire, backed by the skill, to read critically and analytically, with the mind and not just the eye, for pleasure and satisfaction as well as for fact and specific knowledge? The consensus seemed to be that they are not.

In a sense, of course, this criticism was virtually the assumption which gave rise to the conference in the first place, and the task of the individual participants was to try to discover what some of the reasons are. There are many of them, and if a great number of them lie within the schools themselves—in teaching method, in course content, in the kinds of goals that are emphasized throughout the educational system—this is undoubtedly because the schools are a product of a society which is, generally speaking, indifferent to the book and the values it embodies.

Thus an important emphasis in the conference is that which is placed on the social status of reading and the social role of the reader. As Guinzburg points out, "The customs and the habits of students are what we are concerned with," for social pressures are highly important in determining a choice of any activity, whether it be buying a house or taking a trip or reading a book. Until we can increase the repute of the serious student among his fellows, both while in school and after graduation, our colleges will find it difficult to motivate the general run of undergraduates to read. Mr. Angell and others suggested some steps which might give such status to the superior student, but most of them are so completely campus oriented that one must still worry whether the lifetime reading habit can be fostered by them so long as the postgraduate world continues, in Mr. Loewenberg's phrase, to be indifferent to "the humanism of science and the science of art."

Yet if it be true that the schools are shaped by the society, it is also true that the schools are supposed to affect the society in return. The conference did not attempt to establish absolutely which is horse and which is cart, and I will not try to do so in this chapter. But wherever the major flaws lie, their eventual correction will probably have to be accomplished through education, on all its levels. The focus of the conference, therefore, was rightly on the role of the college (and the college library) in the promotion of the lifetime reading interest.

At first glance, one would guess that no better atmosphere than the college campus could be found for fostering habits of lifetime reading on the high level defined in this conference. The stated aims of the institutions of higher learning are almost always those which would best be served by the intelligent use of books and reading. The training of the whole mind; the development of the student's powers of original thinking and analysis; the exercise of the student's imagination; the promotion of sensitivity, aesthetic appreciation and understanding; the recognition of recurring problems of life adjustment; the deepened understanding of one's self and of others; and so on—surely these are aims which transcend the narrow limits of any one discipline and call for training in the use of tools and concepts, techniques and viewpoints which will foster continuing self-education. But the disturbing fact to which the conferees constantly returned is that of the very real conflict which exists between these admirable long-term goals, and the immediate goals of the individual courses.

The reality with which students, faculty members and librarians are all too familiar is that the individual course concentrates upon a narrowly defined body of knowledge or system of analysis with little relevance to other courses and disciplines, and makes but limited and unimaginative use of books. Course content and reading assignments are almost never designed to promote the kinds of book use that would be of value beyond the final examination. The conferees were unanimously agreed, I think, that ideally teachers should be less concerned than they now are with imparting knowledge in a given subject and more concerned with discovering and developing the bit of intellectual curiosity which presumably lies in every student.

These recommendations are admirable but they are guilty to a certain extent of oversimplifying the situation. It is all very well for a group of dedicated book people, removed for the moment from the realities of the classroom, the semester deadline, and the assigned subject matter, to talk glibly of each instructor's obligation to serve the long-time goals of all of education. What they are asking the individual instructor to do, in effect, is to ignore what he would be fired for ignoring: the aims of his specific course. The demands made by this conference upon the instructor, it seems to me, assume that each course in the curriculum should serve all the goals of the total curriculum, whereas the only sensible hope we can hold is that each course will contribute its own small part to a total which is far broader

and deeper than any one course can be. It can hardly be
expected of the instructor of an introductory course in,
let us say, organic chemistry that he shall concentrate at
the expense of the basic principles of organic chemistry on
stressing the broad function of the book in meeting a
variety of aesthetic and personal needs in later life.

What can be expected, however, is that the instructor
will try to demonstrate the ways in which the book can
supplement and enrich the student's experience in his particular subject field. If this were done in each course, and
if each course were designed to relate to the other courses
in the curriculum, the student would come out at the end
of his formal educational program with a sense of how to
adapt particular skills and methods to new situations, with
a permanent interest in ideas, with the ability to read
critically and well in order to serve that interest, and most
especially with a strong realization that college is only the
beginning of an education. He would see that, to continue
his education on the highest plane, he must make intelligent
use of books and reading—a skill which can, beyond any
other, be adapted to a great variety of needs and interests.
In a sense, the individual course would still remain narrow
in that it would concentrate on a particular subject matter,
but that is not really the major problem. The real fault, it
might be said, is not so much that the course is narrow
but rather that the instructor is. If the instructor would
see his course, not as an end in itself but, in relation to other
courses, as part of the student's total educational experience,
even the highly specialized course could be designed to
broaden the over-all intellectual training of the student
rather than to restrict it.

Clearly, then, the individual instructor is a most important factor in the total problem. The role of the
teacher is decisive because of his strategic place in the lives

of the young. From the age of six to maturity, as Angell points out, the growing boy or girl is in contact with teachers, in a relationship which can naturally stress the best use of books and lead by example to their intelligent use. In this sense, the teacher stands in a unique relation to the student, different from that of the parent, the minister, the scout leader, or the librarian, but as authoritative as any of them. One would guess that what the teacher does could make all the difference between making readers or nonreaders of the students in his charge.

And the guess would be right. Mrs. Knapp's report is relevant here, for even at the college level she found that the aims of the particular course and the methods of instruction employed are a more important influence upon reading than is the general subject matter. This supports Mr. Steere's belief that the student of the sciences is no less in need of access to books than is the student of the humanities or of the social sciences. If science students use books less, the fault lies with teaching methods in the sciences, not in the subject matter. By extension then, if the graduates of our colleges generally read but little in their postcollege life, the fault lies with the kind of instruction they have had more than in the substitute interests they pursue. Mr. Loewenberg has said it better than I can: "The problem of the reading of books is the problem of the cultural status of scholarship . . . The answer . . . can only lie in the virility of our education, its meaningfulness, its relevance to the issues of life. It lies ultimately, therefore, in the quality of teaching. If the present system is to be creatively altered, it is the teacher who by his work will alter it."

But while all of the conferees were agreed that this is so, there was far from any agreement on what the appropriate method is for establishing the kind of lifetime reading interest we are all trying to foster. The easy assumption that "free" reading is somehow better than required reading was rejected by many of the speakers. As Dean Odegaard pointed out, random, so-called independent reading may only imply "immaturity of interest and/or an unstimulating curriculum. As a student matures, his interest should become more clearly defined and integrally related to his current curriculum." Thus greater use of "course-related reading" (a term generally preferred by the conferees to "course required") would be an indicator of success in the curriculum.

The group was not unanimous however in holding that guided reading is the best basis for building the lifetime reading habit. It is true that Mr. Brower's "slow-reading" course is based on the belief that intensive, selective reading in certain great texts is the way to stimulate the kind of interest which can lead to continued "good" reading of the type defined in the conference. But despite the specific program described by Brower, he himself points out that there is no single sacred technique for teaching reading, a stand with which—since this is a personal summary—I certainly agree. Both intensive and extensive reading can be useful, and different students react differently to different methods. More than that, different kinds of reading require different approaches even for the same person. Any method that could lead to a lifetime interest in reading should be encouraged; the only question is whether there are approaches which definitely stifle or inhibit the interest in reading and the book.

It seems that there are. It was frequently pointed out that the use made of books in the schools all too often ignores or even precludes an essential in establishing the habit of book use: the fun and pleasure of reading. The conferees rightly rejected the division of college reading into free (good) and required (bad), but clumsy as this approach was, it was trying to distinguish reading-as-pleasure from reading-as-chore. The distinction is one worth making; the error lay in the assumption that assigned reading must, by definition, lie outside the realm of the students' interests. There is a great deal of the reading required of students that could furnish the kind of pleasure that Ellsworth wants reading to represent.

We return, obviously, to the responsibility of the instructor, for he is in a position to make assigned readings exciting and pleasurable and stimulating. When he does not, reading becomes synonymous in the student's mind with "dull stuff that one has to do to satisfy immediate course requirements." In such a context reading is virtually defined as something to be avoided as soon as the outside pressures are relaxed, and this spells death to the lifetime reading habit. The well-documented fall-off in reading which occurs immediately at the time of graduation for the majority of the adult population would seem to demonstrate that this is indeed the view of reading which modern teaching methods have impressed upon today's students.

Here, of course, I am guilty of an oversimplification as great as the one I condemned earlier, for no single factor is uniquely responsible for the current state of reading. The reading experience is a complex one, and the choice of reading as an activity is influenced by many factors. We have spoken of the motivations supplied by the social status of reading, and by the teacher's method of using reading. But even where both of these influences are favorable, other factors may come into play to inhibit reading. It goes without saying, surely, that unless there are books around, students will not read them. It was clear from the conference that, to more or less degree, the books are not around for many students on many campuses. The new

Undergraduate Library at Michigan is a dramatic device for meeting this problem, for it makes books not only available, but really accessible. This distinction between availability and accessibility is an important one, and no better illustrative anecdote is needed than Mr. Steere's description of the awakening represented by his attainment, as an undergraduate student, of a pass to the stacks. There were no more books available after he had his pass than before, but now they were accessible—and this made all the difference.

Mr. Guinzburg's call for a good bookstore on the campus is related to the accessibility factor. So are Mr. Odegaard's and Mr. Heckscher's emphasis upon the importance of books in the home as an influence perhaps far more decisive than any college or library can ever be. The tremendous growth of the paperback, the encyclopedia, and the book club is testimony again to the importance of easy access, for it is the convenience of the rack in the drugstore, the salesman on the doorstep, the book in the mailbox, which as much as anything accounts for their phenomenal success while bookstore sales have progressed so little. Even the simple matter of showing the book to the student in class, advocated by both Professor Angell and Professor Steere, is an aspect of bringing the book within reach, of establishing a physical relationship between exciting ideas and the books which supply them. The problem all too frequently today is that the book is identified in the student's mind with inconvenience, red tape and delay, rather than with ideas, mental challenge or pleasure. To the average student the book means, at the very least, a difficult search through the catalog, a long wait in line, the nuisance of forms to fill out and identification to present, the need to be at a specific place at a given time—and only after all that does it mean the joy of contact with ideas. Accessibility brings

the book together with the ideas, capitalizing on the stimulation of the good classroom presentation, and associating
the book with intellectual pleasures rather than with
physical discomfort and petty irritations.

This kind of conditioning is related also to the physical
environment in which books and reading are made available
to the student. Here again the new Undergraduate Library
serves as Exhibit A: where the surroundings are inviting,
youthful, pleasant, designed with the student in mind, book
use increases. Indeed, Mr. Guinzburg tells us that wherever
libraries or stores are enlarged, improved or made more
attractive book use goes up, and Dr. Ellsworth cites a number of instances of how important a difference the right
setting makes for library use as well.

And it is here, of course, that the good librarian has a
decisive role to play. The teacher can do much to lead
the student to explore the treasures the library holds, but
once the student is in the library and not in the classroom, the guidance falls to the librarian or the assistant
behind the library desk. Even where the reading sought is
only the strictly controlled assigned reading from the reserve book collection, the role of a pleasant and helpful
library worker is important because of the conditioning
process we have just been describing. And when the student begins to seek for his own readings—whether course
related or "free"—the guidance and assistance of the professional librarian can be all important.

Teachers and librarians should be working together on
implementing all aspects of the curriculum, of course, but
nowhere is this co-operation more essential than in the attainment of the long-term goal: the stimulation of the lifetime habit of reading. Co-operation is more than the
mere exchange of essential information: the preparation of
reserve lists, consultation with the librarian when especially

heavy demands on certain titles are anticipated, the mutual agreement on the addition of needed books to supplement the basic assigned readings. It requires also a recognition by the instructor of the part the librarian can play in suggesting additional readings to the student, leading him on to related works, and stimulating his search for supplementary materials. Above all, it requires the acceptance by the faculty of the librarian's competence and responsibility in the realm of "free" and "outside" reading. At present many faculty persons and college administrators who agree that the librarian's role is to support the program and objectives of the parent institution, think of this as meaning merely that the librarian should supply the books for which the professors ask and that is all. That the librarian should take a really active part in initiating the provision of supplementary materials that are course-related—to say nothing of providing extracurricular materials not directly useful to the specific courses—is an idea which is new and unacceptable to many. Yet this whole conference has stressed the point that the objectives of the parent institution are broader than the aims of individual courses and that the establishment of the lifetime reading habit is one of the most important of these. The college library is not exceeding its proper function if it plays a dynamic part in the provision of extracurricular materials and the stimulation of interest in them; it is failing in one of its obligations if it does not.

An important point to make here, it seems to me, is that one of the major needs of present day education is preparation for continuing education beyond the campus. Mr. Lacy stressed this point strongly in discussion and surely there can be no serious disagreement with his observation that college courses as taught in the 1920's—in modern history, in economics, in the sciences, in political science, even in literature and the arts—would not be acceptable preparation for the student of today. The increasingly rapid changes that occur in twentieth century society make it even more obvious that college graduates in the 1950's will be ill-prepared for the responsibilities of citizenship in 1970 unless they have continuously supplemented their formal education. To equip the student to carry on this continuing self-education, ideas and methods are more important than the 1950 facts. Consequently, students should learn to use the library not only to equip themselves to find course readings and to write term papers, or to prepare them for their scholarly research if they should choose to work for an advanced degree. They should learn to use the library because, of all the tools that college provides them, this is the one which they are most likely to be able to use fruitfully no matter how far removed from the academic world their futures may lead them. Similarly, they should learn to know and work with librarians as well as instructors, because once they leave the campus they are much more likely to have the opportunity to turn to a librarian than to a professor for assistance in the intellectual, social and personal problems they will have to face and solve. If the long-term aims of education which are so movingly described in the prospectus of the college are real, then the role of the library and the librarian must of necessity be of an importance equal to that of the classroom and the instructor, for the librarian is freer than any member of the formal teaching faculty to concentrate his attention on the long-term goals of the total educational experience rather than on the immediate goals of a specific course.

That the library and the librarian will become increasingly important in college education seems inevitable. As Heckscher points out, "numbers will force solutions of their own," and as the student population increases the logical

solution will be a greater reliance upon the student's
ability to read and to study on his own even while he is in
college. The President's Committee, quoted by Mr. Guinzburg, has already recommended placing more responsibility
upon the students for educating themselves through independent study. Since it seems highly probable that, no
matter what other means of communication are developed,
the book will for a long time to come be the principal tool
for self-education, the library may soon become in fact
as well as in theory "the heart of the campus."

Man can wait for the inevitable to come upon him, or he
can plan ahead to employ the inevitable in the most ad-
vantageous way. For college administrators who elect the
alternative of planning, several suggestions and implications
appear in the deliberations of this conference.

I address the administrator here because the task of the
future is not just for the librarian or the instructor, but
for the institution as a whole. The good teaching and library
practices which were cited in the conference are heartening
because they demonstrate that something can be done, but
they represent isolated, occasional instances and not the
unified approach to the problem which is the only effective
way to resolve it. The conference calls for the development
of students who will take with them lifetime habits of
curiosity and the knowledge of how to satisfy that curiosity
through reading. Such a goal must be reached *because* of
the administrator's institutional aims and not, as is today
so frequently the case, in spite of them. It requires, in other
words, an integrated, co-ordinated program which reflects
the enthusiastic support and encouragement of the head
of the institution.

The overarching implication for the college administrator is the need for a realistic implementation of the professed objective: the promotion of the lifetime habit of

book use. The discrepancy between the ideal and the real, stressed so frequently in this conference, can be reduced if curriculums and programs are planned from the beginning with the long-term objective in mind. The structure of individual courses should be designed to serve both the immediate goals and the goals for the future, and this can only be done if administrator, instructor and librarian are really convinced of the equal importance of both aims. The nature of the teaching method employed and the kinds of assignments made make the difference between the perfunctory and resigned use of assigned readings which now characterizes so much of current student habits, and the stimulating and challenging enjoyment of the reading experience which occasionally occurs.

If instructors are to be encouraged to redesign their courses and to reappraise their methods of teaching, they will have to see tangible evidence on the part of their schools' administration that this goal is regarded as vital and essential. Recognition by the administration of excellence in teaching, for example, can stimulate the teaching faculty to extend its efforts. An important criterion of such excellence should be the degree to which a teacher inspires the student to seek independently for further knowledge and ideas through wide use of books and reading. Another simple device for convincing the teacher that the college really believes in the importance of books in the advancement of teaching, would be the one suggested by Harold Guinzburg: the provision for the instructor of a special credit at the local bookseller's for the purchase of miscellaneous books. In other words, the college cannot merely say it considers books important; it must overtly give importance to them. On these grounds, Mr. Guinzburg makes an excellent case also for the colleges' assuming some responsibility to see that an adequate bookstore is available on or near the campus.

Similarly, of course, the college must recognize its responsibility for supporting the college library, not only with an adequate budget and a salary scale sufficient to attract professional personnel competent to support the academic program, but also with the provision of quarters and physical facilities which will help to make book use attractive to the student. The Undergraduate Library of the University of Michigan served as an excellent setting for such a discussion, and as a model for the kind of planning and thinking that can make the book a vital and central part of a program of college education.

Adequate support of the library and its program derives from a philosophy of education which sees the librarian in a dynamic role in the teaching program. It seems clear from the discussions that the librarian has a truly integral part to play in the educational experience of the college student, and it seems equally clear that he cannot possibly play the part adequately without the encouragement of the college administration. To promote the co-operation between teacher and librarian which will best serve the goal of lifetime book use, the college must accord to the librarian the status, responsibility and authority which will permit him to make a maximum contribution to the teaching program. This will entail a recognition of librarianship as a kind of teaching; not, as Ellsworth points out, the same kind as the professor does in the classroom, but teaching nevertheless. The librarian can no longer be seen as a passive "handmaiden" who waits to be told which books to buy, and then does no more about them but deliver them across the desk in response to specific requests. He should be involved in curriculum planning; he should have responsibility for supplementing faculty suggestions with his own recommendations for book purchase and the establishment of services; and above all, he should be encouraged to function dynamically in encouraging and stimulating the supplementary independent reading of the student. The library's support of the school's program can no longer be seen as a simple provision of assigned readings; it should include the promotion of book use outside the narrow confines of course requirements to serve the larger and longer-term objectives which transcend the immediate requirements of the individual course and the current academic term.

Again certain simple steps can contribute to the implementation of this ideal. A recognition on the part of the administration, for example, that the knowledge of books is an essential skill of the librarian would suggest that time should be provided within the librarian's working day for uninterrupted reading. The failure of most college libraries to make any room for the sharpening of the librarian's book skill explains why college library service is so frequently technical in nature rather than professional. The librarian has been discouraged, both directly and indirectly, from making it anything more.

In other words, to summarize this summary, public expressions of devotion to the book are not enough; the need is for positive action in its support. Teachers, administrators, librarians and all other bookmen speak readily and lucidly about the role of the book; indeed, this may be a partial key to the problem. For the facility with which the words come has made them an all too easy substitute for action. The teacher who praises the book but fails to use it inventively in his teaching; the administrator who extols the values of reading but fails to support the agencies which supply and distribute books; the librarian who deplores low circulation figures but fails to function as anything more than a counterman in a book cafeteria—none of these has contributed much to the correction of the ills they have identified.

During the course of the conference, a distinction was made between book reading, and book use. The distinction is worth underlining here, in the final sentences of this volume. For even if this book is widely circulated and even if it is widely read, the success of the conference will not necessarily be assured. That can come only through constructive action, action stimulated and given direction by the ideas recorded here. In other words, the ultimate success of the conference really depends upon the readers of this volume and the use they make of it.

APPENDIX

Professor Robert C. Angell
Department of Sociology
University of Michigan

Dr. Lester Asheim
Dean, Graduate Library School
University of Chicago
Chicago, Illinois

Professor Marston Bates
Department of Zoology
University of Michigan

Professor Reuben A. Brower
Departments of English and General Education
Harvard University
Cambridge, Massachusetts

Dr. Paul H. Buck
Director of Libraries
Harvard University
Cambridge, Massachusetts

Mr. Cass Canfield
Chairman, Editorial Board
Harper & Brothers
New York, New York

Dr. Hilary J. Deason
Director, Science Library Program
American Association for the Advancement of Science
Washington 5, D. C.

Miss Margaret Dudley
Executive Secretary
National Book Committee, Inc.
New York, New York

Dr. Ralph E. Ellsworth
Director of Libraries
University of Colorado
Boulder, Colorado

Professor Rudolph H. Gjelsness
Department of Library Science
University of Michigan

Dr. Maxwell H. Goldberg
Executive Director
The Humanities Center for
    Liberal Education
University of Massachusetts
Amherst, Massachusetts

Dr. Mason W. Gross
Provost, Rutgers University
New Brunswick, New Jersey

Mr. Harold K. Guinzburg
President
The Viking Press, Inc.
New York, New York

Mr. Arthur T. Hamlin
University Librarian
University of Cincinnati
Cincinnati, Ohio

Dr. Frederick Hard
President, Scripps College
Claremont, California

Mr. Richard B. Harwell
Executive Secretary
Association of College and Re-
  search Libraries
American Library Association
Chicago, Illinois

Dr. Harlan Hatcher
President, University of Michigan

Dr. Hiram Haydn
Editor-in-Chief
Random House, Inc.
(now: President, Atheneum Pub-
  lishers, Inc.)
New York, New York

Mr. August Heckscher
Director, Twentieth Century
  Fund
New York, New York

Professor Algo D. Henderson
School of Education
University of Michigan

Professor Roger W. Heyns
Department of Psychology
(now: Dean, Faculty of Literature, Science, and the Arts)
University of Michigan

Mrs. Roberta Keniston
Librarian, Undergraduate Library
University of Michigan

Mrs. Patricia B. Knapp
Wayne State University Library
(now: Secretary and Librarian,
  Monteith College, Wayne State
  University)
Detroit, Michigan

Mr. Dan Lacy
Managing Director
American Book Publishers Council
New York, New York

Professor Bert James Loewenberg
Department of History
Sarah Lawrence College
Bronxville, New York

Dr. Howard F. Lowry
President, Wooster College
Wooster, Ohio

Mr. Bob Marshall
Bob Marshall's Book Shop
Ann Arbor, Michigan

Dr. Charles E. Odegaard
Dean, College of Literature,
  Science, and the Arts
University of Michigan
(now: President, University of
  Washington)

Professor William Riley Parker
Department of English
Indiana University
Bloomington, Indiana

Mr. Manning M. Pattillo
Associate Director
Lilly Endowment, Inc.
Indianapolis, Indiana

Dr. Jacob M. Price
Department of History
(Conference Manager)
University of Michigan

Dr. William J. Scarborough
President, Baker University
Baldwin, Kansas

Mrs. Eleanor T. Smith
Superintendent, Work with
  Adults
Brooklyn Public Library
Brooklyn, New York

Professor William C. Steere
Dean, Graduate Division
Stanford University
Stanford, California
(now: Director, New York
  Botanical Garden)

Mr. Robert G. Vosper
Director of Libraries
University of Kansas
Lawrence, Kansas

Dr. Frederick H. Wagman
Director, University Library
University of Michigan

Mr. Frederick L. Wormald
Associate Director
Association of American Colleges
Washington, D. C.